Connecting NetWare to the Internet

Paul Singh

Rick Fairweather

Dan Ladermann

Contributions by:
Leslie Lesnick

NRP
NEW RIDERS
PUBLISHING

New Riders Publishing, Indianapolis, Indiana

Connecting NetWare to the Internet

By Paul Singh, Rick Fairweather, and Dan Ladermann

Published by:
New Riders Publishing
201 West 103rd Street
Indianapolis, IN 46290 USA

Copyright © 1995 by New Riders Publishing

Printed in the United States of America 1 2 3 4 5 6 7 8 9 0

Library of Congress Cataloging-in-Publication Data

```
Singh, Paul.
    Connecting NetWare to the Internet / Paul Singh.
       p.   cm
    Includes index.
    ISBN 1-56205-398-1
    1. NetWare (Computer file)   2. Internet (Computer network)
3. Communications software.   I. Title.
TK5105.9.s46  1995
004.6'7—dc20                                        95-10056
                                                        CIP
```

Warning and Disclaimer

Publisher	Don Fowley
Associate Publisher	Tim Huddleston
Product Development Manager	Rob Tidrow
Marketing Manager	Ray Robinson
Managing Editor	Tad Ringo

Product Director
Julie Fairweather

Senior Acquisitions Editor
Jim LeValley

Production Editor
Sarah Kearns

Editors
John Kane
Cheri Robinson
Lillian Yates

Technical Editor
Rick Fairweather

Marketing Copywriter
Tamara Apple

Acquisitions Coordinator
Tracy Turgeson

Publisher's Assistant
Karen Opal

Cover Designer
Jay Corpus

Book Designer
Kim Scott

Production Team Supervisor
Katy Bodenmiller

Graphics Image Specialists
Clint Lahnen
Dennis Sheehan

Production Analysts
Angela Bannan
Dennis Clay Hager
Bobbi Satterfield

Production Team
Michael Brumitt
Charlotte Clapp
Terri Deemer
Mike Henry
Louisa Klucznik
Kevin Laseau
Erich J. Richter
Susan Van Ness
Mary Beth Wakefield
Jeff Weissenberger

Indexer
Greg Eldred

About the Authors

R. Paul Singh recently co-founded Internetware, Inc.—a company with a mission to make Internet access easy, secure, and manageable for NetWare LANs. Paul Singh has been in the networking industry for over 15 years in different engineering and marketing roles. Prior to co-founding Internetware, he has been an independent consultant for the last two years in the LAN/WAN industry, helping companies develop strategies related to Internet products. Mr. Singh has worked at Telebit Corporation, where he wrote papers and articles on issues related to NetWare IPX protocol in a dial-up environment. Prior to that, he worked at Sun Microsystems, dealing with ISDN and networking issues with multimedia. Mr. Singh has also worked with 3Com Corporation dealing with third-party relations and product management of network servers. Prior to joining the "vendor world," he worked as a Network Engineer at Morrison Knudsen Engineers. He has also taught computing courses at San Francisco City College.

Mr. Singh has a BS in Electrical Engineering from Delhi University, India, and an MBA from St. John's University, New York, specializing in information systems. You can reach him on the Internet at pauls@internetware.com

Rick Fairweather is a Senior Systems Engineer for a Fortune 500 internetworking company located in San Jose, California. He is involved in the technical design and sales of routing and switching solutions for high performance local area networks, large multiprotocol routed networks, the integration of IBM mainframe environments with multiprotocol networks, and wide area networking. Mr. Fairweather has extensive experience with network protocols including TCP/IP, Novell IPX, AppleTalk, DecNet, OSI, Netbios, and SNA. He has also designed and implemented many high performance networks using technologies such as Ethernet, Token Ring, FDDI, Frame Relay, X.25, SMDS, point-to-point leased line services, ISDN, and Asynchronous Transfer Mode.

Dan Ladermann is a co-founder of Internetware, Inc., and also co-founder of The Wollongong Group—a TCP/IP connectivity vendor. He has been in the UNIX, TCP/IP, and Internet marketplace for the last 20 years. He was the Vice President of Engineering at Wollongong, responsible for TCP/IP product development for PCs, VMS, and a variety of UNIX minicomputer systems and mainframes from Amdahl and supercomputers from Cray Research. Starting out his career with the National Security Agency, followed by Ford Aerospace, Mr. Ladermann co-founded The Wollongong Group in 1980 and worked as the engineering lead on the first commercially supported UNIX operating systems for a 32-bit super minicomputer. He has also published many articles on TCP/IP and conducted seminars on TCP/IP protocols in the U.S. and abroad.

Mr. Ladermann has a Masters degree in Computer Science from the John Hopkins University, and a BS in Electrical Engineering from the University of Toledo, Ohio. You can reach him on the Internet at dan@internetware.com.

Trademark Acknowledgments

All terms mentioned in this book that are known to be trademarks or service marks have been appropriately capitalized. New Riders Publishing cannot attest to the accuracy of this information. Use of a term in this book should not be regarded as affecting the validity of any trademark or service mark. NetWare is a registered trademark of Novell, Inc.

Acknowledgments

From Paul Singh:

One of the more pleasurable tasks of being an author is to thank the people who have made this book possible directly, as well as indirectly. My heartfelt thanks go to my wife Suki for her love, understanding, and support, my daughter Tasmin for being so understanding, and my son Zoraver for staying away from my home office on weekends. I also want to thank my parents for teaching me the value of hard work by example.

From Dan Ladermann:

I want to thank my wife, Debbie, for her support and patience during the writing of this book.

From Paul Singh and Dan Ladermann:

First of all, we would like to thank Internetware Inc.'s team for their support. Our special thanks go to Mr. Saroop Mathur of Internetware for reviewing some of the key chapters on protocols. We would also like to thank Mr. Thad Phetteplace at Great Lakes Area Commercial Internet for the contributing section on Web servers in Chapter 6, which helped us stay on course.

We also want to thank all of the Internet access providers that responded to our surveys in time. Our special thanks go to Mr. Bill Yundt of BBN/BarrNet, Mr. B.V. Jagdeesh of Exodus Communications, Mr. Jeffrey Shapard of PSI, and Dr. Hon Chang of Aimnet Corporation for their valuable insights and comments on the book.

We also want to acknowledge the timely help we received from Tim Kehres of IMA, Chris Johnson of Novell, and Donna Loughlin of NetManage.

Our many thanks go to the staff at New Riders Publishing, who made this project possible with their hard work and dedication. In particular, we want to thank Julie Fairweather, who was a constant source of inspiration and support. Sarah Kearns deserves special credit for keeping us in line and helping make the deadlines for this book. We also want to thank Rick Fairweather of Cisco Systems for reviewing technical accuracy of the content and helping us verify some of the facts. In addition, Jim LeValley deserves credit for getting this project started in the first place, and Leslie Lesnick and Andrew Dahl for also providing good support.

Contents at a Glance

Table of Contents

Part II: Communications and Application Software 25

Part IV: Administrative Issues   209

11 Case Studies   211

12 Answers to Commonly Asked "New Internet User" Questions   227

p a r t

I

Internet Fundamentals

Components for Connecting to the Internet

Y ou have been instructed to connect your company

to the Internet, and you are trying to plan out the

resources you will need. One would assume this to

be a fairly easy task simply because of the many

Internet connectivity packages that are available

today, such as "Internet-in-a-box," "Internet in 5

Minutes," and "Quick Internet Access." These

types of Internet connectivity packages, however,

are generally for the single user who needs or

wants an Internet connection.

Internet access for a network is typically much more complex than a single user Internet connection due to the multiplicity of available options. For a network, an Internet connection is independent of the network's topology. Whether you have an Ethernet LAN, a Token Ring LAN, or an FDDI LAN, you can connect to the Internet. Connecting to the Internet, however, may have a different meaning for a LAN than for a single user—what are these differences? This book will help answer this and many other questions, including the following:

→ What does Internet connectivity entail in terms of hardware, software, and services?

→ How is Internet connectivity brought to all LAN users with the least system management?

→ What are the different types of Internet applications available, and how do you decide to use one application over another?

→ How much bandwidth and type of wide area networking service do you need for your LANs?

→ Which service provider should you use for your Internet access?

→ How do you build a business case for Internet connectivity?

What This Book Will Do for You

The objective of *Connecting NetWare to the Internet* is to help LAN Managers, System Administrators, and MIS Managers understand all the components needed to connect their company LANs to the Internet. This book focuses on NetWare LANs, but it will also prove to be equally useful to non-NetWare LAN Administrators.

The intent of this book is not to provide hands-on Internet usage exercises, but rather to bring out information that can help Network managers make the right choice of hardware, software, services, and applications.

Who Should Read This Book

This book will benefit anyone chartered with providing Internet connectivity for LANs. Specifically, people having the following job titles will benefit the most:

→ Network Managers

→ LAN Administrators

→ MIS Managers

→ Network Planners

→ Systems Engineers

→ Certified NetWare Engineers (CNEs)

End-to-End Internet Connectivity

To achieve end-to-end Internet connectivity, you must first be aware of what the Internet can do for you and your company. Chapter 2, "The Internet: Yesterday, Today, and Tomorrow," begins with a historical overview of the Internet and follows its development through today, showing how companies are maximizing their usage of the Internet for business purposes. Emerging uses of the Internet are also discussed, followed by a detailed cost and benefit analysis on how you can justify your Internet connection.

True end-to-end Internet connectivity requires additional software, hardware, and services at both the sender and the receiver's end. Some of the existing software and hardware used for UNIX computer access may be usable for Internet access, while new software and hardware may have to be acquired for transparent Internet access for all LAN users.

Figure 1.1 shows all of the components needed to connect a network to the Internet. Similarly, a mirror image of this figure would represent the other end of the Internet connection.

The Internet connectivity matrix, shown in figure 1.2, is another representation of the Internet connectivity components depicted in figure 1.1. Because this book is organized around this matrix, the remainder of this chapter focuses on each level of the matrix to lay the groundwork for future chapters.

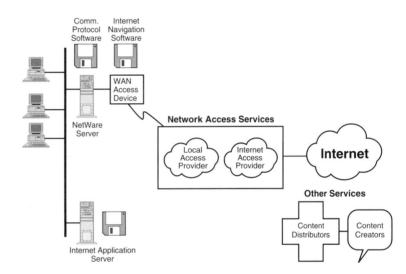

Figure 1.1

Internet connectivity components.

Figure 1.2

The Internet connectivity matrix.

Layer 7   SECURITY AND MANAGEMENT

Layer 6	Internet Access Providers (Regional, National, International)
Layer 5	WAN Access Devices (Routers, Modems, DSU/CSU)
Layer 4	WAN Access Services (Analog, ISDN, Leased, Switched 56, Frame Relay)
Layer 3	Internet Application Servers (E-mail servers, News servers, Web servers)
Layer 2	Internet Navigation Software (E-mail, FTP, Telnet, Mosaic)
Layer 1	Network Communication Protocols (IP, IPX, AppleTalk)

Network Communication Protocols

The communication protocol understood by the Internet is *Internet Protocol* (IP), whereas NetWare communicates using the *Internet Packet Exchange* (IPX) protocol. This is like having two people in a room, with one speaking Chinese and the other speaking English. The only solutions are to either hire a translator or teach each person the other's language. To help you understand this relationship between IP and IPX, Chapter 3, "Understanding TCP/IP," provides an overview of the IP protocol, while Chapter 4, "Adding TCP/IP to NetWare LANs," discusses the issues related to communication between the IP and IPX protocols. Appendix B, "IP Subnetting and Binary Conversion Tables," is referenced frequently throughout Chapter 3; it provides valuable information about IP addressing that can be referenced, utilized, and applied in your own environment.

Internet Navigation Software

The Internet is like a country without road signs. People who have been traveling on the Internet for some time know of many back alleys and short-cuts, but those less familiar with it tend to get lost. These old-timers also tend to use archaic navigational aids, which are command-line-oriented applications. Many people, however, are now contributing to the development of much-needed maps to make it easy for everyone to navigate the Internet. Many new tools have thus been developed to facilitate Internet navigation, with Mosaic perhaps being the most well-known tool. Similarly, FTP and Telnet tools are becoming more graphical and easier to use. Other navigational aids such as Archie, WAIS, and Gopher are making it easier to find resources on the Internet. These tools are collectively called *Internet applications*. Chapter 5, "Internet Applications," discusses the various Internet applications that are needed by end-users to navigate the Internet.

Internet Application Servers

How are your users going to get their e-mail? Where is the e-mail going to be stored? In what format do your users use e-mail today? How can our Lotus cc:Mail users send and receive mail from the Internet? The answers to these and similar questions might indicate the need for an e-mail server. Where should that server be located—at your site or the Internet access provider's site? The same questions need to be answered for News servers or Web servers. Chapter 6, "Internet Application Servers," provides the answers to these questions by examining issues involving the various Internet servers and offering different alternatives for diverse situations.

WAN Access Services

The next level on the Internet connectivity matrix is selection of the WAN services. In most cases, you can find an Internet Access Provider within your local telephone calling area. Therefore, you need to be concerned only with WAN service from your local telephone company. How much bandwidth is required by the LAN users? What is your monthly budget for access services? What kind of bandwidth pattern do you expect on your WAN? If your bandwidth requirement is 56 Kbps, what types of services are available and how do you decide between each of the services? Chapter 7, "WAN Access Services," addresses these and many other similar issues, and provides an overview of different

WAN services, such as analog dial-up, digital dial-up, and dedicated lines.

WAN Access Devices

Specific hardware devices are needed to connect a network to the appropriate WAN access service. This WAN device might be just a modem, a router with a modem, an ISDN terminal adapter, or a leased line DSU/CSU. Chapter 8, "WAN Access Devices," covers the details related to WAN access devices, and defines which options are appropriate for different situations.

Internet Access Providers

In order to access the Internet, you need to have an *Internet Access Provider* (IAP). It is similar in concept to the long-distance service provider needed for your telephone service. Chapter 9, "Internet Access Providers," discusses the criteria for selecting an IAP, and Appendix A, "Examining Internet Access Providers," provides a list of the IAPs. Chapter 9 also examines the type of services offered by the IAPs, a cost range for these services, and what to expect from your service provider.

Security and Management

Internet security is a key issue that should be a proactive part of planning the Internet connection, rather than a reactive part or merely an afterthought. Security issues should not be restricted to just controlling access from the outside, but they also should focus on controlling access from the inside to provide management information and details of Internet connectivity. Chapter 10, "Network Security," discusses the issue of security and management tools for NetWare-centric LANs, as well as mixed UNIX and NetWare LANs.

Case Studies

Clearly, there are many issues to address and many decisions to make when establishing an Internet presence for your company. With the large number of organizations already connected to the Internet today, you might be wondering how they arrived at their decisions and why they made specific selections over other available alternatives. Chapter 11, "Case Studies," provides a forum for which to learn more about these Internet connectivity issues, and portrays in detail how corporations are making the choices that are appropriate for their individual environments.

Benefits of LAN-Based versus Single-User Internet Access

Do you let your LAN users attach a modem to each individual PC for remote access? Do you let your LAN users connect to other LANs over modems attached directly to their computers? Do you let your LAN users have a FAX modem in each of their own computers? Most likely, you probably answered "No" in each case. The most common reasons for this are as follows:

→ Reduced costs by sharing the telephone lines

→ Reduced costs by sharing modems and other hardware

→ More controlled and secure access

→ Easier to manage and administer

Do you know how many users on your LAN already have a dial-up Internet access account? It is time to think of providing Internet access to all LAN users before dial-up single-user access gets out of hand.

These same reasons can be applied to the issues surrounding Internet access that affect your network users. Unfortunately, many companies today are letting users connect directly to the Internet with a modem on their desktop. This method can be both inefficient and expensive if the goal is to give all employees Internet access. It is best to consider providing Internet access to all of the users on your LAN with usage permission restrictions in place, which provides more management leverage and control. More importantly, however, is that appropriate bandwidth can be allocated, depending on the total concurrent usage. Therefore, with the benefits of a LAN-based Internet connection in mind, go now to Chapter 2, "The Internet: Yesterday, Today, and Tomorrow," where you will continue to learn more about the components for connecting NetWare to the Internet.

2

The Internet: Yesterday, Today, and Tomorrow

It is very difficult to define the Internet—it means different things to different people. For some people, it is an online service that offers entertainment and educational value. For others, it is just another wide-area network that provides an economical means for both inter- and intra-company electronic communications. The Internet has also been called an online library of software and ideas, as well as published materials such as books and magazines. Technically, the Internet is the largest *Transmission Control Protocol/Internet Protocol* (TCP/IP) internetwork in the world.

The following all describe the concept of the Internet from different perspectives:

→ Internet = Inter + Net = Connection of different nets = The Net

→ Collection of computers linked together in one large network

→ World's largest bulletin board

→ World's largest electronic mail network

→ World's largest online service

The Internetworking Concept

It is much easier to understand the concept of the Internet by comparing it to an internetwork. An *internetwork* is a group of network nodes communicating over the same or different physical medium (such as twisted-pair wiring or fiber wiring) or topologies (such as Ethernet or Token Ring) that are linked together with a bridge or a router. *Bridges* or *routers* can be thought of as traffic cops in the sense that they direct the data from one network to another. The internetworking of LANs that are geographically separate is done using a *wide area network* (WAN) service, such as a dedicated service (T-1, Frame Relay, or 56/64 Kbps links) or a switched connection (Dial-up Analog, ISDN, or Switched 56). Once an internetwork is in place, users are able to access resources on any of the other LANs, provided those users have the appropriate access privileges.

Figure 2.1 shows an internetwork of a company with three geographically separate LANs connected together to form a large virtual LAN. These LANs are connected over a dedicated wide area network.

The Internet—the Internetwork of Networks

The Internet is a large internetwork comprised of many LANs and computers. Unlike the internetwork of a company that only connects its own offices together, the Internet connects networks and computers from any number of organizations. These networks and computers can be located anywhere in the world. If you have access to the Internet, therefore, you can connect to another host computer on the Internet that may be located next door to you or in a foreign country thousands of miles away. This, of course, all occurs behind the scenes and is transparent to the user.

As shown in figure 2.2, the Internet is very similar in concept to the internetwork of a company like that shown in figure 2.1. The only difference is that the Internet is larger than any single internetwork, is open to anyone, and may cross many more LANs to get to the destination.

It is estimated that over 3 million hosts are connected to the Internet, and these hosts are located in more than 50 countries. The number of users now using the Internet is estimated to be anywhere from 10 million to 35 million.

Figure 2.1

Internetworking makes all LANs appear as one.

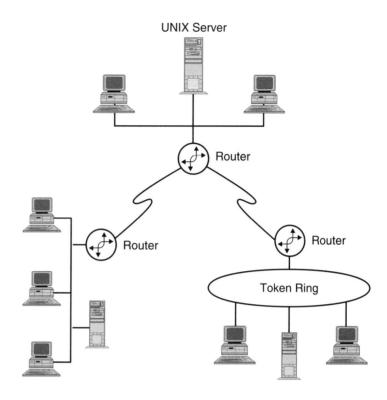

One might expect such a large internetwork to be controlled and managed by many network managers. Despite being the largest internetwork in the world, the Internet is virtually anarchic and runs without any centralized authority or management, with the exception of the InterNIC. In order to understand how this large and very public

internetwork functions efficiently without any central management, let us first look at a brief history of the Internet.

n o t e As defined by the InterNIC, an Internet *host* is a computer or a collection of computers directly connected to the Internet, which enables network users temporary access to its services. The computer acts as "host" to one or more public services and the users accessing those services.

n o t e The *Internet Network Information Center* (InterNIC), or simply *The NIC*, is an organization that provides information and registration services to Internet users. One of the primary responsibilities of the InterNIC is assigning IP addresses and domain names to new Internet sites and keeping track of these Internet addresses to avoid duplication. The NIC is also responsible for maintaining and distributing *Requests for Comments* (RFCs)—technical reports that document protocols, standards, and policies on the Internet.

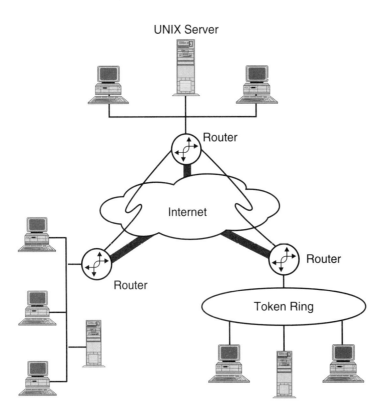

Figure 2.2

The Internet is an
internetwork of com-
puters worldwide.

History of the Internet

The Internet was called ARPAnet at the time of its origination in 1969. The *Advanced Research Project Agency* (ARPA) is an agency of the U.S. Department of Defense that contracted with *Bolt, Beranek, and Newman* (BBN) to set up a WAN to connect four university sites for research purposes—Stanford, UCLA, UC Santa Barbara, and the University of Utah. The *Internet Protocol* (IP) was born out of the ARPAnet project. In the early 1980s, the Department of Defense separated out MILNET, the military portion of the ARPAnet, and left the remainder of the ARPAnet for use by the Universities.

The *National Science Foundation* (NSF), another agency of the U.S. government, laid the foundation for the modern-day Internet when it decided to build its own network to connect six supercomputer centers. NSF used ARPAnet's IP to build its network, which was connected using 56 *Kilobits per second* (Kbps) links. The usage of the NSFnet started increasing as many local schools connected to their nearest supercomputing center for access to the Net. In 1987, NSF awarded a contract to Merit Networks Inc., which ran Michigan's educational network in partnership with IBM and MCI. This contract was meant to upgrade the network to a high-speed (T1-1.544 *Megabits per second* or Mbps) backbone. As the traffic increased, NSF upgraded its backbone to T3 (45 Mbps) speeds in 1992. NSFnet completely phased out ARPAnet in the early '90s as the U.S. Department of Defense started using MILNET for classified purposes, while all other traffic from ARPAnet migrated to the NSFnet.

 n o t e The six supercomputing centers linked initially by NSF were as follows:

→ Cornell National Supercomputer Facility, Cornell University

→ The Scientific Computing Division of the National Center for Atmospheric Research, Boulder, Colorado

→ San Diego Supercomputer Center, University of California

→ National Center for Supercomputing Applications, University of Illinois

→ John von Neumann National Supercomputer Center, Princeton, New Jersey

→ Pittsburgh Supercomputer Center, operated jointly by Westinghouse Electric Corp., Carnegie Mellon University, and the University of Pittsburgh

Use of the NSFnet for commercial purposes initially created a huge controversy because it was originally founded for research purposes only. Now that the U.S. government's funding of the NSFnet has expired, however, both commercial and noncommercial traffic can be carried freely and without dispute on the NSFnet, now known as the Internet.

Internet Access Providers

All Internet subscribers pay for the Internet in the form of monthly fees to their particular *Internet Access Provider* (IAP). The IAPs buy their communication circuits from telephone companies and also buy access to a Network Access Point where they can connect to the Internet. A Network Access Point is a tap into the Internet backbone that provides worldwide connectivity. Alternatively, IAPs can pay a yearly fee to *Commercial Internet Exchange* (CIX) for carrying commercial traffic among providers. The CIX charges every Internet access provider an annual fee of approximately $10,000.

 n o t e CIX was formed by three IAPs—CERFnet, PSInet, and Alternet—with an objective to provide commercial high-speed networking services without using the NSFnet. It is not a requirement for an IAP to be a CIX member.

The Internet Access Provider industry began as a cottage industry, with many Internet operators working out of their living rooms using just a few UNIX workstations and modems. Because Internet access is now becoming mission-critical for many companies, however, IAPs are being asked to provide a much greater level of service to their customers than ever before. The Internet industry therefore is evolving, resulting in fewer but larger IAPs that are better equipped to provide more reliable service. Many of the telephone companies, such as Sprint, AT&T, and MCI, are now providing Internet access, making it a very competitive market. In addition, all of the online service providers, such as CompuServe, Prodigy, and *America Online* (AOL), are starting to offer direct Internet services. All of these changes will make the Internet very different than what it is today.

Development of Internet Standards

The *Internet Society* (ISOC) is a nonprofit voluntary member organization that promotes the Internet and its technologies. The Internet Society appoints a council of invited volunteers, which form what is known as the *Internet Architecture Board* (IAB). IAB's charter is to deal with standardization and long-term directions for the Internet.

The Internet provides its users with an opportunity to express their opinions and get involved through the *Internet Engineering Task Force* (IETF). The IETF is a voluntary organization—anyone can attend its meetings. The IETF has published many standards to help the networking industry develop interoperable products. The IETF sets up working groups to address specific issues. Generally, when there are at least eight volunteers from different companies to research a topic, a working group is formed. In the end, most working groups publish a document known as *Request for Comments* (RFC), which becomes a standard. Over one thousand RFCs are available on many different topics, including SNMP, TCP, IP, UDP, PPP, and many more. These RFCs can be obtained from the InterNIC by way of U.S. postal mail, electronic mail, or with an Internet file transfer program.

The Internet Today

The number of hosts on the Internet has been growing at an estimated rate of 10–20 percent per month from early 1993 to 1995. Figures indicate that the number of Internet hosts exceeded 3 million at the end of 1994, as shown in figure 2.3. Assuming an average of 10 users per host, this points to over 30 million possible users. Another Internet growth indicator is the increased amount of traffic, which is measured in gigabytes on a monthly basis by the Internet Society. Figure 2.4 displays a graphical representation of Internet traffic patterns.

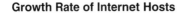

Growth Rate of Internet Hosts

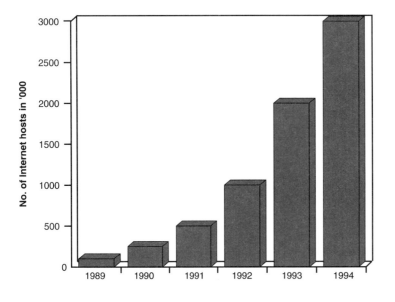

Figure 2.3

The growth rate of Internet hosts.

Figure 2.4

*Traffic growth on the
Internet.*

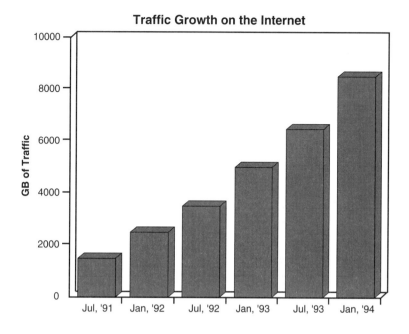

Even though the United States accounts for over 50 percent of Internet hosts, European and Asian hosts are also growing at a rapid rate, as shown in figure 2.5. As stated previously in this chapter, over 50 countries have host computers on the Internet. Universities are often the first to get connected to the Internet in these countries. Developing countries, however, face great obstacles to such growth. As an example, one of the primary obstacles to Internet growth in developing countries is the lack of reliable telephone service. If this were not an issue, you would see a much greater growth rate in the number of Internet hosts worldwide than what you have seen thus far.

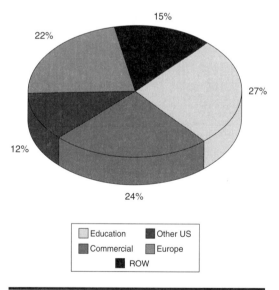

Figure 2.5

The distribution of current Internet hosts.

Business Uses of the Internet

The Internet is used in the corporate environment in a variety of ways. The following discussion relates some of the most important uses to date, including electronic mail, research, and technical support.

Electronic Mail

The most common application for which people are using the Internet is e-mail. The only universal standard for exchanging e-mail among heterogeneous mail systems is the Internet mail standard, called *Simple Mail Transfer Protocol* (SMTP). Even when you send an e-mail message from CompuServe to a user on a different online service, such as America Online, you still use the Internet to exchange e-mail. The following example depicts this usage well.

It is 9:00 a.m. in New York, and you want to make sure that your vendor in California gets your message as soon as he arrives at the office. You could wait and call him when it is 9:00 a.m. in California, but you have a lunch meeting at that time. Another option would be to leave him a voice mail message, but the details of your message are too complicated. Thus, the best solution is to leave him an electronic mail message with all the details. Despite the fact that your vendor uses a different electronic mail system and is not directly connected to your LAN, you can still communicate with one another by using the Internet and/or Internet mail protocol.

Just as FAX numbers on business cards are considered a necessity today, an Internet e-mail address will be a must within the next 12–18 months. Most companies in the high-technology business already include an Internet e-mail address on their employees' business cards.

Research

The amount of material available on the Internet well exceeds that of many libraries, and a common complaint has been simply the difficulty in finding that information. However, this problem is resolving itself with the newer Internet tools that are becoming available. One of the most important tools in this category is a program called Mosaic, which allows a point-and-click search of Internet information. These types of tools definitely provide an advantage to the user and make the job of finding information on the Internet much easier. Again, an example of this Internet usage method follows.

You have been assigned the task of evaluating different routers for your company, and you have a week to complete the project. You recall several articles in a recent trade magazine, but you can't locate the magazine. Because you have an Internet connection, however, you can view all previous issues of the magazine online, find the articles for which you are searching, and print the ones you need. To get a copy of one of the vendor's product brochures, you can get back on the Internet and browse for the information from the vendor's Web server. Now, in just a matter of hours, you have all the basic information to get started with your evaluation.

Electronic Technical Support

Many companies, including Cisco, Microsoft, and Novell, are using the Internet as a technical support vehicle for customers. In essence, customers can use the Internet in lieu of making a telephone call to get marketing information, software updates, and other types of technical support from an organization. This type of usage is very similar to the services provided by vendor bulletin boards and CompuServe forums, with the major differences being economics and accessibility. Internet access is more universal than CompuServe, and it is in many situations much cheaper to set up a company's bulletin board on the Internet than on CompuServe. Using the Internet for technical support enables companies to provide services that they could not otherwise offer.

The various ways in which technical support is being provided by companies include the following:

→ **E-mail**—Using e-mail, phone tag can be avoided, offering customers a timely response to their requests.

→ **FTP**—FTP access means that a company can offer both the textual and binary files for downloading by its customers. For example, Novell offers bug fixes for their software via FTP.

→ **Web servers**—Web servers are primarily being used to provide information rich with text, graphics, and multimedia. Unlike FTP access, where one file at a time is loaded and then viewed at the customer site, Web servers enable customers to view the document before making a decision on whether they should download that information.

Emerging Uses of the Internet

One of the emerging uses of the Internet is electronic telemarketing, which provides an alternative to traditional telemarketing. As shown in figure 2.6, traditional telemarketing is very expensive, especially for a small company—the result is either losing customer calls or employing more staff than needed. Also, traditional telemarketing uses the same skill-level person to answer technical questions as it does to take down a name and send literature.

Figure 2.6

Traditional telemarketing.

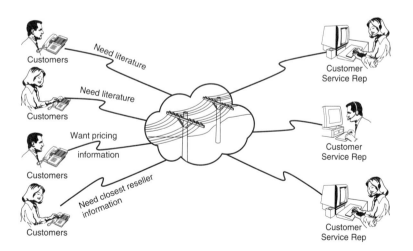

As it enters the electronic age, a company provides all its literature and other pricing-related information on a Web server, which provides customers with the chance to browse and download the desired information instead of making a telephone call to get answers to specific questions. Therefore, electronic telemarketing complements traditional telemarketing, reducing the cost of doing business (see fig. 2.7). Electronic telemarketing will enable smaller companies to offer as high a quality of service as any large company.

Another emerging use of the Internet is that it is becoming a de facto WAN for small and mid-size companies that cannot afford to have their own private network. In this case, small companies receive the same benefit of interconnectivity that large companies have enjoyed for years. For the Internet to become such a de facto WAN, however, issues such as security and privacy need to be addressed. These issues will be covered in more detail in Chapter 10, "Network Security."

Electronic commerce will begin to evolve as standards for digital cash and secure transactions are accepted by developers and users of the Internet. Some rudimentary form of electronic commerce is already emerging on the Internet, where products can be ordered over the Internet once the account information has been verified using the traditional methods of a person-to-person call.

Lastly, some other emerging uses of the Internet appear in the area of video conferencing techniques, as well as multimedia commercials and product advertising on the Internet. Companies with Web sites are already starting to implement intensive graphics on their home page to make their site more appealing to the public, as well as to better sell their products to customers.

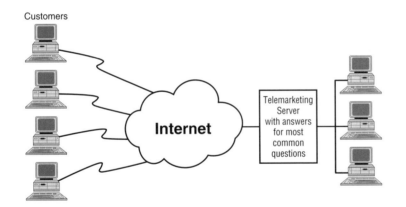

Figure 2.7

Traditional telemarketing, as supplemented by electronic telemarketing.

Justifying Internet Connectivity in Your Corporation

With the emerging uses of the Internet essentially upon us, there is a mad rush in the corporate world to establish Internet presence—this means different things to different people, however. For some companies, getting a company domain name is the highest priority; for others, it is using a public e-mail system; and for others, establishing their own Web server on the Internet is a priority.

The first task is to analyze the needs for the Internet connection by considering the following questions:

➜ What will the Internet do for me?

➜ Why should I connect to the Internet?

Second, the benefits from the Internet connection must be evaluated. The benefits achieved will vary from company to company, but can essentially be clarified by asking the following questions:

➜ What tangible benefits can be gained by connecting to the Internet? The primary measurement here is financial. In this section, the cost benefits obtained from the Internet connection are discussed.

➜ What intangible benefits can be gained by the Internet connection? While these are often the most difficult benefits to measure, they may in fact be the determining factors that justify the Internet connection. A number of these intangible benefits are discussed later in this chapter.

Third, the cost for the Internet connection must be considered. There are many options to be factored into this portion of the analysis. Many Internet Access Providers have varying service offerings and costs. These issues are discussed in Chapter 9, "Internet Access Providers." In addition, many options are available for connecting to the Internet. The connection may be via analog dial-up using a modem connected to a standard telephone line, circuit or digital switched services such as ISDN or Switched 56 Kbps, point-to-point dedicated circuits such as a T1 circuit, or packet switched services such as Frame Relay. In Chapter 7, "WAN Access Services," a detailed presentation of each technology, its benefits, and respective costs will be discussed in detail.

Finally, these three areas must be considered in whole to determine if the Internet connection is feasible. It is unlikely that the tangible cost benefits of the Internet connection will equal or exceed the costs involved. However, by evaluating the needs and the overall benefits of connecting to the Internet, you, like many organizations throughout the world, may determine that the Internet community is one of which you need to be a member.

In the remainder of this chapter, a presentation of the justification of the Internet connection is provided, with emphasis in the following areas:

➜ Cost savings

➜ Improved customer service

➜ Information access

Cost Savings

Cost savings are typically the first argument in favor of an Internet connection. Before the cost savings can be measured, however, you must assess how exactly the connection is to be used.

Using the Internet for Electronic Mail

One of the most common uses for the Internet connection is electronic mail. Assessing the cost savings of an Internet connection by taking advantage of electronic mail is very straightforward. To assess this benefit, you must first estimate the costs and characteristics of traditional means of communication, including mail via the United States postal system, overnight mailing via providers such as Federal Express and United Parcel Service, and voice communications—particularly long distance communications.

 It must be emphasized that electronic mail should not be considered as a replacement for all written and verbal communications within an organization and externally to customers, vendors, or business partners. Electronic mail should be used where appropriate and not considered as a replacement for traditional means of direct, personal communication.

For example, one organization provided the following information, which was gathered through interviews with departmental representatives and analyzing expenses related to postage, overnight letter shipments, and long distance phone calls. Each department was asked to monitor what percentage of their mailings, overnight mailings, and telephone costs could be made effectively and appropriately by way of electronic mail. Over a ninety-day period, the following average expenses, representing the amounts which could potentially be saved with electronic mail, were demonstrated:

Mail postage	$325
Letters via overnight services	$140
Paper savings (stationery, etc.)	$78
Long distance telephone expenses	$225

Using this organization as an example, an Internet connection could provide for a tangible cost reduction in these expense categories in excess of $750.

However, there are also intangible cost advantages in using electronic mail, particularly when compared to the U.S. postal mail system. Electronic mail is delivered virtually immediately, whereas traditional mail may require several days to even a week to be delivered. Will your customer benefit by receiving your information that same day, while your competitor's information may not arrive for a week? Will your sales representative in a remote sales office benefit from receiving new pricing information immediately without having to wait several days? Will informing your employees of new procedures and policies reduce costly mistakes in manufacturing? Frequently, the intangible benefits will provide savings that may even exceed those that can be directly measured.

Using the Internet as a Wide Area Network

Perhaps the second most used feature of the Internet is its use as a *wide area network* (WAN) for a corporation with geographically dispersed locations. Many organizations may choose to build a private WAN using services and circuits provided by one of many WAN service providers. The primary benefit of this approach is security—the private WAN is isolated from other WANs. The issue of security is discussed in detail in Chapter 10. Yet while this isolation provides strong security benefits, it may also be its greatest limitation. A private WAN will not facilitate communications with people outside of the company WAN, such as customers, vendors, and business partners.

Using the Internet as a WAN will facilitate communication with other organizations and individuals that are connected to the Internet. Furthermore, the Internet connection may in fact present cost savings when compared to building a private wide area network.

Improved Customer Service

In today's ever-competitive business environment, customer service and customer satisfaction are often considered as critical to an organization's success as the financial indicators. In the eyes of many companies, customer satisfaction and financial success often go hand in hand. But how can the Internet be used to improve customer service?

Consider the example of a company whose primary business is the manufacturing and sales of computer networking equipment. Traditionally, technical support for this type of company is accomplished by staffing a help desk or technical support center with technically qualified personnel to assist in answering questions and resolving problems for its customers. The cost of this approach is fairly easy to assess. Personnel costs and related expenses such as telephone services can be tracked very accurately, and can also be readily used in the financial justification of an Internet connection. Using the Internet as a means to provide customer assistance and support, an organization can realize savings by controlling telephone expenses, as well

as functioning with less staff than otherwise required.

A customer would contact this support center with the expectation of prompt and accurate information. If this information can be provided to the customer electronically via the Internet, information and solutions can be provided immediately. Chapter 5, "Internet Applications," presents a number of Internet access methods, including Telnet access, Web servers using HTTP, and file transfer using FTP. For example, access to a database application providing technical information, tips, and product information could be provided to customers using Telnet. This same information could also be provided using a highly graphical interface using *HyperText Transfer Protocol* (HTTP) by providing access from Web browsers, such as NCSA Mosaic or Netscape. Required files, such as software updates and bug fixes, could be transferred using FTP.

But what are the benefits? First, the obvious benefit would be a tangible financial benefit to the company. Customers that use these online services to obtain their information would not require the involvement of an individual from the technical support and the related costs with traditional forms of support, such as telephone expenses.

Finally, let's review the effectiveness of the preceding example. The organization discussed previously indicated that the applications that have been developed for Internet access are utilized on average 1,300 times per week, while the average contact when using traditional telephone support is 12 minutes. This would provide for an elimination of more than 100 person-hours in support costs per week. Additionally, whereas software might have been provided to the customer via overnight mail, the customer can now download the required files through the Internet, eliminating overnight mailing charges. Clearly, this is a considerable savings.

But even more important is the benefit to the customer. Accessing an application via Telnet or HTTP in real time enables a customer to obtain information immediately. This information could be accessible 24 hours per day, even when support personnel are not available. Customers can receive the resolution they require promptly without the time constraints of when the support center is open or when a representative is available to assist them. The organization discussed previously has realized a 20 percent increase in customer satisfaction survey results in the first year alone.

Information Access

One of the most rapidly growing uses of the Internet is for the sales and marketing of products and services. As more individuals and organizations connect to the Internet, the Internet becomes an increasingly viable and productive medium for communications.

Perhaps one of the most significant driving factors for this growth is the expanding use of Web servers and browsers. Through the use of a Web server, these applications enable a company to provide information to its customer in a highly graphical format that is easy to use.

Many companies in the computer system and networking market, such as Apple Computers, Cisco Systems, Hewlett Packard, IBM, Microsoft, Novell, Sun Microsystems, 3COM, and many others, are currently using Web servers to communicate infor-

mation to their customers and prospects. Technical associations such as the InterNIC, the *Internet Engineering Task Force* (IETF), the Internet Society, and the ATM forum are using Web servers to make their information available to a large audience. Many computer magazines today are being presented electronically via Web servers. Demographic data, financial market indicators, corporate financial information, and endless other topics are being presented on the Internet using Web servers. It should be no surprise that the Internet is sometimes referred to as the "library of the future."

A Web browser enables the user not only to access these graphically based servers, but also to search the Internet for sources of information. Using the online directories and various search tools discussed in Chapter 5, you can search the Internet for information on any number of topics.

There are benefits to this growth both for the organization providing the information, as well as to those who access it. Using this technology enables a company to make its marketing literature, product announcements, and public pricing available to a large audience without the costs associated with printing and distributing written information. Changes to this information can be made immediately without the costs and delays involved with printed materials.

The benefit to the user is the immediate accessibility of information. There is a vast amount of information on the Internet, and the tools available today make this information very accessible.

Evaluating the Issues

The first step to justifying an Internet connection is performing a needs analysis, which should include the factors that are demanding the services that will be made available from the Internet, the type of connection to the Internet that will be required, and the equipment that will be required. These issues will be discussed in depth in Chapters 5, 7, 9, and 10. By measuring the benefits that will be derived from the Internet connection, the feasibility of connecting to the Internet can then be properly evaluated.

Summary

The Internet is over 25 years old, but its commercialization and thereby explosive growth has occurred only in the last few years. E-mail continues to be the number-one application for the Internet. Using the Internet for research is getting easier with a new class of point-and-click Internet navigational tools, such as Mosaic. The Internet is being used by many companies for providing better service to their customers at a cost lower than the traditional methods. Justifying an Internet connection is best accomplished by first performing a needs analysis, and then by measuring the costs and benefits that will result from connecting and not connecting to the Internet. It is likely that when you compile all of the tangible and intangible benefits, they will outweigh the costs of an Internet connection in today's ever-competitive business environment.

Communications and Application Software

chapter

3

Understanding TCP/IP

Transmission Control Protocol/Internet Protocol
(TCP/IP) is essentially the exclusive communication
protocol used on the Internet. In order to understand how the Internet works, a basic knowledge
of the TCP/IP protocol is essential. This chapter
provides a basic understanding of TCP/IP, along
with some of the important issues such as network
addressing, naming, and connection protocols used
over serial links. If you are already familiar with
TCP/IP, you may skip or scan this chapter.

The following topics are discussed as you set out on the task of understanding TCP/IP:

→ What is TCP/IP?

→ The historical development of TCP/IP

→ The layers of TCP/IP

→ Addressing in a TCP/IP network

→ Naming in a TCP/IP network

→ Future directions of TCP/IP

TCP/IP has become a universal communication protocol not only on the Internet and wide area networks, but also is becoming increasingly common on local area networks. The key factors that have contributed to TCP/IP becoming a universal protocol are the following:

→ TCP/IP is based on open and well-published standards, thereby making it easy to write applications based on TCP/IP protocols for any type of operating system.

→ TCP/IP is not dependent on any specific operating system, and has therefore been implemented for all types of computers—from PCs to mainframes.

→ Many TCP/IP protocol implementations and applications are available in public domain, thereby reducing the cost of implementation for the user.

→ TCP/IP operates effectively and efficiently over a variety of *local area network* (LAN) technologies (i.e., Ethernet, Token Ring, and FDDI) and *wide area network* (WAN) technologies (i.e., T1, Switched 56 Kbps, Frame Relay, X.25, ISDN, SMDS, ATM, and analog dial-up services).

→ TCP/IP provides a common set of standard applications to provide services such as electronic mail, file transfer, and remote access to computers. These applications are discussed in Chapter 5, "Internet Applications."

 This chapter focuses on layer 1 of the Internet connectivity matrix.

7   SECURITY AND MANAGEMENT
6   Internet Access Providers
5   WAN Access Devices
4   WAN Access Services
3   Internet Application Servers
2   Internet Navigation Software
1   Network Communication Protocols

What is TCP/IP?

TCP and IP, two of the most popular communication protocols today, allow different kinds of computers using different operating systems to communicate with each other over a LAN and/or a WAN. The term TCP/IP is frequently used to refer to the collection of communication protocols that make up the full TCP/IP protocol suite.

Some of the other protocols in the TCP/IP protocol suite include the following:

→ *Universal Datagram Protocol* (UDP)

→ *Internet Control Message Protocol* (ICMP)

→ Routing protocols such as *Routing Information Protocol* (RIP)

→ Application protocols such as *File Transfer Protocol* (FTP), Virtual Terminal Protocol (Telnet), and *Simple Mail Transport Protocol* (SMTP)

These different protocols are covered in more detail later in this chapter.

The TCP/IP protocol suite is constantly evolving. In the last few years, a whole new class of application protocols, such as Gopher and *HyperText Transport Protocol* (HTTP), have emerged. This has resulted in the most popular Internet application—Web browsers. Some of the well-known Web browsers include Mosaic and Netscape, which are covered in Chapter 5.

Historical Development of TCP/IP

TCP/IP is the result of over 25 years of research and development. An earlier generation of TCP/IP called *Network Control Protocol* (NCP) was first used to build the *Advanced Research Projects Agency Network* (ARPAnet). *Defense Advanced Research Projects Agency* (DARPA) is the agency of the U.S. Department of Defense responsible for the development of new technology for use by the military. DARPA, formerly known as ARPA, was responsible for funding much of the development of the Internet. In the late 1970s and early 1980s, Mr. Vinton G. Cerf and Mr. Robert E Kahn, working for DARPA, developed the core TCP/IP protocols. For a number of years, the ARPAnet used both TCP/IP and NCP protocols; in 1983, however, the ARPAnet switched over fully to TCP/IP.

In 1982, the TCP/IP protocol was integrated in the Operating System of *Berkeley Software Distribution* (BSD) UNIX. This work was also being funded by DARPA. Most of the early commercial versions of UNIX were based on BSD UNIX, or they at least used the TCP/IP implementation from BSD UNIX. Historically, TCP/IP has thus been considered an integral part of UNIX.

In the mid to late 1980s, a number of commercial companies, including The Wollongong Group and FTP Software, created TCP/IP solutions for personal computers. Products such as these have brought Internet applications such as FTP, Telnet, and electronic mail to personal computer users.

The past few years have seen an exponential growth in the use of TCP/IP software on PCs for two main reasons. First and most obvious, Internet access requires TCP/IP; therefore, if you are using a PC and want to connect to the Internet, you must utilize the TCP/IP protocol. Second, the advent of client-server computing, as well as the move to UNIX servers for database access, has affected the PC market as it relates to TCP/IP—both require that the client (PC) communicating with the server use the same communication protocol, which in this case is TCP/IP.

TCP/IP, unlike NetWare, has had a universal addressing scheme from the beginning, where each host computer has a unique address. Also, as discussed later in this chapter, addressing in TCP/IP networks allows for the creation of addressing hierarchies using subnetting.

This hierarchy is similar in concept to the zip codes used by the United States postal system. The first characters in the zip code identify the general region where the letter is destined. Reading into the zip code further identifies the destination more precisely, and finally identifies the local post office that will receive the letter and coordinate delivery to your home.

TCP/IP, therefore, is well-suited for building large internetworks such as the Internet. Increased sophistication brings increased complexity for the network administrators, however. Some comparisons to NetWare addressing are illustrated to help make TCP/IP addressing easier to understand.

 The explosion of the Internet has made TCP/IP even more successful in the last few years. Its success, however, is getting in the way of its growth. The increased number of TCP/IP-based networks is quickly growing beyond the expectation and design considerations built into the addressing scheme—the pool of available IP addresses is rapidly nearing exhaustion. Standards for the next generation of IP—*IP next generation* (IPng)—are currently being developed. IPng is being designed to address this problem, and will expand the address space to handle future needs.

For more information, please see the section, "Future Directions of TCP/IP," toward the end of this chapter. There are also ways to connect your LANs to the Internet that can significantly reduce the number of IP addresses that you need. See Chapter 4, "Adding TCP/IP to NetWare LANs," for further discussion.

For a network administrator chartered with providing Internet access, many new tasks and technologies must be understood. The critical foundation to understanding these technologies is the seven-layer

OSI model, which is covered in the next section. This model provides a framework on which to organize the various protocols discussed in this chapter.

Overview—The Layers of TCP/IP

In order to understand TCP/IP, it is best to compare it with the OSI model. The *Open Systems Interconnections* (OSI) model was developed in 1978 as part of the *International Standardization Organization* (ISO) standards activities. As shown in figure 3.1, the OSI reference model provides a tool and framework for discussion of different protocols and communications systems.

| Application |
| Presentation |
| Session |
| Transport |
| Network |
| Data Link |
| Physical |

Figure 3.1

The OSI reference model.

The TCP/IP protocol suite can be compared to the OSI model, but like several other communications protocols, its layers don't correspond exactly to the OSI's seven layers. Figure 3.2 shows the TCP/IP protocol suite, which is best described as a five-layer model.

Figure 3.2

The TCP/IP protocol suite.

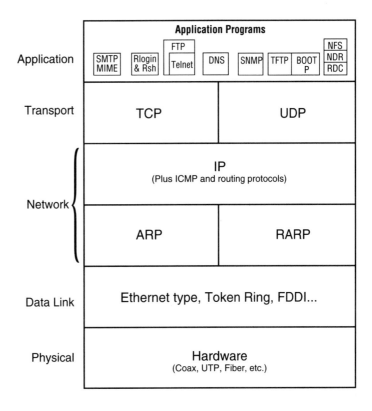

In the TCP/IP protocol suite, there are no layers that map to the Session and Presentation layers of the OSI reference model. Each layer in the protocol suite builds on the layer below it and provides additional capabilities to the layer above it, while hiding the complexities of the underlying mechanism. The five layers of TCP/IP are as follows:

→ Physical

→ Data Link

→ Network

→ Transport

→ Application

Physical Layer

The physical layer is responsible for bit transmission between one node and the next. It is the actual cabling (or wireless carrier) that connects the nodes. This layer deals with issues related to interfacing to the transmission media, encoding of the data signal, voltage, current, connector sizes, shapes, and pinouts. The physical layer is not actually part of the TCP/IP protocol suite.

TCP/IP is media-independent, and one of its key strengths is its ability to run over almost any type of media. The flexibility that is built into the TCP/IP suite allows it to perform well on a broad range of media—from slow speed dial-up serial lines to very high speed fiber-optic cables. Because of its media independence, you will find TCP/IP running over all types of physical media, including coaxial cable, twisted-pair cable, fiber-cable, packet radio, satellite, etc.

Data Link Layer

Layer 2, the data link layer, controls the access to the physical medium. It contains the protocols appropriate to the various physical layers. Following are some examples of these protocols:

➜ Ethernet protocols that define the format of data as it is sent over the various media supported by it, including coaxial cable, twisted pair, and fiber-optic cable

➜ Token Ring protocols that define transmission over shielded and unshielded twisted pair cabling

➜ X.25 or HDLC running over high-speed serial lines

➜ FDDI protocols for running over fiber-optic cable

The data link layer sends and receives information in logical units called *frames*. At the data link level, frames are marked with special bit patterns that identify the beginning and end of the frame. As discussed in the section, "Understanding SLIP and PPP," later in this chapter, some media-like, serial lines don't send data in frames—the framing must be created by the software. Most data link layers also provide some error control that detects errors in the data frame.

Ethernet Frames

As an example, let's look at an Ethernet frame. Figure 3.3 shows the fields of the Ethernet frame. The number above each field indicates the number of bytes in that field. The preamble field alerts all stations on a bus that a message is coming. The source address and destination address are used for station-to-station communication. This source and destination addresses, often described as the hardware or MAC address, are addresses that are typically burned into the memory of the network interface card. In Ethernet, the first six characters of the address are assigned by the *Institute of Electronic and Electrical Engineers* (IEEE) to a manufacturer, while the next six characters are assigned sequentially to each new board or interface. This guarantees that each interface has a unique Ethernet address, and also provides indication of the vendor who manufactured the board or interface. For example, the address 0000.0c08.9f04 identifies that this device was manufactured by Cisco Systems because the first six characters of the address, 0000.0c, identify the address prefix assigned to Cisco Systems.

8	6	6	2	46-1500	4
Preamble	Destination Address	Source Address	Type or Length	Data	FCS

Figure 3.3

The Ethernet frame.

n o t e A listing of current hardware vendor codes is published in RFC 1700.

In the case of Ethernet, two types of packets can be used—Ethernet_II (or version 2) packets and IEEE 802.3 packets. The significant difference between these two formats is apparent in the next field: Type or Length.

In Ethernet_II, this field represents the protocol type, such as TCP/IP or DECnet, for data in the data field. This identifies to the layer above—the network layer—what network protocol is being used.

In IEEE 802.3, this field represents the length of the data field. In IEEE 802.3, a *Service Access Point* (SAP) field in the data section identifies the data type. The SAP identifies the network protocol in use for 802.3 packets.

This difference causes an incompatibility between IEEE 802.3 and Ethernet_II. In order for two devices to communicate with each other on the same network, they must use the same frame type. However, the good news is that software drivers have the ability to identify and distinguish between the types of Ethernet frames because of the fact that all of the Ethernet-II data types are invalid lengths for the 802.3 length field. For this reason, a single interface can support both types of packets. TCP/IP uses Ethernet_II frames, while IPX defaults to IEEE 802.3 framing, but can actually use either type of framing. It is very common to configure a NetWare client workstation to utilize ODI drivers with Ethernet 802.3 framing for IPX and Ethernet-II framing for TCP/IP.

Understanding SLIP and PPP

Serial Line IP (SLIP) and *Point-to-Point Protocol* (PPP) are both layer 2, or data link layer, protocols. They deserve special attention here due to their newfound importance and recent large-scale acceptance in the wide-area networking environment.

SLIP and PPP enable any stand-alone or networked computer to connect directly to the Internet over serial communication lines. As discussed previously in the section on the data link layer, most data link media sends information in frames and provides some error-checking mechanisms. This is not true of serial lines. Serial lines only transmit one byte at a time with no framing. SLIP, available only for asynchronous connections such as analog modem communication, is a very simple framing scheme for putting IP packets on a serial line. It can only transmit IP, however, and therefore cannot be used by other network protocols such as IPX, as shown in figure 3.4. Because of its simplicity, it does not provide any features required to troubleshoot connection problems. Detailed information on SLIP can be found in RFC 1055.

PPP, on the other hand, is a full-featured serial-line protocol that works on both asynchronous and synchronous links, indicating that PPP can be used not only for dial-up analog connections, but also for dial-up digital links such as ISDN and dedicated connections such as point-to-point circuits. Unlike SLIP, PPP can work with other protocols besides IP at the layer 3 level, including NetWare's IPX protocol (see fig. 3.4). Detailed information on PPP can be found in RFCs 1661, 1662, 1663, and 1618.

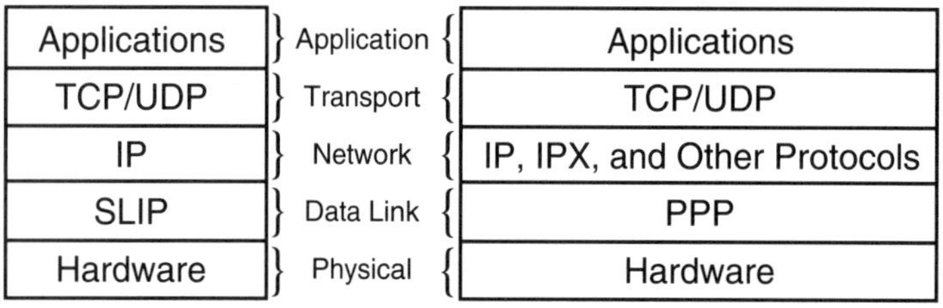

Applications	} Application {	Applications
TCP/UDP	} Transport {	TCP/UDP
IP	} Network {	IP, IPX, and Other Protocols
SLIP	} Data Link {	PPP
Hardware	} Physical {	Hardware

Figure 3.4

SLIP and PPP protocols in the five-layer TCP/IP protocol suite.

In addition to offering specific security options over SLIP, PPP also offers flexible mechanisms to implement a wide variety of address assignment policies. Dynamic address assignment is a major issue for IAPs. For these reasons, many IAPs are moving away from SLIP and are only offering PPP access, especially over analog dial-up links.

Network Layer

The network layer, which is often referred to as the internetwork layer, is the most important layer in the TCP/IP protocol suite. In the TCP/IP protocol suite, IP is the main protocol at this layer. This layer implements all of the IP addressing and routing. These addresses, as you see later in this chapter, are assigned by the network administrator and not related to the hardware or MAC address. In addition, other protocols—including ARP and RARP, which deal with lower-level issues and routing protocols—are also implemented at this layer.

The routing of packets across networks occurs in this layer, with packets being the primary information unit. Packets are routed based on a device's network address, which is different than the physical address (i.e., Ethernet address), as defined in the data link layer.

Internet Protocol

The *Internet Protocol* (IP), the main protocol in the network layer, routes packets sent to it by the higher-layer protocol (TCP and UDP) through an internetwork, which may consist of many different kinds of data-link and physical layers. The IP protocol is characterized by the following three features:

→ It is connectionless.

→ It is unreliable.

→ It offers best-effort delivery.

IP is called *connectionless* because each packet is treated independently from others. IP adds necessary header information to allow each packet to be correctly routed to its destination. Imagine a workstation retrieving files from a server using FTP. If a workstation sends three packets, for example, they may travel over different paths and get reassembled at the final destination, as shown in figure 3.5.

The IP service is *unreliable* because it does not guarantee delivery. The packet might be lost, duplicated, delayed, or delivered out of order. The IP service does not detect these conditions, nor does it inform the sender or the receiver about them.

Figure 3.5

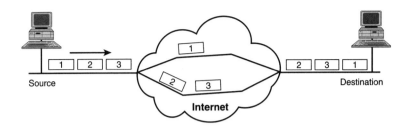

Connectionless delivery
of IP datagrams.

The IP service's delivery is considered *best-effort* because it does not discard packets at will. It only makes an attempt to deliver, and when underlying networks fail or become too congested, the result is unreliable transmissions.

The closest analogy in everyday life of the IP service is third-class mail from the U.S. postal service. In most cases, third-class mail reaches its destination, but the U.S. postal service does not guarantee delivery. If the recipient has changed his or her address, the U.S. postal service does not inform the sender that the delivery of mail didn't occur.

Services Provided by IP

IP provides the following basic services:

→ It defines the exact format of data as it passes through a TCP/IP network.

→ It breaks up (fragments) and reassembles the packets if needed to meet the requirements of the underlying data link layer.

→ It performs the routing function, which means choosing the most efficient path over which to send the data.

→ It specifies rules as to how hosts and gateways on the Internet should handle packets, how and when to generate error messages, and the conditions in which packets can be discarded.

IP Packet Structure

Figure 3.6 shows the IP packet structure. The Version field specifies the IP version number. The current IP protocol version is 4—most of the current TCP/IP products on the market today are compliant with this version number. The next generation IP, typically referred to as IP next generation or IPng, will be version 6 or 7.

 Just like in an ordinary letter, the most important information in an IP packet is the source and destination address.

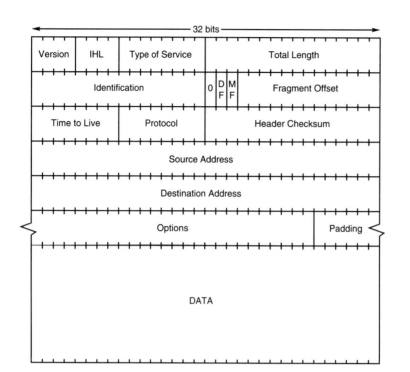

32 bits

Version	IHL	Type of Service	Total Length		
Identification			0 DF MF	Fragment Offset	
Time to Live	Protocol		Header Checksum		
Source Address					
Destination Address					
Options				Padding	
DATA					

Figure 3.6

The structure of the IP packet.

Understanding IP Addressing

Every computer or device connected to the Internet and running TCP/IP protocol has a unique address, referred to as its *IP address*. A computer or device could be a multi-user system like a UNIX or mainframe computer, a personal computer, or a hardware device like a router. If a computer or device has more than one network interface, each interface will have an IP address. IP addresses, like telephone numbers, are unique. IP addresses make network addresses independent of the underlying topologies or hardware addresses.

Like all network layer addresses, an IP address is generally divided into two parts—the network number and the host number, as shown in figure 3.7.

The network number must be unique within the internetwork in which you will be communicating. In the case of NetWare, for example, IPX numbers must be unique within an internetwork of NetWare servers and clients.

The same is true with the Internet—the network address must be unique. The unique IP network number is assigned by InterNIC Registration service. You may get your IP network number directly from the InterNIC or from your Internet Service Provider. See the section, "Obtaining an IP Address and Domain Name," later in this chapter for details on the InterNIC and obtaining unique network numbers.

IP addresses are 32 bits long, and are broken down into four octets or bytes. The IP protocol regards these addresses as binary numbers, with each of

Figure 3.7

Network layer addresses have two parts—a network number and a host number.

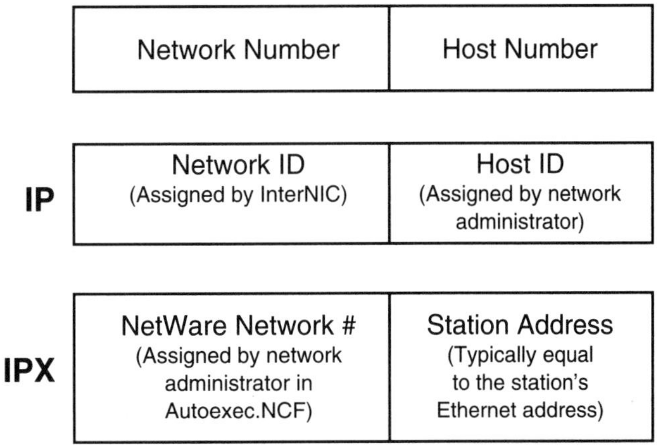

Network Number	Host Number

IP

Network ID (Assigned by InterNIC)	Host ID (Assigned by network administrator)

IPX

NetWare Network # (Assigned by network administrator in Autoexec.NCF)	Station Address (Typically equal to the station's Ethernet address)

these bytes having eight bits. As binary numbers, these bytes or octets range from 00000000 to 11111111. Table 3.1 illustrates the value of each of the digits in a binary number.

In decimal representation, the binary number 00000000 is 0 and the binary number 11111111 is 255. A table has been provided in Appendix B, "IP Subnetting and Binary Conversion Tables," to assist in the conversion of binary numbers to and from decimal representation.

 n o t e As an example, the binary number 10101111 can be represented in decimal format by adding the values of each of the characters of the binary number that have a value of 1. The binary number 10101111 has a 1 in the 1st, 3rd, 5th, 6th, 7th, and 8th characters. The values of these characters are 128, 32, 8, 4,

2, and 1. If you add these together, you have the value 175. Therefore, the binary number 10101111 in decimal representation is 175.

Unfortunately, working with numbers in binary is not a familiar task for most network administrators. For simplicity, IP addresses are stated in what is referred to as *dotted decimal format*, which is a series four numbers (0 to 255) separated by decimal points. Therefore, the lowest possible Internet address is:

0.0.0.0

while the highest possible address is:

255.255.255.255

Table 3.1 Determining Decimal Values of Binary Numbers

Binary Number	1st	2nd	3rd	4th	5th	6th	7th	8th
Decimal Value	128	64	32	16	8	4	2	1

In order to rationalize assigning the Internet addresses to companies of all sizes, the original designers of the TCP/IP protocols have broken IP addresses into different classes, as discussed in the next section.

Classes of IP Addresses

As mentioned earlier, an IP address consists of two parts—the network number (net ID) and host number (host ID). In order to make effective use of the IP address space, different classes of IP addresses have been created. There are five classes of Internet addresses, depending on the available network address range, as shown in figure 3.8.

Class A addresses have a 7-bit network ID and a 24-bit host ID. Thus, there can only be 127 ($2^7 - 1$) class A addresses, which have been exhausted long time ago. The networks with class A can have maximum of 16,777,216 (2^{24}) hosts, but two of the possible numbers (all 0s and all 1s in binary) are reserved (see the section on reserved addresses later in this chapter). This allows for a maximum of 16,777,214 hosts.

Class B addresses, suitable for large companies, consist of a 14-bit network ID and a 16-bit host ID. There can be a maximum of 16,383 ($2^{14} - 1$) class B addresses. Class B networks can have a maximum of ($2^{16} - 2$) 65,534 possible hosts. Most of the class B addresses have also been exhausted, leaving class C as the only choice for companies that are now seeking Internet addresses.

Class C addresses consist of 21-bit network ID and 8-bit host ID. Therefore, there can be a maximum of 2,097,152 (2^{21}) class C addresses, with only 254 ($2^8 - 2$) host addresses.

Class D and E addresses are not assigned, with class D reserved for multicasting and class E reserved for future use.

The following table summarizes the number of networks and host addresses in each of the three assignable network classes.

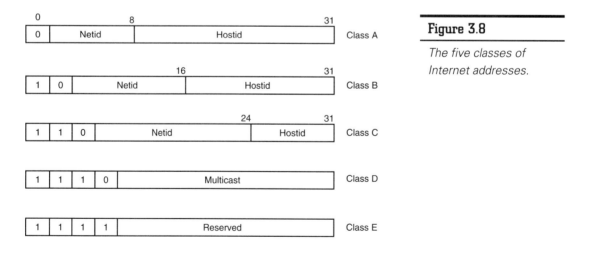

Figure 3.8

The five classes of Internet addresses.

Communications and Application Software

Table 3.2 Class A, B, and C Addresses—Number of Networks versus Number of Nodes

Address Class	First Octet Range(Decimal)	Number of Networks	Number of Nodes
A	1-127	127	16,277,214
B	128-191	16,383	65,534
C	192-223	2,097,151	254

Figure 3.9 shows an example of IP addressing for two hypothetical networks. Network Alpha has a network address of 192.42.5 assigned to it, while Network Beta has the address 129.85 assigned to it.

Table 3.3 shows that when you convert the dotted decimal format of the network address to binary format, you can tell from the high order bits (shown in **bold type)** what IP address class each address is. Given its particular address class, the underlined portion is the network ID portion, while the *italic portion* is the host ID portion.

Figure 3.9

Sample IP addresses for two hypothetical networks.

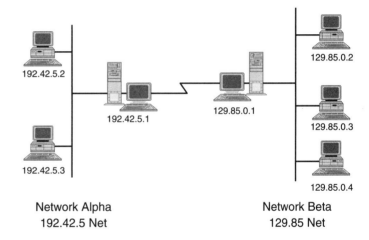

192.42.5.2

192.42.5.1

192.42.5.3

129.85.0.1

129.85.0.2

129.85.0.3

129.85.0.4

Network Alpha
192.42.5 Net

Network Beta
129.85 Net

Table 3.3   Addressing Configuration for Networks Alpha and Beta

Network	Network Alpha	Network Beta
Address in dotted decimal format	192.42.5.0	129.85.0.0
Address in binary format	**110** 00000 00101010 00000101 *00000000*	**10** 000001 01010101 *00000000 00000000*
IP address class	Class C	Class B
Number of hosts possible	254	65,534

Thus, the Network Beta 129.85 can grow to 65,534 nodes, while the Network Alpha, like most other class C addresses, can only grow to 254 hosts. If you apply for an IP address, you are most likely to get a class C address, which is limited to 254 hosts.

All devices on a physical network must have IP addresses using the same net ID, but a unique host ID. Therefore, all of the devices on network Beta would have an IP address beginning with 129.85. It is highly unlikely, however, that a network would be implemented with 65,534 devices on a single network segment, particularly if this network was spread out among a number of geographically dispersed locations. Instead, this internetwork would be made up of a number of individual networks. A mechanism known as *subnetting* is thus employed to further divide its assigned address space into multiple logical networks.

Subnetting

Subnetting allows an organization to further divide the host ID portion of its assigned address space into separate logical networks. The *assigned address space* is the range of allowable addresses

within the assigned network address. For example, if your assigned address is 192.42.5, then the allowable address range is 192.42.5.0 to 192.42.5.255. For organizations with more than one physical network, subnetting is required to make the networks appear as one to the outside world. For organizations with only one physical TCP/IP network, however, subnetting is not needed.

For example, the Network Beta from figure 3.9 may have three separate Ethernet networks—this is illustrated in figure 3.10. In this case, the organization may choose to use the third octet (the high byte of their host ID) to represent which Ethernet network a host is on. By doing this, it can now have 254 subnets, with up to 254 hosts on each subnet (see fig. 3.10).

Subnetting has no significance for people on the outside of the local network. The outside systems only see Network Beta as one network with a network address of 129.85. When an organization subnets its address space, it can select the number of bits to allocate to the subnet space and the host space. There are several guidelines which must be considered in subnetting your address space.

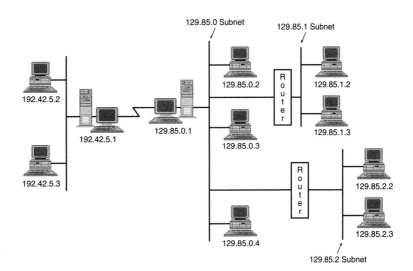

First, you need to determine how many of the host bits should be used for subnetting. Appendix B provides tables indicating the suitable number of subnet mask bits, the number of subnets each option will allow for, and the number of hosts or IP devices that can be on each subnet.

Second, in selecting what subnet numbers can be used, it is suggested that a subnet address of all 0s and all 1s be avoided. By doing this, you will avoid specific addresses that are reserved. These reserved addresses are discussed in detail in the section titled "Reserved Addresses—Broadcasts and Subnet Addresses."

Network Beta could have been subnetted to have seven bits of subnet space and nine bits of host space. This would allow for 126 subnets, with 510 hosts each. A *subnet mask* is used to identify what portion of the address is to be used as the logical network address (network plus subnet portion). In the example in figure 3.10, Network Beta's subnet mask would be 255.255.255.0. This specifies that the last octet is the host name, and that the first three octets make up the net and subnet portion.

Let's look at another example. You have been given a network ID of 202.192.156 from the InterNIC. This is a class C address, so it has eight bits of host ID space that you can subnet. Your company has only two locations with three workstations each, but is expected to grow to about 10 locations in the coming years. It is also expected that there will be less than 14 addressable IP nodes at any single site. The first task is to decide the network mask, which in this case could be the first four bits of the host ID available (see fig. 3.11).

Therefore, subnet A's address bits could be 0001, which will mean that your company's first location will have the address of 202.192.156.16. All other nodes can be assigned addresses with the last four bits varied. Similarly, subnet B's address bits could be 0010, giving an address of 202.192.156.32. The other nodes can be assigned addresses again by varying the last four bits. The subnet mask in this example would be 255.255.255.240. This specifies that the last four bits of the octet is the host name, and the first three octets and the first four bits of the last octet make up the net and subnet portion. (Binary 1111 0000 equals 240 decimal.)

Figure 3.11 shows the 202.192.156 network connected to the Internet via a gateway and the two subnets.

```
202.192.156.  0000  0000
                ↑
              Subnet
```

Subnet-A
```
202.192.156.  0001  0000 = 202.192.156.16
```

Subnet-A's node addressing
```
202.192.156.  0001  0001 = 202.192.156.17
202.192.156.  0001  0010 = 202.192.156.18
202.192.156.  0001  0011 = 202.192.156.19
                     1111
```

Subnet-B
```
202.192.156.  0010  0000 = 202.192.156.32
```

Subnet-B's node addressing
```
202.192.156.  0010  0001 = 202.192.156.33
202.192.156.  0010  0010 = 202.192.156.34
```

Figure 3.11

Subnet and network addressing.

Reserved Addresses—Broadcasts and Subnet Addresses

Addresses of all 0s or all 1s (binary) have special meaning in IP addresses. A host address of all 1s, which would be 255 in decimal representation in the case of a class C address, or a class B address with an 8-bit subnet, indicates a "broadcast." If the broadcast address is used, data is sent to all hosts on the subnet. All 0s are reserved for machines that do not know all or part of their own host address. For example, a diskless workstation might send out an address request to a bootP or address server using an address of all 0s. The server would then respond and provide the TCP/IP address for the diskless workstation. In some past implemen-tations, all 0s were also used for broadcast addresses. For these reasons, host addresses should never be all 0s or 1s.

Mapping IP Addresses to Physical Addresses (ARP and RARP)

As you saw earlier in the section, "Understanding IP Addressing," each host is assigned a 32-bit address that is used when sending and receiving packets. The IP address hides the complexity of the hardware address from the upper layer. However, there has to be a way to map the physical hardware addresses to the network address. As you know, Ethernet has a 48-bit physical address assigned by the manufacturer of the Ethernet NIC. To map the 48-bit physical address to the 32-bit IP address, the *Address Resolution Protocol* (ARP) was implemented. ARP enables a host to find the physical address of a target host on the same physical network if only the target's IP address is known. ARP hides the network physical address from the IP layer, enabling you to assign any IP address without consideration for the physical address. A diskless workstation can use the *Reverse Address Resolution Protocol* (RARP) to determine its IP address. RARP communicates with the server through the workstation's physical address to obtain its IP address.

Role of the Domain Name System

Which is easier to remember—1-800-IWARECOM or 1-800-492-3266? What about this—204.156.137.36 or internetware.com? "Internetware.com" is the domain name for an equivalent IP address of 204.156.137.36. Domain names are English names that have been mapped to an IP address. Every machine on the Internet has a domain name address, just like it has an IP address.

The domain name is comprised of a minimum of two parts, with each part being separated by a period. The last part indicates a group to which the domain belongs, such as .com, or .edu. The second-to-last part indicates the company or an institution name, such as Novell in novell.com or Stanford in stanford.edu.

A machine's domain name, for example, may be pauls@mktg.abc.com. This indicates that the machine's domain name is pauls, and that it belongs to the marketing group at ABC company, which is a commercial organization (see fig. 3.12). A standard electronic mail address includes the recipient's name, along with the host name and domain name. For example, margief@dvlpmnt.mafrdlds.com indicates that margief is the mail recipient at the host dvlpmnt at mafrdlds, which is a commercial organization.

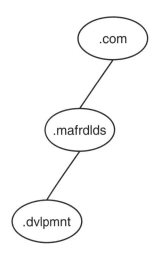

Figure 3.12

The domain name hierarchy.

The domain name could be maximum of 255 characters, with each part not to exceed 63 characters. Domain names can have any number of parts, as long as they do not exceed these limits. The domain names are not case-sensitive—in fact, it is customary to write domain names in small letters. The domain names are categorized based on geography, as well as industry segments. In the U.S., geographical categorization has not been very popular; however, most non-U.S.-based organizations do use geographical schemes, such as .ca representing Canada and .jp representing Japan.

With the geographical categorization, a domain name may look like this:

stevef@abc.redlands.ca.us

which indicates the user is stevef, who works at ABC company, which is located in Redlands, which is a city in California, which is a state in the U.S.

The following lists the most common domain names used in the U.S., along with some examples of international domains:

edu	Institutes of higher education
com	Commercial firms
gov	Government agencies
mil	U.S. military
org	General non-commercial organizations
net	Computer networks
int	International organizations
us	United States (not widely used)
uk	United Kingdom

ca	Canada
ja	Japan
au	Australia
cn	China
fl	Finland
fr	France
de	Germany
hk	Hong Kong
in	India
kr	South Korea
kp	North Korea
mx	Mexico
nl	Netherlands
nz	New Zealand
sg	Singapore
es	Spain
se	Sweden

By looking at someone's IP address, it is impossible to derive their domain name, or vice versa, because no direct correlation exists between the IP addresses and domain names. The one exception is that they are linked through an entry in a database stored on a DNS server. This is similar to people's names and telephone numbers—there is no direct relationship between people's names and telephone numbers, but you could consult a white or yellow page directory to find out the telephone number for any individual or business that has a phone.

A *Domain Name Server* (DNS) is used to map the domain names with the IP addresses. DNS is a dis-

tributed directory service, which means that no one machine stores all of the domain name to IP address mapping information. Each domain name server only contains information about mappings of the domains one level below it. There are separate root servers for the groups, such as .com or .edu. These root servers are duplicated and maintained at different locations with a full backup at all times (as a standard part of DNS).

 There is no relationship between a four-part IP **t i p** address to that of a four-part domain name.

To demonstrate this process, let's use a simple example. If you send an inquiry about a particular domain name like www.Novell.com, the first request goes to the .com root server. The .com root server then sends the inquiry to Novell's domain name server, which in turn is aware of and recognizes its www server address. As shown in figure 3.13, User A's request goes first to the .com root server, which knows of Novell's DNS server. The root server sends a request to the DNS server, which knows the location of the www.Novell.com server. From this point on, User A's workstation knows the address of the server www.Novell.com, and so all queries are redirected directly to that server.

In most cases, you will find DNS lookup to be very fast, which is due to caching of the most frequently used remote names in the domain name server of the local site. In addition to IP address information, DNS servers also store special information about mail users, which are discussed further in Chapter 6, "Internet Application Servers." For example, the message for pauls@mktg.abc.com will also get to him if it was addressed as pauls@abc.com. The

Figure 3.13

*A DNS request from a
user to a server.*

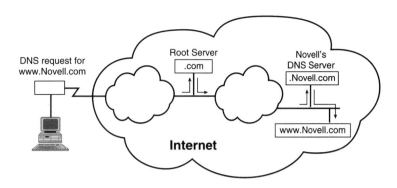

reason is that ABC company also maintains a do-main name server that is aware of all of its internal names.

Does this mean that every company with an Internet address of its own requires a DNS server at its site? Not necessarily! Please see the next section for details.

Where to Locate Your DNS Hardware

It is not always essential or advisable to have your own domain name server. Many IAPs offer DNS services whereby they may advertise for your company's domain name. For example, assume a company called IWare with a domain name of iware.com wants its IAP to host its domain name server.

As shown in figure 3.14, if Alan at abc.com sends a packet for pauls@iware.com, then the first domain request is made to the root .com server, which contains the IAP's domain name server address. The IAP's domain server would then resolve the IP address mapping for iware.com. Once Alan's workstation gets the IP address for iware.com, the communication can occur just as it would on any WAN.

For smaller companies, it is a common practice to host the domain name service at the IAP's site. This way, the local site does not need to run and administer a DNS server that is normally UNIX-based. Most IAPs have high-speed communications connections such as T1 or even T3 circuits to the Internet, and can resolve names even if your site or server is down.

Figure 3.14

*A DNS server at the
IAP's site.*

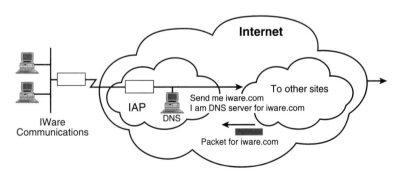

For companies with larger networks or multiple locations and only one gateway/router advertising the address, it is best to host the Domain Name Server at the central site. Figure 3.15 shows a more complex network, where the domain name server is located at the local site. The DNS server can be hosted on a NetWare server or UNIX server. The most common and well-known implementations of DNS are available on the UNIX operating system. With NetWare/IP, Novell also offers DNS server as an NLM.

Routing of IP Datagrams

Routers are the most common gateways in use today. A *gateway* is a device that connects two or more networks. A *network*, in this case, could be a *local area network* (LAN) segment or a complete *wide area network* (WAN). A host, on the other hand, usually connects directly to one physical network. A *host* is any computer connected to the Internet that has an Internet or IP address and can host Internet applications.

The Internet is composed of multiple physical networks interconnected by gateways. All of the gateways on the Internet form a cooperative and interconnected structure. Datagrams pass from one gateway to another until they reach a gateway that can deliver the datagram directly. Therefore, all the gateways maintain IP or Internet routing tables. The routing tables of a company's internal network can be very complex, depending on the size of the network.

Connecting a small network to the Internet is simple, however—this is because the complexity of building the routing information is transferred to the IAP's *Point of Presence* (POP), as shown in figure 3.16. The POP is the physical facility used by the IAP to connect your network. When a user sends an IP datagram from the source address—destined for another network (the destination address)—the original network's router, G1 in figure 3.16, sends the datagram to the next nearest router, G2. This router is located at the IAP's POP. At the POP is another router that forwards this packet through other intermediate gateways, if needed, until the packet reaches its destination.

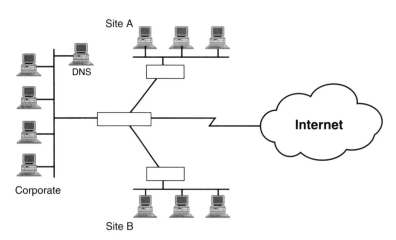

Figure 3.15

A DNS server at the company site.

Figure 3.16

IP datagram delivery.

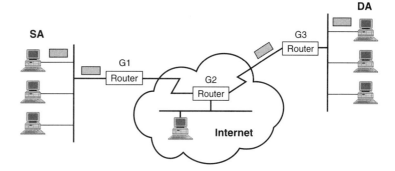

 There are many routing protocols in TCP/IP, such as *Routing Information Protocol* (RIP) and *Open Shortest Path First* (OSPF), which are used to exchange routing table information between gateways and hosts. These protocols are beyond the scope of this book. Please consult any of the books on routing for details on these protocols. Most NetWare administrators that are only concerned with connecting to the Internet don't require expertise in protocols such as RIP and OSPF. NetWare administrators involved with setting up routers for private networks need an extensive knowledge of these technologies, however.

Internet Control Message Protocol

The *Internet Control Message Protocol* (ICMP) is an integral part of IP and travels in the data portion of the IP datagrams. If every gateway on the Internet worked all the time, communication would occur flawlessly. If a gateway cannot route or deliver a datagram, however, it needs to instruct the original source to take action to avoid or correct the problem. ICMP enables gateways to send error or control messages to other gateways and hosts. One of the most frequently used debugging tools in the

Internet is called *Ping*, which is basically an ICMP echo request and reply message. With Ping, you can determine whether the host is reachable or not.

Obtaining an IP Address and Domain Name

Domain names are assigned on a first come, first serve basis. Therefore, if your company has not applied for a domain name yet, it should do so now before someone else claims the same name that your company has requested. The famous case of MTV claiming its mtv.com domain while someone else had already gotten that name is a clear indication to companies that they should stake claim to their domain name before it is taken to avoid costly legal battles. At the time of this writing, there is no charge for obtaining a domain name, but this might change by the time this book is published. Because of an extensive backlog of domain name requests, it now takes in excess of six weeks to register a domain name.

There are two ways to obtain domain name and IP addresses within the U.S., as follows:

→ Get your IAP to apply for you

→ Contact InterNIC via e-mail, FAX, or mail at the following address:

Via electronicmail: H O S T M A S T E R @ INTERNIC.NET

Via telephone: (703) 742-4777

Via facsimile: (703) 742-4811

Via postal mail: Network Solutions
InterNICRegistration
Services
505 Huntmar Park Drive
Herndon, VA 22070

If you are new to the Internet, it is strongly suggested to leave the task of applying domain names and IP addresses to your IAP. In many cases, the IAP may provide IP addresses from its own pool, rather than getting separate IP addresses for you. Before you use the IP addresses provided by the IAP for your internal network, please make sure that you will be able to use the same addresses if you had to change your Internet access provider for any reason at a later date.

Transport Layer

The two most important protocols in layer 4, the transport layer, are the *User Datagram Protocol* (UDP) and the *Transmission Control Protocol* (TCP). Both protocols use IP as their network layer protocol. UDP is a connectionless protocol that is useful when an application does not require sequencing of packets or 100 percent reliability of delivery of packets, or is willing to provide these in the application. Examples of applications that use UDP are Sun's *Network File System* (NFS) and *Domain Name System* (DNS).

TCP is used by most applications because it provides a reliable data stream. When an application sends data to the TCP layer, it knows that the data sent to the destination will be correct 100 percent of the time. Applications that use TCP include *File Transfer Protocol* (FTP) and Virtual Terminal Protocol (Telnet).

User Datagram Protocol (UDP)

UDP, like IP, is also a connectionless and best-effort delivery system that uses IP to transport messages among machines. UDP adds the capability to differentiate among multiple destinations within a single computer. In addition to the IP destination address, UDP uses a set of abstract destination points called *protocol ports*. When a UDP message arrives, it also contains destination and source port numbers. The TCP/IP standards define certain ports, whereas others are assigned dynamically. Table 3.4 provides a list of well-known UDP ports. A complete list of all assigned port numbers is included in RFC 1700, which is published by the *Internet Assigned Numbers Authority* (IANA). IANA is the central coordinator for the assignment of unique parameter values for Internet protocols. The IANA is chartered by the *Internet Society* (ISOC) and the *Federal Network Council* (FNC) to act as the clearinghouse to assign and coordinate the use of numerous Internet protocol parameters.

Table 3.4 Common UDP Port Numbers

Port Number	Application	Description
7	ECHO	Echoes back the state
11	USERS	Provides list of active users
43	NICNAME	Provides "who is" service
53	DOMAIN	Domain Name Server (DNS)
67	BOOTPS	Bootstrap protocol server
68	BOOTPC	Bootstrap protocol client
69	TFTP	Trivial File Transfer Protocol
111	RPC	NFS is built on top of this Remote Procedure Call (RPC) port
161	SNMP	Simple Network Management Protocol (SNMP) net monitor

UDP provides multiplexing and demultiplexing functions for multiple applications running on a host.

UDP expects application software to add reliability mechanisms if it requires it. For some applications that do not require reliability, or that can add a simple reliability scheme, UDP is preferable because it is faster than TCP and requires less overhead due to not needing to set up a session prior to sending data. Many applications don't implement all of the necessary reliability and error-checking and correction mechanisms. Therefore, applications written to UDP may work well in small networks, but may fail or behave differently on a large network such as the Internet, where additional errors and packet loss could occur.

Transmission Control Protocol

Transmission Control Protocol (TCP) is the transport protocol of choice in the TCP/IP protocol suite because it provides reliable, full-duplex, and virtual connections. Unlike UDP, it is connection-oriented and therefore sets up a session between two machines before transmission. To achieve reliability, TCP uses a technique called *positive acknowledgment with retransmission*, which means that if data became lost in the transmission process, TCP would recognize the delivery failure by the acknowledgment (or lack thereof) and would retransmit the data.

TCP provides multiple virtual-circuit connections between two TCP hosts. The source port and destination port numbers identify the end-point processes in the TCP virtual circuit. Port numbers less than 256 are specified in the RFC 1700—their ports are called *well-known ports*. The rest of the ports can be assigned by applications on an as-needed basis. TCP and UDP ports share some common port numbers. In establishing security, users often use port numbers to restrict inbound and outbound access based on applications. Table 3.5 contains a list of some well-known TCP ports.

Some of the applications use UDP, while others use TCP protocol. Domain Name Server is the only application that can use either of the two protocols. Most Internet applications use TCP protocol because TCP takes care of error checking and retransmission. However, TCP adds more overhead than UDP, is slower than UDP, and is a lot more complex than UDP.

Table 3.5 Well-Known TCP Port Numbers

Port Number	Application	Description
7	ECHO	Echo data
20	FTP_DATA	File Transfer Protocol (FTP) data
21	FTP	FTP control
23	TELNET	Terminal connection program
25	SMTP	Simple Mail Transfer Protocol
43	WHOIS	Who Is
53	DOMAIN	Domain Name Server
79	FINGER	Finger protocol
103	X400	X.400 Mail service
119	NNTP	Network News Transfer Protocol
80	HTTP	HyperText Transmission Protocol

Application Layer

Up to this point, all of the layers of TCP/IP deal with getting raw data from one computer to another. No direct interaction with the user takes place until you reach the application layer. At the application layer, there are two types of applications—client applications and server applications. It is the client applications, like FTP, Telnet, and SMTP, with which users interact. Most TCP/IP applications operate in the client-server model. For example, the user runs an FTP application on a local machine, referred to as the FTP client, that connects to an FTP server on a remote machine. The client applications know how to contact servers based on the assigned protocol port number, such as 21 in the case of the control connection for FTP (see table 3.5).

Because many important applications and servers exist, Chapter 5, "Internet Applications," has been dedicated to the discussion of applications, and Chapter 6, "Internet Application Servers," covers details on some of the known servers.

The Future of TCP/IP

Due to the complexity of the TCP/IP protocol, address assignment and system management are time-consuming and requires a fair amount of expertise. A new standard called the *Dynamic Host Configuration Protocol* (DHCP) has been proposed to alleviate some of TCP/IP's address management and assignment complexities. DHCP is in its early stages, however, and suffers from lack of interoperability between different implementations and DNS. Microsoft has implemented DHCP in its Windows NT 3.5 systems, and that is integrated with its proprietary WINS names database. DHCP, an important milestone for making TCP/IP address-

ing easier, may not emerge as the panacea for dynamic addressing in the near future, as it requires changes to all of the TCP/IP client software.

The success of the Internet and thereby TCP/IP is creating a new problem—IP address depletion. As discussed before, it is highly unlikely that a company will be able to obtain a class B address. Obtaining a class C address is much more probable, but even then there is a restriction of 254 host addresses. To solve this problem, the next generation IP (IPng) has been proposed. It is anticipated that IPng specifications will be finalized later this year. IPng will overcome many limitations of IP and will have some enhanced features, such as the following:

→ Large available addresses—it will have 16-byte addressing

→ Automatic address assignment

→ Security with built-in encryption

→ Traffic prioritization

IPng, however, will have incompatibilities with the current version of IP. The most significant issue will be addressing—IPng will have a completely different addressing scheme than existing versions of TCP/IP. Part of the standards activities for IPng is planning the transition from the current version. There are still many details that need to be worked out. IPng is still very much in the design phases and will likely not have mass market acceptance until 1997.

Until IPng is released, therefore, you must implement the current version of IP. With proper planning, however, you can design your network so that you will be able to easily accommodate the next generation of IP.

Summary

You should now have a basic understanding of the important issues of IP addressing and domain naming. These are important to understand when connecting your Novell network to the Internet. Also covered in this chapter was a brief overview of the layers of the TCP/IP protocol suite, SLIP/PPP, and the future directions of TCP/IP. If you desire more in-depth information on these topics, there are numerous books that cover this information in detail.

With this basic information covered, the next chapter, "Adding TCP/IP to NetWare LANs," compares TCP/IP to the Novell SPX/IPX protocols and discusses adding TCP/IP to your Novell network.

4

Adding TCP/IP to NetWare LANs

T he language of the Internet is *Transmission Control Protocol/Internet Protocol* (TCP/IP), while the language spoken in NetWare LANs is *Sequenced Packet Exchange/Internetwork Packet Exchange* (SPX/IPX), even though NetWare servers also come bundled with TCP/IP protocol stack. For NetWare workstations to communicate with the Internet, therefore, they either need to learn TCP/IP or use a translator within the NetWare server to facilitate communication of NetWare workstations with the Internet.

The purpose of this chapter is to present and compare different alternatives for integrating TCP/IP into the NetWare environment so that all of the NetWare workstations can transparently connect to the Internet. This chapter also provides a brief comparison of TCP/IP and SPX/IPX protocols, in addition to information on a Windows Sockets programming interface called WINSOCK. This chapter is organized in the following manner:

➜ TCP/IP versus SPX/IPX protocols

➜ Understanding WINSOCK

➜ Bringing TCP/IP into NetWare LANs

➜ Criteria for selecting TCP/IP products

 note This chapter focuses on layer 1 of the Internet connectivity matrix.

7 SECURITY AND MANAGEMENT
6 Internet Access Providers
5 WAN Access Devices
4 WAN Access Services
3 Internet Application Servers
2 Internet Navigation Software
1 Network Communication Protocols

TCP/IP versus SPX/IPX Protocols

It is difficult to compare networking protocols without the interference of individual biases. TCP/IP experts tend to put down SPX/IPX because they feel it is proprietary. Even though SPX/IPX is on 60 percent of LAN-connected desktop workstations, many argue that TCP/IP will become the de facto desktop protocol because Microsoft is now bundling TCP/IP in its operating system, in addition to the SPX/IPX protocol. This simply means, however, that both services are now available to the end user. Microsoft and others recognize that the cost of migration for any NetWare site from SPX/IPX to TCP/IP is often prohibitive, especially when hundreds of workstations need to be upgraded.

SPX/IPX was originally derived from the *Xerox Networking Protocol* (XNS), which also formed the basis for 3Com's 3+ LAN operating system. TCP/IP, on the other hand, was originally developed by DARPA and is a well-published and open standard. It has been ported, therefore, to many computer systems. Novell bundles TCP/IP in the NetWare servers, but bundles SPX/IPX for both the NetWare servers and workstations. Both TCP/IP and SPX/IPX protocols have their own pros and cons, however—IPX is better suited for the LAN environment, whereas IP works extremely well for large, internetworked WANs.

Figure 4.1 provides a comparative overview of the TCP/IP and SPX/IPX protocols in relation to the OSI model.

These protocols can be compared at the following levels based on their similarities and differences:

➜ Data link and physical layers

➜ Network layer

➜ Transport layer

➜ Application layer

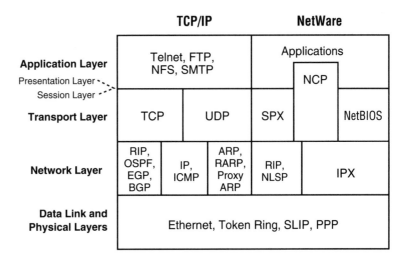

Figure 4.1

A comparison of TCP/IP and SPX/IPX protocols.

	TCP/IP			NetWare		
Application Layer	Telnet, FTP, NFS, SMTP			Applications		
Presentation Layer					NCP	
Session Layer						
Transport Layer	TCP		UDP	SPX		NetBIOS
Network Layer	RIP, OSPF, EGP, BGP	IP, ICMP	ARP, RARP, Proxy ARP	RIP, NLSP		IPX
Data Link and Physical Layers	Ethernet, Token Ring, SLIP, PPP					

Data Link and Physical Layers

At the data link and physical layers, TCP/IP and SPX/IPX are similar. Both protocols now work with the most common network topologies, such as Ethernet, Token Ring, FDDI, and others. There are four types of Ethernet packets: Ethernet-II, IEEE 802.3, IEEE 802.2, and SNAP Ethernet. Until NetWare 4.x, the default for IPX was 802.3 packets (Novell's modified version of IEEE 802.3), even though it could be configured to work with any of the packet types. With NetWare 4.x, the default Ethernet packet type for IPX is IEEE 802. IP, on the other hand, is primarily used with Ethernet-II type packets.

Network Layer

In addition to the core IP protocol, the network layer in the TCP/IP protocol includes address resolution protocols like *Address Resolution Protocol* (ARP) and *Reverse Address Resolution Protocol* (RARP), Internet message control protocols like *Internet* *Control Message Protocol* (ICMP), and routing protocols like *Routing Information Protocol* (RIP) and *Open Shortest Path First* (OSPF) Protocol.

There is no equivalent of ARP in the NetWare environment because IPX workstations, unlike IP, take their address from the physical address. See the section, "IP versus IPX Addressing," later in this chapter for more details. There is also no equivalent of ICMP in the NetWare environment.

IP versus IPX

At the network level, both IPX and IP possess the same characteristics. Both are connectionless datagram services on top of data link protocols, such as Ethernet and Token Ring. Both IP and IPX protocols expect their higher-level protocols or applications to provide the required error checking and correcting mechanisms. The addressing schemes for IPX and IP are very different, and their differences are discussed in the next section of this chapter. Both of these protocols have similar routing protocols, as discussed next.

Routing Protocols

The *Routing Information Protocol* (RIP) is the most commonly used routing protocol on both IPX and IP networks. Routing protocols such as RIP and OSPF are used to exchange routing table information between gateways and hosts. Routing tables help routers direct a packet to the right destination. RIP is suitable for small size networks because it imposes a large overhead in updating routing information among different routers.

RIP on IPX is different from that on IP networks, however, and no interoperability exists between these two RIPs, even though RIP on both protocols was derived from the XNS protocol. Although the IP protocol has many other routing protocol choices besides RIP, Novell has implemented a new routing protocol called the *NetWare Link State Protocol* (NLSP) to address some of the shortcomings present with RIP. NLSP is an enabling technology for building large internetworked NetWare LANs, and is being used as the basis for the joint Novell AT&T Network Connect Services, which will compete with the Internet and other online services. NLSP is available with version 4.02 of NetWare, and is similar in concept to the OSPF protocol.

Transport Layer

At the transport level, the TCP/IP protocol suite offers TCP and UDP protocols, while the SPX/IPX protocol suite offers SPX and NCP protocols.

TCP versus SPX

At the transport level, SPX and TCP possess similar characteristics. Both provide connection-oriented reliable services, for example, on top of their connectionless counterparts—IPX and IP respectively. Not all NetWare applications use SPX, just as not all IP applications use TCP. Applications written to TCP and SPX, however, don't have to deal with providing reliability mechanisms because that function is taken care of by these protocols. Some of the well-known applications such as FTP and Telnet use TCP, while Btrieve, a database bundled earlier with NetWare, is an example of a well-known application that uses SPX. Both TCP and SPX add additional overhead on the system, and are therefore not as fast as other protocols at this layer, such as UDP and NCP.

UDP versus IPX

The *User Datagram Protocol* (UDP) offers an alternative to the other transport layer protocol, TCP. UDP is a connectionless protocol, much like IPX, that is used in place of TCP in cases where either performance is more important than reliability, or reliability with UDP is easier to implement than with TCP. As discussed in Chapter 3, "Understanding TCP/IP," UDP provides an application port *multiplexing function*—a function that is performed by IPX in the NetWare environment. Even though UDP and IPX are not equivalent, UDP's multiplexing function is performed by IPX, eliminating the need for such a protocol in the NetWare environment.

NCP

The *NetWare Core Protocol* (NCP) provides its own reliability mechanisms, such as session control, error detection, and retransmission. NCP can thus work directly on top of IPX. In addition, NCP is used to implement NetWare's file services (file sharing, file locking, permissions), and print services (printer sharing, printer redirection).

There is no direct equivalent service to NCP in the IP protocol suite. *Network File System* (NFS) in the TCP/IP protocol provides some of the same services as NCP. NFS in the TCP/IP protocol model belongs to the application layer, while NCP extends into both the transport and application layers. The next section discusses the application layer differences between SPX/IPX and TCP/IP protocols.

Application Layer

The applications at this layer are not the same as the everyday applications for word processing and spreadsheets. This layer deals specifically with application protocols such as FTP, Telnet, NCP, NFS, SMTP, and MHS.

There is no real equivalent to nor a need for most of the Internet applications, such as FTP or Telnet, in the NetWare-only environment. As discussed in Chapter 5, "Internet Applications," Telnet is a terminal emulation application that is used only in multiuser operating systems like UNIX or DEC VMS. File transfer within the NetWare environment is handled by NCP, while TCP/IP uses FTP for that purpose.

The need for FTP and/or Telnet, however, arises in heterogeneous networks, wherein NetWare users must be able to access applications from UNIX or other multiuser hosts, as well as the Internet. Until recently, the only way for NetWare users to access FTP, Telnet, and other Internet applications was to load TCP/IP protocol on every NetWare workstation. Some innovative vendors like Internetware, however, are changing that by enabling NetWare users to run Internet applications on top of SPX/IPX. See the section, "Two Distinct Server-Based Approaches," later in this chapter for details.

The only application protocol for which there is some equivalency between TCP/IP and SPX/IPX is in the messaging protocols, which are discussed next.

Messaging Protocols

Both TCP/IP and SPX/IPX protocols have their own messaging protocols, called SMTP and MHS respectively, at the application layer. *Simple Mail Transfer Protocol* (SMTP) and *Message Handling System* (MHS) are equivalent in that both offer messaging services like message delivery, propagation, and messaging *Application Programming Interfaces* (API) for software developers to write messaging-enabled applications. SMTP is the mail standard for all Internet communication. All communication taking place between users on the Internet must therefore utilize the SMTP protocol. SMTP is also becoming a standard for corporate e-mail backbones. MHS, on the other hand, is a standard on all NetWare LANs because it is bundled with the NetWare software. Not all e-mail packages for NetWare LANs use MHS, however. Instead, e-mail systems like Lotus cc:Mail and Microsoft Mail have their own proprietary messaging standards. Chapter 6, "Internet Application Servers," provides more details on various e-mail systems and their Internet communication systems.

IP versus IPX Addressing

From detailed discussions of IP addressing in Chapter 3, it is obvious that IP addressing is fairly complex. In comparison, IPX addressing is almost automatic to the point that a detailed understanding is not critical for most NetWare administrators, except in cases of very large NetWare networks. This section discusses some similarities and differences between the IP and IPX protocols in the following areas:

→ Address size

→ Relationship to hardware addressing

- ➜ Address complexity
- ➜ Address registration service
- ➜ Address format

Address Size

IP addresses are 32 bits (4 bytes) long. Every node on the IP network, whether it is a server or a workstation, has a unique 32-bit address of its own. As discussed in Chapter 3, this address is comprised of net ID and host ID. On the other hand, IPX network addresses are 10 bytes long, with a 4-byte (32 bit) network number and a 6 byte (48 bit) node address. The possible pool of addresses in IPX is therefore much higher than in IP.

Relationship to Hardware Addressing

The 32-bit IP addresses have no direct correlation to the physical hardware addresses, which are 48 bits long. Therefore, the address resolution protocol is needed in IP to map hardware addresses to IP addresses. On the other hand, the IPX node address *is* the 48-bit physical hardware address. Therefore, every node on the NetWare LAN acquires the address of its hardware, making addressing simpler for NetWare nodes.

Addressing Complexity

Even though IPX addresses are longer than the IP addresses, they are much simpler to set up and manage. NetWare is a client-server system, where each node automatically gets its node address from its physical address, and its network number from its server. The network number for NetWare is much simpler to allocate than with IP—all of the 48-bit address space is available for the use of servers at a company because there is no central registration service. Even with a site that has 1,000

NetWare servers, it is much easier to find 1,000 unique network numbers.

Address Registration Service

For IP sites that want to connect to the Internet, a unique IP address is needed—this can be acquired from InterNIC, as discussed in Chapter 3. Unlike IP, NetWare has no such thing as universal addressing and registration. Novell has recently introduced a NetWare registry service; however, it is unlikely that most NetWare sites will rush to acquire a unique address because this requires changes to routing tables and server addresses.

Address Format

IP addresses are stated in dotted decimal format, while IPX addresses are stated in hexadecimal format. For example, an IP address may look like 209.154.50.5, while an IPX address may look like 01500003 or 1 or 1A.

Even though IP and IPX are two separate protocols, each with its own personality, it is possible to combine some layers of one protocol with the other. An example would be running all of the TCP/IP application protocols on top of the SPX/IPX transport or network layers. WINSOCK is one such specification that has been used by some vendors to provide interoperability of IPX with the TCP/IP applications. In fact, since WINSOCK has emerged as a standard for writing Windows applications in the TCP/IP environment, the next section is devoted to understanding WINSOCK.

Understanding WINSOCK

Windows Sockets, or WINSOCK, is an API defined at the session layer that simplifies the development of TCP/IP applications in the Microsoft Windows environment. WINSOCK is similar to the NetBIOS interface to which many networking applications have been developed. WINSOCK is derived from Berkeley Sockets network interface, as defined in version 4.1c of BSD UNIX. WINSOCK specification is endorsed by all major software vendors, including Novell and Microsoft.

WINSOCK is implemented as a *dynamic link library* (DLL) in a Windows environment, and it therefore does not require any conventional memory (DOS memory between 0 to 1 MB). DLLs are libraries of executable functions that link with a network application at the time of executing an application, rather than when the application is created, thus separating the application from the API.

As shown in figure 4.2, WINSOCK mediates between the TCP/IP applications and the TCP/IP protocol stack (transport and network layers). Therefore, WINSOCK is intended to make it easy for the TCP/IP application vendors to be compatible with different TCP/IP protocol stack implementations, as long as they are also WINSOCK-compatible. This is similar to the introduction of *Open Data-link Interface* (ODI) by Novell, which made it easy for the hardware vendors and TCP/IP protocol stack (transport and network layers) vendors to integrate their products with the NetWare environment.

Also shown in figure 4.2 are the other two standard driver interfaces—*Network Driver Interface Specification* (NDIS) and Packet driver. NDIS is another specification proposed by Microsoft that can be a substitute for ODI. Packet driver is a specification that is similar to ODI, and has been in use for TCP/IP solutions for PCs even before ODI was developed.

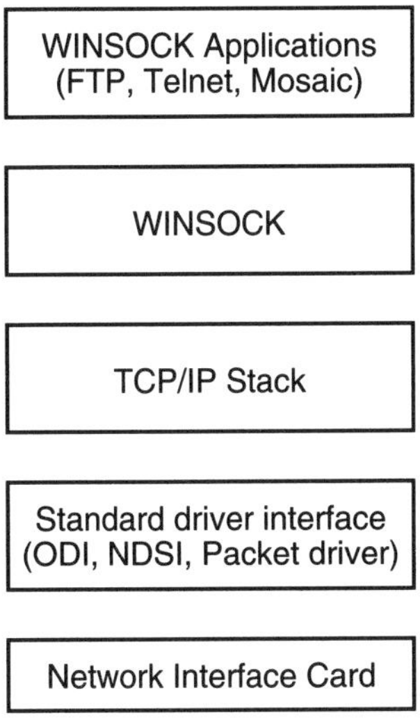

Figure 4.2

WINSOCK and TCP/IP protocols.

Even though WINSOCK's broad goal is to be protocol-independent, its current version 1.1 is implemented mainly for TCP/IP only. WINSOCK benefits end users and software developers alike by making software developers' jobs easier and offering freedom of choice to end users.

The Benefits of Using WINSOCK— End Users

Before the advent of WINSOCK, users were locked into buying the TCP/IP application and protocol stack from the same vendor. WINSOCK offers freedom of choice to end users, meaning that they can mix and match applications and TCP/IP protocol stacks from different vendors, as shown in figure 4.3. Therefore, a user can standardize on any TCP/IP protocol stack vendor and choose WINSOCK-compatible TCP/IP applications from another vendor or from the public domain. As new applications are introduced or improved upon, WINSOCK enables users to swap out the old or just add on new applications without changing TCP/IP stacks. For example, when Mosaic (a Web browser application discussed in Chapter 5) was introduced in the public domain, users running WINSOCK TCP/IP stacks didn't have to make any changes in their set up to run Mosaic.

The Benefits of Using WINSOCK— Software Developers

Before the advent of WINSOCK, applications had to be developed and tested specifically for each vendor's TCP/IP protocol stacks. Therefore, database vendors might have to develop ten different versions of their software to accommodate ten different TCP/IP vendor's products. WINSOCK offers a standardized programming interface so that application software developers—for example, software developers for TCP/IP applications such as FTP, Telnet, and Mosaic—can develop applications

independent of the TCP/IP protocol stack. An application such as Mosaic will thus work on TCP/IP stacks from Novell, Microsoft, and all other vendors of WINSOCK-compatible stacks.

You can obtain a copy of the WINSOCK API by attaching as an anonymous user and downloading it from one of the following FTP sites:

> sunsite.unc.edu:/pub/micro/pc-stuff/ms-windows/winsock
>
> microdyne.com:/pub/winsock

WINSOCK Limitations

Like many other early stage standards, WINSOCK is still evolving and has some glaring limitations, including the following:

→ Incompatibility

→ Lack of raw socket support

→ Lack of multiprotocol support

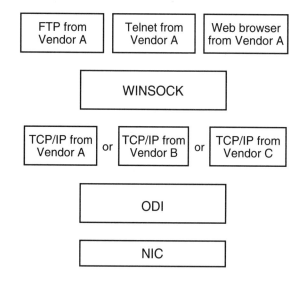

Figure 4.3

WINSOCK offers freedom of choice to end users.

In a perfect world, all applications will work with all protocols, and all vendors will cooperate to interoperate their applications and protocol stacks. In a real world, however, there are many incompatibilities between the implementations of different vendors. You should ask your TCP/IP vendors, therefore, if they have tested their applications on other vendors' WINSOCK interfaces, and also if they have tested other vendors' applications over their TCP/IP protocol stack.

Some of the applications that use the ICMP protocol are not supported by WINSOCK at this time. Ping is one such application, which is used to check if a particular host is dead or alive.

A third limitation of WINSOCK is that the current version of WINSOCK does not address multiple protocols. These multiple protocols are scheduled to be in WINSOCK 2.0, which is likely to be accepted by vendors by the end of 1995. If compatibility with WINSOCK 1.1 is any indication, don't expect to see any large-scale availability of WINSOCK 2.0 applications before the end of 1996.

Bringing TCP/IP into NetWare LANs

Since TCP/IP is the protocol for the Internet, it must be incorporated into the NetWare environment to enable all NetWare network users to connect to the Internet. The two broad approaches for bringing TCP/IP into NetWare LANs are as follows:

→ Loading TCP/IP at every NetWare workstation

→ Loading TCP/IP in the NetWare server

Using the analogy from Chapter 1 of two people who speak different languages, but somehow have to communicate with each other, the first approach (loading TCP/IP at every NetWare workstation) is equivalent to teaching both languages to each individual. The second approach (loading TCP/IP in the NetWare server) is equivalent to hiring a translator. If, instead of only two people, there were hundreds of people involved, the task of teaching another language to every individual would be more complex and time-consuming than hiring a translator.

Some of the technical details of both approaches, and criteria for choosing products in each case, are discussed in the following sections.

Loading TCP/IP at Every Workstation

One of the most common approaches used in the industry today to implement TCP/IP into NetWare LANs is to load TCP/IP at every workstation, in addition to NetWare's SPX/IPX protocol (see fig. 4.4). This approach was made possible with the advent of ODI, which permits multiple protocols to share the same hardware. This architecture is equivalent to having two separate networks—one IPX-based and the other IP-based—share the same physical media. In this manner, the IP network works in its traditional peer-to-peer fashion with no regard for the NetWare server, whereas the IPX network works in the client-server fashion with no regard for the presence of IP at the workstation.

There are many different products that provide TCP/IP protocols and applications that work in parallel with NetWare workstations. This section, focused at providing you the information to make a right decision for your network, is divided into the following areas:

→ Underlying technology terms, such as TSR, DLL, and VXD

- → Overview of Novell's TCP/IP products

- → Other commercial implementations

- → Information needed to configure TCP/IP

- → Criteria for choosing TCP/IP products

- → Advantages and disadvantages of loading TCP/IP at every workstation

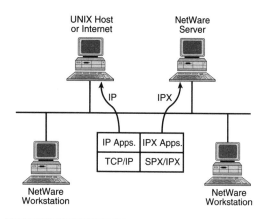

Figure 4.4

Loading TCP/IP at every NetWare workstation is like having two parallel networks.

TSR, DLL, and VXD

A *terminate-and-stay resident* (TSR) program is one that loads into memory upon execution and remains active until it is manually unloaded. A Windows DLL is a program that is only active when Windows is running. Unlike TSRs, DLLs are dynamically loaded and unloaded as needed by Windows. A *virtual device driver* (VXD) is an architecture recommended for implementing network protocol stacks within Windows because it provides network services to Windows and DOS applications simultaneously.

The network protocols can be implemented as TSR, DLL, or VXD. TSR resides in real-mode addressable DOS memory, and thus consumes memory from the limited conventional memory of 0 to 1 MB. DLL, on the other hand, doesn't consume any conventional DOS memory, but DLL-based protocols are not available to DOS. This may not be an issue for customers with Windows-only workstations. VXD-based protocols give you the best of both worlds—they work in both DOS and Windows environments without consuming conventional memory. VXD-based protocols are likely to outperform DLL-based protocols. Please also note that VXD is not a replacement for DLLs in general, but only presents a better alternative for implementing lower-level services like network protocols.

In choosing a TCP/IP at the NetWare workstation, it is important to decide whether the TSR, DLL, or VXD approach best meets your needs. If your environment includes many DOS workstations, TSR may be an acceptable approach, but if your environment is primarily Windows, DLL or VXD will both meet your needs. VXD is preferred over DLL if everything else (i.e., applications) is equal.

At this point, a review of different products offered by Novell would be helpful.

Overview of Novell's TCP/IP Products

Novell sells many products to interconnect NetWare and TCP/IP networks, such as UNIX and the Internet. For customers that want to run both NetWare IPX and TCP/IP at every workstation, Novell sells two main products, as follows:

- → LAN WorkPlace for DOS

- → LAN WorkGroup

Essentially, both products offer the same features for the end users, and provide a parallel TCP/IP stack, as discussed previously. LAN WorkPlace is installed and executed at every client and is available in single-user and multi-user licenses. In comparison, LAN WorkGroup is installed in the NetWare server, but executed at every client—it is not available in single-user packs. LAN WorkGroup provides server-based installation, centralized network administration, and an ability to monitor application usage.

Even though most of the desktop environments have moved to Windows, LAN WorkPlace and LAN WorkGroup (of which the current version is 4.2) still have their roots in DOS. In addition, the TCP/IP protocol in both products is implemented as a TSR, thereby requiring conventional DOS memory. Figure 4.5 shows the memory consumption at the workstation with LAN WorkPlace loaded.

Novell also supplies the WINSOCK DLL with LAN WorkPlace and LAN WorkGroup. In addition, both LAN WorkPlace and LAN WorkGroup include Windows applications such as FTP and Telnet. (see Chapter 5 for a discussion of Internet applications). The Windows applications are not WINSOCK-compatible, and therefore would not work on third-party TCP/IP stacks. By the time of publication of this book, Novell is likely to have shipped Version 5.0 of the LAN WorkPlace and LAN WorkGroup products, which will have WINSOCK-compatible applications.

In addition to Novell, there are many other implementations of TCP/IP that are compatible with NetWare. The next section discusses some of the other well-known commercial TCP/IP implementations.

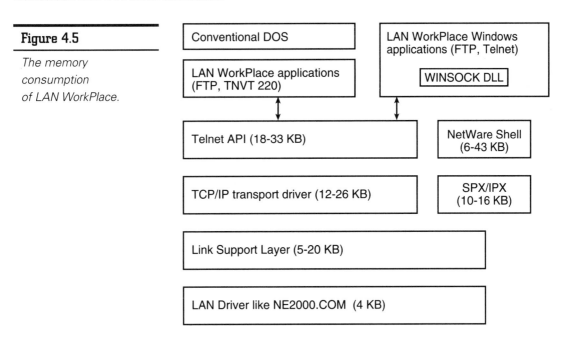

Figure 4.5

The memory consumption of LAN WorkPlace.

Other Commercial Implementations of TCP/IP

Microsoft has released a TCP/IP stack with Windows for Workgroups and Windows NT. It is possible to configure NetWare workstations to use this TCP/IP stack. Microsoft also will bundle TCP/IP with Windows 95, wherein the TCP/IP stack has been implemented as a VXD. It should also be noted that both Windows 95 and Windows for Workgroups contain IPX protocol stacks.

In addition to Novell and Microsoft, many other TCP/IP players in the market supply both TCP/IP stacks and applications. These players include Beame & Whiteside, Distinct Corporation, Esker Corporation, Frontier Technology, FTP Software, IBM, IP Switch, Net Manage, Walker Richer Quinn, and The Wollongong Group. Despite the presence of WINSOCK DLL and WINSOCK-compatible applications, the majority of vendors have not developed install routines that simplify mixing and matching protocol stacks and applications from different vendors. Many vendors are realizing the significance of this issue, however, and are starting to make it easier to run their applications on TCP/IP stacks from other vendors.

Regardless of which vendors' TCP/IP protocols you choose, TCP/IP has to be configured at every workstation. No vendor has yet achieved a plug-and-play solution for configuring TCP/IP because it requires information that has to be supplied by the installer.

Configuring TCP/IP at Every Workstation

The information needed to configure TCP/IP at every workstation is no different than that required to configure a pure TCP/IP network with UNIX hosts. In general, the following information is needed to configure TCP/IP stacks at every workstation:

→ Depending on the class C address obtained from the InterNIC, plan for an internal addressing scheme and the allocation of IP addresses for each workstation. If you are using a private IP address scheme and are now connecting to the Internet, you must change your IP address scheme to correspond to the Internet assigned address.

→ Similar to the IP addresses, the subnet mask also is specified in dotted decimal format with a binary 0 used for the host and a binary 1 used for the network. A subnet mask of 255.255.255.0, for example, means that the last eight bits are assigned to the host ID and the remaining 24 bits are used for the network ID.

→ In all IP networks, it is common to have one IP router that knows of other IP nodes on the local network. This IP router could be a stand-alone router, another UNIX computer, a NetWare server, or a network card in one of the computers. See Chapter 8, "WAN Access Devices," for a discussion of different router choices.

→ In addition to knowing your domain name, you have to specify your domain name server and its IP address. The domain name system translates IP addresses to English-like names. The *Domain Name Server* (DNS) can be hosted at your site or at your Internet Access Provider's site. See Chapter 3, "Understanding TCP/IP," for a discussion of DNS.

Criteria for Choosing TCP/IP Products

If you have decided to use a TCP/IP stack at every workstation, the following are some of the criteria you should use in evaluating different vendors' offerings:

- Many vendors offer only NDIS-based drivers that can be made to work on NetWare, but impose additional installation overhead. Therefore, make sure that the vendor has a native ODI driver available for its TCP/IP stack.

- You must ensure that the documentation discusses special settings for making the TCP/IP protocol stack work on a NetWare LAN.

- The TCP/IP stack could be implemented as a TSR, DLL, or VXD. If you are using a Windows environment, TSR implementations are not highly desirable as they consume conventional DOS memory. The VXD approach is slightly better than DLL-based protocol stacks, and will become a standard way for implementing protocol stacks in the future.

- There are two levels of WINSOCK compatibility—one at the protocol layer and the other at the application layer. It is important that the protocol stack be WINSOCK-compatible and provide a WINSOCK DLL file that is compatible with WINSOCK 1.1 specifications. You should also ensure that all of the TCP/IP applications supplied by the vendor are WINSOCK 1.1-compatible. In fact, you should ask if their applications and stacks have been tested for interoperability with other vendors' applications and stacks. This will become more important as operating systems start bundling TCP/IP protocols for free.

- Most TCP/IP vendors are trying to differentiate their products by bundling more applications. Unfortunately, most of these applications are not integrated with each other, and in this case more is not always best. You must evaluate your needs rather than choose a package due to its large application count. Surprisingly, many public domain applications are as high in quality as some commercial packages. If your LAN users are new to the Internet and you have already established an e-mail standard, the Mosaic Web browser from the *National Center for Supercomputing Applications* (NCSA) or Netscape from Netscape Communications might be sufficient for most users—they provide point and click access to FTP, Gopher, World Wide Web servers, and newsgroups. Some power users might require separate FTP and Telnet applications. Once again, see Chapter 5 for details on the Internet applications.

- Most TCP/IP vendors still license their software on a per computer basis rather than a concurrent user license basis. You should insist on concurrent user licensing, however, as it enables you to load software in the server and pay for active users rather than total possible users.

Advantages and Disadvantages of TCP/IP at Every Workstation

Loading TCP/IP at every workstation has its advantages and disadvantages. It depends on your requirements, familiarity with UNIX, and size of the network. Therefore, you should measure these advantages and disadvantages, discussed in the following, in relation to your requirements.

Advantages For a UNIX-centric network that also has some NetWare servers, loading TCP/IP at every workstation might be advantageous because UNIX system administrators are already experienced in TCP/IP protocols. The access to various internal and external systems can be achieved directly over the TCP/IP protocol, which is the default operating system for UNIX and the Internet.

Disadvantages For most NetWare-centric networks that either have few UNIX hosts or which are seeking Internet access, however, the following issues must be carefully weighed before putting TCP/IP at every workstation:

→ TCP/IP addressing is complex, and the allocation and management of TCP/IP addresses for every workstation therefore adds administrative overhead.

→ The TCP/IP address pool is dwindling, and getting the class B address needed by most networks with over 255 nodes is nearly impossible. Therefore, you will have to contend with multiple class C addresses if your network has more than 255 nodes, making management even more complex.

→ Loading TCP/IP at every workstation also makes each workstation a peer node on the Internet with an IP address, thereby enabling hackers to access every workstation unless firewalls are put in place.

→ Just like any peer-to-peer LAN, no centralized control or record of user activities for audit trial or billing is available with this approach. Loading TCP/IP at each workstation can emulate the pre-LAN times when there was very little centralized control and management of PC software or hardware.

Before discussing an alternate method of bringing TCP/IP into the NetWare environment by way of a NetWare server, it is important to understand various server based TCP/IP products from Novell.

Novell's Server-Based TCP/IP Products

Novell has many products that use or provide server-based TCP/IP to NetWare LANs. Even though not all of the products facilitate Internet access,

this section will help clarify any confusion regarding different server products from Novell. The server-based TCP/IP products from Novell include the following:

→ TCP/IP protocol stack in the server

→ NetWare FLex/IP

→ NetWare NFS

→ NetWare/IP

TCP/IP Protocol Stack in the Server

Every NetWare server, including NetWare 3.1 and above and NetWare 4.0 and above, includes a TCP/IP protocol stack as a *NetWare Loadable Module* (NLM) in the form of a TCPIP.NLM file. NLMs are software tasks that run in the NetWare server, and can be dynamically loaded or unloaded from the server console. TCPIP.NLM requires that STREAMS, CLIB, and SNMP NLMs be loaded before it. If these NLMs are not loaded beforehand, they are automatically loaded when TCPIP.NLM is loaded. With TCPIP.NLM loaded in the NetWare server, it can be used as an IP router and also provides transport services for TCP/IP applications that can run at the server.

NetWare FLex/IP

NetWare FLex/IP provides a way for UNIX and NetWare users to share printers and files. It lets UNIX users submit print jobs to printers attached to NetWare servers. It also allows UNIX or TCP/IP users to access NetWare servers using the FTP commands. Therefore, NetWare FLex/IP provides FTP server services as an NLM. Because its main goal is to make NetWare server access easy for UNIX users, NetWare FLex/IP is not very useful for

Internet access, except for the case when you also want to make your NetWare server an FTP host server. Unlike the TCP/IP stack in the server, this is an option that has an additional cost and must be purchased separately.

NetWare NFS

NetWare NFS, like NetWare FLex/IP, is also targeted at helping UNIX and TCP/IP users access NetWare servers. In addition to the FLex/IP features, it also provides an NFS daemon, which lets UNIX and other NFS clients access NetWare volumes using the standard UNIX/NFS MOUNT command. NetWare NFS does not help NetWare LAN users access the Internet any more than the TCP/IP stack in the server. Like NetWare FLex/IP, NetWare NFS also involves an extra cost.

NetWare/IP

NetWare/IP enables TCP/IP workstations to access NetWare's NCP protocol. This takes NetWare a step closer to having a pure IP network. NetWare/IP requires both a client software with TCP/IP loaded at every client and a server component. Contrary to popular belief, NetWare/IP does not let companies run only with IP protocols.

None of these Novell products discussed in this section solve the Internet access problems for NetWare workstations if TCP/IP is not loaded at every workstation. However, Novell's bundling of the TCP/IP protocol in the server is being used to facilitate Internet access for NetWare users, as discussed in the following section.

Loading TCP/IP in the Server

As mentioned previously, loading TCP/IP at every workstation is not an optimal alternative for many sites. Another alternative is now gaining recognition, however—loading TCP/IP only in the server. In this method, all of the NetWare workstations continue running IPX protocols at the workstation level, while using the TCP/IP protocol loaded at the server level to access all TCP/IP resources, such as UNIX servers and the Internet. This can be accomplished with a client-server architecture, wherein workstations still use IPX to access the NetWare server, and the server performs the IPX to IP conversion as needed. Figure 4.6 shows details on the architecture of a network with TCP/IP loaded in the server.

Figure 4.6

A server-based TCP/IP architecture.

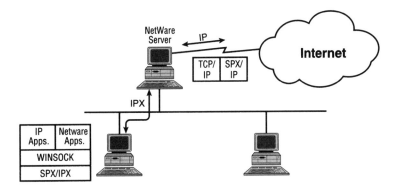

In this architecture, control is returned to the NetWare server. All TCP/IP communication occurs through the NetWare server, which acts as an IP-to-IPX gateway. Also, because all the workstations use the IP address of the server, only one IP address is needed per server. To run all the standard IP applications, WINSOCK is the only available standard. Therefore, it is possible to extend WINSOCK to work over SPX/IPX and use the NetWare server as the gateway to the IP world. The same is not possible for DOS workstations because there is no such standard as WINSOCK for DOS, and hence applications written for one interface will not work with the other.

This section, which provides information to help you make the right decision for your network, is divided into the following areas:

→ Server-based TCP/IP products

→ Information needed to configure TCP/IP

→ Criteria for choosing server-based TCP/IP products

→ Advantages and disadvantages of loading TCP/IP at the server

Server-Based TCP/IP Products

Two types of broad server-based approaches, each with its own merits and demerits, are possible to achieve the same result. These approaches are as follows:

→ Using third-party TCP/IP in the NetWare server

→ Using Novell's TCP/IP in the NetWare server

The following section describes the two approaches and the available products in each category.

Using Third-Party TCP/IP in the NetWare Server The only vendor shipping a product that uses third-party TCP/IP in the NetWare server is Firefox, a United Kingdom-based company. Its product, Novix, includes a TCP/IP stack in the server as an NLM, TCP/IP applications, and its own interface for the workstations. Many of the NetWare networks are already configured with using Novell's TCP/IP in the server for routing, UNIX file and print access, and/or SNMP management. In the networks that are already using Novell's TCP/IP, two choices are available for customers who want to use this approach, as follows:

→ **Replace Novell's TCP/IP server stack with Firefox's TCP/IP.** This alternative might be acceptable to some customers, but not acceptable to those who like Novell's TCP/IP features and want to depend on Novell to provide future upgrades consistent with its operating systems.

→ **Put two network interface cards in the NetWare server and bind each card to a different TCP/IP stack—one from Novell and the other from Firefox.** This alternative may be acceptable for sites that want to continue using Novell's TCP/IP; however, this alternative adds too much systems and management overhead because two separate TCP/IP NLMs from two vendors now have to be managed.

Using Novell's TCP/IP in the NetWare Server As mentioned earlier, Novell supplies a complimentary TCP/IP protocol stack as an NLM with NetWare 3.x and 4.x. The stack is useful when using the NetWare server as a TCP/IP router, however, as well as for other functions. Internetware, Inc., a company based in Sunnyvale, California, supplies a product called IWare that uses Novell's TCP/IP stack and extends it in the manner shown in figure 4.6. IWare extends the WINSOCK interface to run over SPX/IPX, and therefore enables all WINSOCK-compatible IP applications to run over SPX/IPX. IWare sends all requests generated by IP applications, such as FTP, Telnet, and Mosaic, to the NetWare server over IPX, which then redirects them to the Internet over IP. Similarly, IWare accepts input from the Internet over IP and passes responses back to workstations over IPX. At this time, IWare's limitation is that it does not work in DOS.

By using Novell's TCP/IP stack, you are assured of compatibility with Novell's other TCP/IP-based NLMs that also use Novell's TCP/IP stack. These include products in NetWare FLex/IP and NetWare NFS.

Configuring a NetWare Server with TCP/IP

The information needed to configure TCP/IP in the server is the same as that for configuring TCP/IP at every workstation. The difference is that only one IP address is needed for the server, rather than an individual IP address for every workstation. In addition, there is no need to configure every workstation because all configuration can be done at the server.

Criteria for Evaluating Server-Based TCP/IP Products

If you decide to use the server-based TCP/IP solution, some of the criteria you should use in evaluating different vendors' offerings are as follows:

→ Integration with NetWare's bundled TCP/IP stack—Tighter integration with NetWare TCP/IP reduces your management overhead.

→ Server management tools—Because you chose this alternative to gain server management, all

the desirable server-management tools like access control, viewing, and reporting should meet your needs.

→ WINSOCK compatibility—Check for interoperability of third-party applications on vendors' interfaces so that you can choose any commercial or public domain third-party applications.

→ Applications—This is similar to the criterion discussed in the section, "Criteria for Choosing TCP/IP Products," found earlier in this chapter.

Advantages and Disadvantages of Using Server-Based TCP/IP

Two server-based approaches for providing TCP/IP in the server have been discussed in this chapter. No matter which approach is used, server-based TCP/IP offers both advantages and disadvantages over loading TCP/IP at every workstation. The decision should be made, however, based on your requirements and NetWare expertise.

Advantages to Using TCP/IP on the Server For NetWare-centric sites that have few UNIX hosts and need Internet access, using server-based TCP/IP is the most advantageous approach. It offers the following advantages:

→ TCP/IP addressing becomes more simplified.

→ All workstations have only IPX addresses, which are advertised only to devices on that workstation's own physical network. Internet users on the outside thus cannot break into the NetWare workstations because there are no known addresses for the workstations. Therefore, this architecture provides a security firewall. The NetWare server, however, should still be secured against attack by intruders. One caution that can increase security on the

NetWare servers is to not load any server daemons such as FTP and NFS. See Chapter 10, "Network Security," for a detailed discussion of security issues.

→ All TCP/IP communication goes through the NetWare server, thereby enabling control of TCP/IP access from the NetWare server. IWare enables network administrators to restrict access to the Internet by user, by group, by time of day, or by applications such as FTP, Telnet, newsgroups, and World Wide Web, for example. Figure 4.7 shows a representative menu from the IWare product.

→ With a server-based approach, it is possible to capture the access information and present it to the network administrator for audit trail and for billing purposes. Figure 4.8 shows another example of the IWare product, which offers this feature.

Disadvantages to Using TCP/IP on the Server For a UNIX-centric site whose servers have expensive firewall and access control software, TCP/IP addressing and management might not be as important as they are for NetWare-centric sites. For UNIX sites, however, the following might be disadvantages:

→ Server-based performance is always less than in the case of a native TCP/IP implementation. The performance can vary from anywhere between 70 percent to 90 percent of that of the native implementation. The performance degradation, however, is only noticeable in a LAN environment at 10 Mbps.

 n o t e   For Internet access, the bottleneck is the WAN connection speed, which in most cases is 56 Kbps. In such an environment, no performance degradation is noticed.

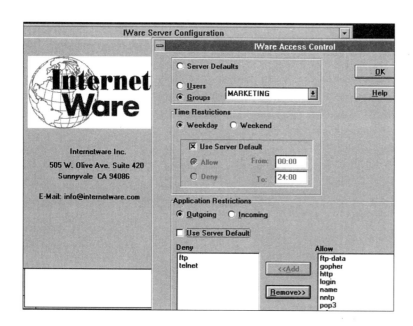

Figure 4.7

Server-based TCP/IP enables control of Internet access.

→ For some applications such as Ping, WINSOCK specifications do not yet exist; therefore, the implementation might be proprietary to the vendors.

Criteria for Selecting TCP/IP Products

Figure 4.9 summarizes the complete selection matrix discussed in this chapter.

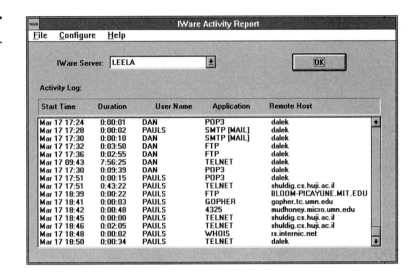

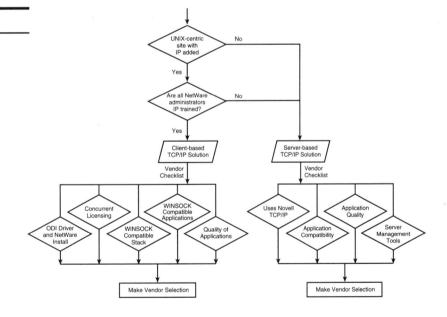

Summary

In order to connect to the Internet, TCP/IP protocols have to be integrated within the NetWare environment that uses SPX/IPX protocols. One of the
ways to integrate TCP/IP is to load TCP/IP at every
workstation, in addition to the SPX/IPX protocol. This
alternative increases management overhead, requires a separate IP address per each workstation,
and makes your network vulnerable to hacker attacks from the Internet. The other alternative is to
use server-based TCP/IP. One of the server-based
approaches is to use a third-party TCP/IP stack in
the server, while the other approach is to use
Novell's server TCP/IP that comes free with
NetWare 3.x and 4.x networks. The server-based
TCP/IP approaches work best for NetWare-centric
sites because they reduce management overhead,
require only a single IP address, and allow access
control, management, and reporting of the Internet
access not easily possible with the alternative of
loading TCP/IP at every workstation.

Once you have integrated TCP/IP in your NetWare
environment for Internet access, you can now begin considering the types of Internet applications
that you would like to offer to your users. The next
chapter, "Internet Applications," provides a foundation for understanding the various types of applications that can be implemented, which will in turn
help you determine which ones are best suited for
your particular environment.

5

Internet Applications

To facilitate communications between Internet users, as well as make the process of finding and accessing Internet data easier, a number of core applications have been developed. *Electronic mail* (e-mail), *File Transfer Protocol* (FTP), and Virtual Terminal Access (Telnet) have been the most prevalent Internet applications used over the last decade. In addition to providing access through standards-based applications, some online services and Internet access providers also offer their own unique applications to access information on their service and the Internet.

With the recent development and widespread use of the *World Wide Web* (WWW), however, Web browsers that integrate many of the latest navigational tools are becoming the standard user application for Internet access. The one thing that all of the latest generation of Internet applications have in common is a much easier point-and-click, drag-and-drop user interface. With the emergence of these more user-friendly applications, the Internet is much less intimidating than it used to be for novice users, which is one of the reasons for its recent growth.

Most services offered on the Internet are based on the client-server model and are composed of two components—a client portion and a server portion. The client portion is the application that runs on the user's local PC, with which the user interacts directly. The client application connects to a server application that normally runs on a larger machine. The server application could be running on a server machine on the local LAN or on a remote machine on the Internet.

This chapter focuses on the different Internet client applications that are available today. The next chapter, "Internet Application Servers," examines the server components. The objective of this chapter is to increase your understanding of these applications so that you can choose the correct applications for your environment. Although it is not the intent of this chapter to focus on application usage, some interactive sessions with different applications are provided.

All of the software applications discussed in this chapter are available from a wide number of commercial vendors, including NetManage, Spry, The Wollongong Group, Frontier, and FTP Software. In addition, there is a wide variety of excellent software available for free over the network. At the end of the chapter is a section that lists which applications are available from the different vendors, and where you can you can look on the network to find the free software.

The various applications discussed in this chapter include the following:

→ E-mail

→ FTP

→ Usenet newsreaders

→ Web browsers

→ Gopher

→ Internet indexing tools, such as Archie, Veronica, and WHOIS

→ Telnet

 n o t e This chapter focuses on layer 2 of the Internet connectivity matrix.

7	SECURITY AND MANAGEMENT
6	Internet Access Providers
5	WAN Access Devices
4	WAN Access Services
3	Internet Application Servers
2	Internet Navigation Software
1	Network Communication Protocols

E-Mail

Electronic mail has become a universal communication tool for organizations. Most users on NetWare networks use a LAN-based e-mail system, such as Lotus cc:Mail, Novell's Groupwise, or MS Mail, to communicate electronically. All of the online services (CompuServe, Prodigy, America Online, and so on) provide Internet gateways for their users to enable communication between different types of e-mail systems. In fact, for many organizations, the Internet is used as an e-mail backbone, whereby they can easily and economically communicate with customers and vendors. Generally, most companies start using the Internet primarily for e-mail purposes, gradually discover the full power of the Internet, and then start using other tools. *Simple Mail Transport Protocol* (SMTP) is the Internet mail protocol that is used by millions of users all over the world to exchange e-mail. A pair of *Request For Comment* (RFC) documents (RFC 821 and RFC 822) define the way mail is exchanged between servers and the format of the mail messages respectively. The details on SMTP servers are covered in Chapter 6, "Internet Application Servers." This section focuses only on end-user tools and some of the important issues related to e-mail.

Components of E-Mail Systems

In general, e-mail systems can be split into three broad components, as follows:

→ Local e-mail server, message transfer agent, or post office server—all are terms describing the server component of the mail system.

→ E-mail reader, user agent, or client e-mail programs—all are terms describing the client component of the mail system, including applications such as Eudora, Pegasus, Lotus cc:Mail, or MS Mail.

→ Mail gateway or mail relays—both terms describe devices used to send e-mail from a non-SMTP mail system, such as Lotus cc:Mail, to the Internet.

Figure 5.1 illustrates these three main components. The local e-mail server provides local mail storage and mail communications for the e-mail readers (user agents) that run on the user's workstation. The Internet gateway server is responsible for mail communication between the local e-mail server and the Internet. Mail servers and gateways will be covered in more detail in Chapter 6. This chapter looks at the mail solution from the mail reader perspective.

Figure 5.1

The three e-mail components.

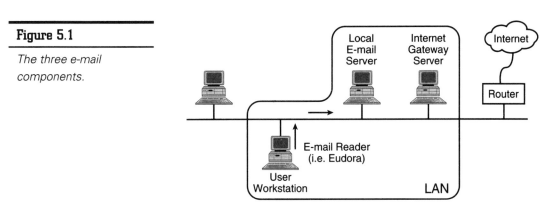

If you already have chosen the mail reader for your LAN, you may not have a choice of the server. Most e-mail packages have not yet moved to a true open standards-based client-server architecture, where you can choose a mail server separate from a mail reader. The most commonly used packages in this case are Lotus cc:Mail or MS Mail. Novell has established *Message Handling System* (MHS), however, as its messaging standard that comes with every NetWare server. Many e-mail readers, therefore, depend on the NetWare server for providing the MHS services. Some of these readers include Pegasus and DaVinci e-mail packages.

If you already have an established a LAN-based system that you intend to use, you will have two alternatives to access Internet mail. The first is to use a mail gateway that allows mail from your local mail system to be exchanged with the Internet. Mail gateways are covered in the next chapter, along with mail servers. The second option is to continue to use your existing mail system for local mail, and to use a separate mail client for Internet mail. In this case, the client application and issues are the same as if you were only using an Internet-based mail system for both your local and Internet mail. This section focuses on mail clients that are based on the TCP/IP standards.

The traditional Internet mail system, which is based on SMTP, is really a peer-to-peer mail system. It was designed with multiuser systems such as UNIX in mind, and it also assumes a direct and permanent connection to the Internet and other SMTP servers. Two protocols, *Post Office Protocol* (POP) and *Interactive Mail Access Protocol* (IMAP), have created a client-server type of environment for the Internet mail system. POP and IMAP enable PC users, who may not always be connected to the Internet or able to always be running a SMTP application, to retrieve their mail from the server or post office at their convenience. This is similar to people that travel a lot and are not always home to receive their U.S. mail. These people often get a post office box, where the mail is stored until it is convenient for them pick it up. Most mail clients today implement the *POP version 3* (POP3), which is the current standard. IMAP is a newer protocol than POP and not widely implemented today. The client applications that have implemented IMAP also support POP for compatibility with existing servers. Mail originated on the client is sent to the server by using the SMTP protocol.

The e-mail client-server model shown in figure 5.2 depicts the complete mail process. Internet mail, which is based on the SMTP protocol, is retrieved from the e-mail server by the POP or IMAP-based e-mail reader or client to which the Internet mail is addressed. Internet mail to be delivered is sent using SMTP to the e-mail server, which in turn communicates with other e-mail servers on the Internet.

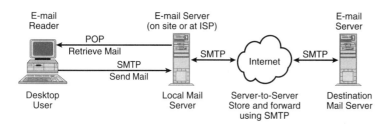

Figure 5.2

The Internet e-mail client-server model.

Communications and Application Software

Mail servers are discussed in detail in Chapter 6, "Internet Application Servers."

E-Mail Reader

For every mail transaction, a mail reader or a composing program must be present. The mail reader or composer program, which can be a simple command-line interface or a Windows-based *graphical user interface* (GUI), is simply software that is loaded at the end-user's desktop. This software enables users to retrieve their e-mail from the server or to send e-mail to someone with an Internet mail address. Many mail readers provide mail management features, such as the capability to organize mail into folders and subfolders. *Mail filtering*, a feature that enables users to "screen" incoming messages based on selected criteria, also is becoming an increasingly important addition to e-mail programs, considering the high volume of mail exchanged in organizations today.

Some of the most popular POP mail readers include Eudora and Pegasus. Eudora is public domain software and can be downloaded from the Internet at no cost. A newer and commercially supported version is available from Qualcomm for a small fee. Pegasus, on the other hand, has the distinction of being the only mail reader that can also access Novell MHS Servers and POP3. Like Eudora, Pegasus is also public domain software.

 See table 5.4, at the end of this chapter, for a list of what applications are available from both commercial software vendors, along with free software that can be obtained off the Internet. A list of network sites is also provided, enabling you to look for free software.

 Almost all of the commercially available TCP/IP software packages, such as FTP Software, Frontier Software, and NetManage, include a POP mail reader.

Before selecting a mail reader, much time should be spent planning your organizational e-mail needs and comparing these needs to features and capabilities of various mail readers on the market. Ease of use, mail management capabilities, and mail filtering options are all important features to look for in an e-mail system. Because end users develop an affinity to a particular mail reader after only a short time of use, it is very difficult to change e-mail systems once implemented. Proper planning up front increases the likelihood of selecting an appropriate mail reader for your organization the first time.

Internet Message Anatomy

Every message contains two parts: a header and a body. The body of the message is generally text in the ASCII format. Due to the ASCII format requirement for data, non-ASCII data must be encoded before it can be sent with SMTP. Files that are attached to e-mail messages therefore must be encoded because they are not in ASCII format. In the past, uuencoding—which can be quite complex—was the most common way of attaching binary files to e-mail messages. It is now becoming easier, however—most e-mail packages today enable users to automatically uuencode and decode their own messages.

 First developed on UNIX systems, uuencoding is a method for encoding a binary data file into a data file that only contains ASCII characters. The encoded file can then be transported by systems only capable of handling text-based data files. A uuencoded file can be converted back to its original binary file by doing a uudecode.

BinHex is another popular encoding scheme used for sending files over the Internet. Because of the lack of standards for incorporating encoding instructions in SMTP, however, interoperability problems began to occur between mail clients. As a result of this interoperability, MIME emerged. *Multipurpose Internet Mail Extensions* (MIME) builds on the existing SMTP message format by standardizing additional fields for mail message headers that describe new types of content and organization for messages.

MIME enables you to easily attach binary files to an e-mail message without complex user interaction. Most of the new Internet e-mail reader software is MIME-compatible. Because these different readers all implement the same MIME standard, there is full interoperability between different MIME-compliant e-mail readers. You can attach images, audio, video, and multimedia files to your e-mail messages, in addition to executable programs and binary documents. Network administrators should, however, advise their users to use caution when sending file attachments. If a file is too large, it will increase the load on your network, draining file server resources and decreasing network performance.

Sending Messages

RFC 822 specifies the format of each of the e-mail messages, including the exact syntax of the headers. E-mail clients such as Eudora interact with the user to gather the needed information and create a mail message that conforms to the RFC 822 specifications.

 n o t e RFC 822 is the Internet standard that specifies the format of an SMTP mail message. Its companion document, RFC 821, defines the actual protocol that is used to exchange RFC 822-formatted messages between mail systems.

Figure 5.3 shows a message being composed with Eudora e-mail. Eudora gives the user a form that allows fields in the header—such as the "To:" field—to be filled in. Other header fields—the "From:" field, for example—are automatically filled in by the mail system.

The following headers are most commonly used in all Internet e-mail systems during composition of a message:

➜ To: In this field, specify the e-mail address of the message recipient(s), such as dan@internetware.com.

➜ From: This field represents your e-mail address, such as pauls@mango.com, which is generally filled in automatically by the e-mail program being used. In most e-mail systems, this information is given to the e-mail system at setup time, when it is first configured or installed. In figure 5.3, the real name "Paul Singh" is treated by the e-mail system as a comment and not used by the e-mail system for message routing. You can, therefore, use almost anything in its place. The normal convention is to use your full name, but you can also put in your nickname or any other string that you like.

➜ Subject: It is not mandatory to put information in this field, but it is recommended—it gives your e-mail recipients an idea of the content of your message. For example, "Test message" is the subject in the example in figure 5.3.

➡ Cc: This field is optional as well, but if filled, it must contain the individual(s)' e-mail address in a format similar to that specified in the To: field.

➡ Attachments: This field indicates the files that are attached to the e-mail message. Most of the Internet mail packages today enable you to attach files in the MIME format or uuencoded format. MIME readers are quickly becoming universal. The message in figure 5.3 shows that an attachment, C:\EUDORA\CHAP03AR.DOC, has been added to the mail message.

➡ Body: The text of the message is placed in this field. Technically, there are no restrictions on this section, but from a social standpoint, an e-mail message should be treated no differently than a written letter or a face-to-face conversation—it is merely another medium for message transfer and communications. Even though it is quite easy to create and send e-mail messages, however, you should be careful not to get careless with your writing.

➡ Signature: An e-mail signature is similar to a return address label on a mail envelope. Rather than typing your name, company name, mailing address, and telephone and fax numbers at the end of each message, you can use the Signature field to define these variables once. After that, simply insert the signature at the end of each message you send. This field should be restricted to four lines. In figure 5.3, the Signature field can be added just by selecting the signature box. In most e-mail packages, the actual signature doesn't display for the sender, but it appears in the recipients' e-mail copy.

Figure 5.4 shows an example of a message composition window of Pegasus, another popular e-mail package for NetWare sites. The general concepts are the same as with Eudora, but, as with all e-mail packages, Pegasus offers its own style of graphical user interface with a unique blend of features. Because the underlying message format and protocols are the same for all Internet mail packages, they all have the same basic capabilities. Additional

Figure 5.3

Composing an e-mail message with Eudora.

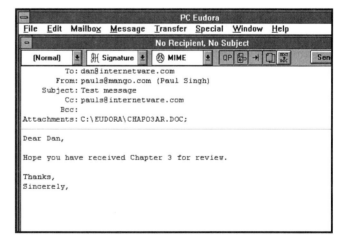

facilities such as spell checking, text editing, mail folders, and filing systems all vary from application package to application package. In addition, the vendors are continually upgrading the features of their packages capabilities. The choice is often just a matter of personal preferences.

Receiving Messages

Figure 5.5 shows the mailbox screen of the inbox (IN) folder with two messages. The beginning of a message received from the Internet by using the Eudora mail reader is also displayed. It contains the same type of information as the messages you send. In addition, it also contains the date and time, which indicates when the message was originally sent. This message contains details pertaining to the different e-mail systems it traversed while enroute to its destination; however, this information generally has no relevance to the message recipient.

Figure 5.5 also shows a message received from a MIME package that contains some file attachments. If your e-mail reader is MIME-compatible, all of the file attachments are automatically put in the directory specified in the e-mail program settings. MIME mail readers warn you, however, that the message is coming from a MIME e-mail package and may or may not be readable. Generally, the text portion of the message can be read by different e-mail systems, whereas the file attachments are retrieved only if there is a MIME-compatible e-mail reader available at the receiver's end.

Internet Mailing Lists

You can subscribe to over 10,000 mailing lists on the Internet. Some of the mailing lists are open to everyone, but others are restricted by the owners of the mailing lists. Many of the networking companies have their own mailing lists, but restrict the access to their users. Most mailing lists are set up to send out messages automatically to the list. These mailing lists are also known as *mail reflectors* because every message sent to one person is reflected to the entire list.

Figure 5.4

Sending e-mail with Pegasus.

Figure 5.5

Displaying an e-mail message with Eudora.

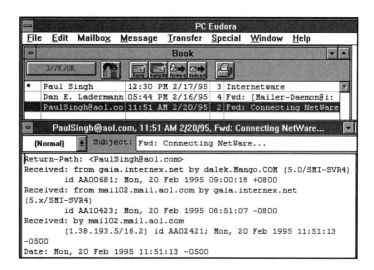

If you are interested in getting current mailing lists, you can obtain additional information by way of anonymous FTP (discussed later in this chapter) from the following FTP site:

rftm.mit.edu

Current mailing lists are located in the directory called "/pub/usenet/news.announce.newusers" as the file name Publicly_Accessible_Mailing_Lists.

t i p

Sites that make general information available to the public have been know to reorganize the information and change the names of files. If you are looking for a particular file, but are having difficulty finding it, you may need to "browse around" in the site by retrieving other files to determine how information is organized at that site. Helpful files to look for are those containing the phrase "readme" or "info."

Table 5.1 lists some of the mailing lists that may be of interest to networking professionals.

Table 5.1 Mailing Lists

Mail List Name	Subject
novell@suvm.sys.edu	NetWare for higher education
novops@suvm.sys.edu	Novell technology operations list
srvreq-l@miamiu.muohio.edu	Forum for network servers
novttp@suvm.syr.edu	Novell technical transfer partners list
vtnovell@vtvmi.cc.vt.edu	Virginia tec Novell users

To subscribe to one of the mailing lists, send an e-mail message to the "request" address listed for the mailing list. For example, if you want to subscribe to the tennis@hobby.com mailing list, you can send an e-mail message to tennis-request@hobby.com to subscribe to the list. Note that this rule may not work all of the time. If it doesn't, check the request address listed for that particular mailing list—it may specify a different request method. Before you subscribe to any list, however, be ready for an increase in your e-mail traffic, sometimes by as much as hundreds of messages a day per list.

 Don't make the mistake of sending the subscription message to the mailing list. A message addressed to the mailing list gets read by everyone on the list and is generally very annoying to list members.

Common Questions Regarding E-Mail

New Internet users or system administrators are sure to have questions regarding e-mail on the Internet. This section addresses some of the most common questions that arise at new installation sites.

What Kind of Reliability Can be Expected from an E-Mail Package?

Most of the Internet e-mail packages try to deliver the message and return an error message to the sender if the delivery does not occur. This accountability may not be true of e-mail messages that go through various gateways that convert messages from a proprietary format to SMTP.

How Can You Exchange E-Mail with CompuServe Users?

The address for CompuServe users becomes the first five numbers of their CompuServe ID, followed by a period and @compuserve.com. A user with a CompuServe address of 76545,72, therefore, is addressed as 76545.72@compuserve.com.

Is There a Size Limitation to the E-Mail Message?

The e-mail specification does not limit the size, but most of the network providers tend to limit the size of the message. Some of the online services such as CompuServe and America Online restrict the Internet messages to less than 60 KB. It is advisable to restrict the e-mail size to within 30 KB, if possible. There is no way to tell in advance if you will reach this limit. If you do, you may get a message back reporting a delivery error, or the entire mail message may not be delivered.

How Do I Find Someone's E-Mail Address on the Internet?

One way to find out an individual's e-mail address is to simply call and ask the person. Better yet, you can have the person send you an e-mail message, which will automatically give you the appropriate e-mail address. Unfortunately, a complete White or Yellow Pages directory of personal e-mail addresses does not exist.

Other documents are available on the Internet, however, which provide more help on topics such as e-mail addressing and mail servers. One way to get that information via e-mail is as follows:

→ To get general information on using the mail-server, send a request to "mail-server@rtfm.mit.edu" with a body of: help.

→ For a listing of top-level files and directories available at this site, send a message to "mail-server@rtfm.mit.edu" with a body of: index.

Can E-Mail be Used as a Vehicle to Download Files?

Many sites enable you to request files via e-mail. Most of these files tend to be ASCII format files. For example, the previously mentioned file for finding individual e-mail addresses can be downloaded via FTP and can also be obtained via e-mail. FTP, however, is a better application to use to download the files. With an e-mail request, you send the request and then must wait for an e-mail message to be sent with the reply. With FTP, you can connect directly to the site, view what documents are available, and download one or more documents. FTP is discussed in detail in the next section.

File Transfer Protocol

File Transfer Protocol (FTP) is the most widely used Internet application after e-mail. FTP enables you to transfer or download a single file, multiple files, or entire software packages from Internet sites offering these files to your own computer. FTP, an interactive access protocol that works on top of TCP, is based on a client-server model that makes these file transfers between computers possible. Thus, the site offering the files must be set up with an FTP server software, whereas the computer receiving the file download must be set up with an FTP client software.

Most FTP servers run multiuser operating systems, with UNIX being the most common. The FTP client can run on any operating system. In fact, the Windows and Macintosh GUI-based FTP implementations are used universally by most PC users. These implementations have made FTP a much more user-friendly application than it used to be.

 t i p In addition to being available as a separate user application, basic FTP capability is automatically built into Web browsers. This capability makes for easy downloading of files when surfing the Internet.

On a NetWare network, users are constantly performing file transfers from the file server. Most of these file transfers in NetWare are hidden and totally transparent to the users. Despite the fact that FTP is now easier to use, however, the same transparency is not true of file transfers on the Internet. The following sections discuss some basics of FTP. If, after reading this section, additional information on using FTP is desired, you can refer to the documentation that came with your software. You can also download the following guidelines with FTP from the Internet:

> ftp.sura.net

The current guide is located in the following directory:

> "/pub/nic/network.service.guides" as the file how.to.ftp.guide

Authorized versus Anonymous FTP Access

FTP is an *authenticated protocol*, which requires that you authenticate yourself before being granted access to a site with FTP. You must have a user name and password that are valid and known to the host before an FTP access is permitted.

Many files that are offered to the general public for free, however, do not require authentication. In this instance, authentication is waived with a scheme called *anonymous FTP*. With anonymous FTP, the user name is "Anonymous" and the password may be optional—usually "Anonymous," or "Guest."

 Many sites are starting to require users to enter their e-mail addresses as passwords so that the sites can maintain a record of user access.

Types of FTP Files

FTP differentiates between an ASCII and a binary file transfer. ASCII is the default mode of transfer in most FTP packages. Most of the files with .TXT extensions or READ.ME files are text files that can be transferred in the ASCII mode. Microsoft Word or WordPerfect files, on the other hand, contain non-ASCII data and must be transferred in binary mode.

Almost all other files except ASCII files should be downloaded in the binary mode. Binary data files such as executable programs, which have a .exe or .com extension, should always be transferred in binary mode. Before transferring binary files, make sure that your program is set to the binary mode. Some FTP software programs automatically recognize the file type and do the download accordingly in the correct mode. This is also helpful when you highlight many files at the same time and download with one drag-and-drop command. Some programs have a configuration option where you can have it automatically set ASCII or binary mode, based on the extension of each individual file. The remainder of the FTP software programs require you to specify, normally by a selection button, the mode of transfer you desire.

One of the most common binary transfers performed on the Internet is the downloading of software applications. Most of the software programs need more than one file. To make downloading of multiple files easier and faster, it is a common practice to provide the files compressed and archived in a single file. The most common utility used for PC programs is called PKZIP (a shareware offering from PKWARE, Inc. based in Brown Deer, Wisconsin), which enables compression and combination of multiple files into one file. Generally, a .ZIP extension is added to the files that you compress with PKZIP. You use PKZIP's PKUNZIP command to extract the files. More and more programs are now offered as a self-extracting archive, which when executed, implodes all the files to their original state. PKZIPed files should always be downloaded in binary mode.

Requirements for Using FTP on the Internet

In addition to having the FTP software, you must be connected to the Internet either as a SLIP or PPP account or through your LAN. If you are connected with a Shell interface, you can't transfer files directly to your computer. In that case, the files must first be transferred via FTP to the host computer (where your Shell account is, which will generally be at the IAP site), and then downloaded to your computer by using a dial-up communication program such as Procomm or Delrina Wincomm Pro. In general, most LANs are connected with the PPP interface; therefore, all LAN users can do FTP directly to their computers. From the end user point of view, all of the Internet hosts appear the same as local UNIX hosts.

Basic FTP Commands

In your typical use of your computer, you most likely do file transfers by using the DOS COPY command or by using Windows File Manager's drag-and-drop features. On your Novell network, the file transfers can be local to your computer (such as COPY C:\AUTOEXEC.BAT C:\AUTOEXEC.SAV). The file transfers also can occur between your local computer and the server (such as COPY C:\AUTOEXEC.BAT F:\AUTOEXEC.SAV, where F: is a directory on the server).

With FTP, you must first connect to the remote machine. In a simple line mode FTP, this is done with the Connect command. In Windows GUI-based FTP clients, this is typically done by selecting connect or selecting New from the File menu. You must then enter your user name and password in the appropriate fields on the screen, or you will be prompted to do so. FTP then connects you to the remote machine. Once connected, you can issue commands to move around in the file system tree, transfer (get and put) files, and manage directories. For most Windows-based graphical user interface FTP programs, most of the FTP functions can be accomplished by point and click or drag-and-drop operations. Table 5.2 gives you the base FTP commands, their closest equivalent in DOS, and a basic description of each command.

Table 5.2 Basic FTP Commands

FTP Command	Equivalent DOS Command if any	Description	Notes
ascii	None	Set transfer mode to ASCII	Causes end-of-line translation to take place on transfer
binary	None	Set transfer mode to binary	No translation during transfer
cd	cd or chdir	Change directory on remote machine	Similar to changing the directory on the NetWare server
lcd	cd	Change directory on local machine	Similar to changing the directory on a PC workstation
del	del or erase	Deletes remote file	Similar to deleting a file on the NetWare server
dir or ls	dir	Lists contents of remote directory	May give information in remote system format (UNIX format)

continues

Table 5.2, Continued

FTP Command	Equivalent DOS Command if any	Description	Notes
exit	None	Close connection and exit FTP	Will happen automatically if you quit the FTP application
get	copy	Gets file from remote machine	Transfers in ASCII or binary based on previous specification
put	copy	Puts file to remote machine	Same as for "put"
mkdir	mkdir or md	Makes directory on remote machine	Similar to creating a directory on the NetWare server

Downloading Netscape—An Interactive Session

The following sequence illustrates the downloading procedure for acquiring Netscape—a Web browser—by using The Wollongong Group's FTP client from its PathWay product. The Netscape Web browser is the client application users can use on their local workstation to access the *World Wide Web* (WWW). Web browsers are covered in more detail in the next section.

1. After starting the FTP application, but before you make a connection to an FTP server, your initial FTP screen should appear as displayed in figure 5.6. In order to create a new connection to a server, the user would select "new" from the "File" menu. After selecting "new," the connection and login screen appears (see fig. 5.7).

2. The user is presented with a form to fill in.

For this example, the following information is filled in for Netscape:

→ Host name—ftp.mcom.com

→ User name—anonymous

→ Password—e-mail address (note that, for security reasons, asterisks display in this field instead of the legible password)

→ Host operating system—UNIX (note that some FTP clients automatically detect a host's operating system type)

Figure 5.7 shows the screen display after all the fields have been filled in. Once all the information is completed, the user clicks on the Connect button.

3. Once you click on the Connect button, the FTP application makes the connection to the selected server using the provided user name and password. As shown in figure 5.8, the FTP

application then displays the remote machine's directories. Like using Microsoft Windows File Manager, the user can select different directories by clicking on the desired directory. If the directory path is known, it can also be filled in directly by typing into the box next to the word "Remote."

4. Once the correct directory has been located (in this case, /netscape/windows), you can use the mouse to drag and drop the desired file from the remote machine to the local machine directory C:\TMP. The Wollongong PathWay drag-and-drop feature works just like it does in Windows File Manager.

Figure 5.9 shows the file transfer in progress. The bottom of the window shows the number of bytes transferred thus far.

5. In figure 5.10, the file transfer has been completed and the local directory screen updated. The Netscape file, ns16-100.exe, has been downloaded.

Figure 5.6

The initial FTP screen.

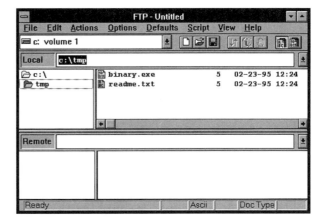

Figure 5.7

The connection and login screen.

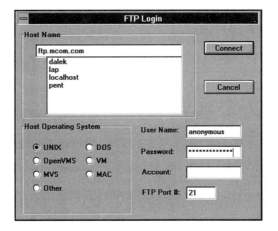

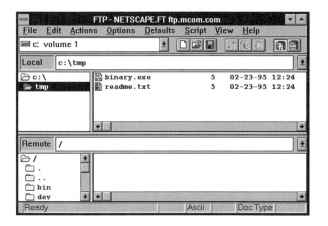

Figure 5.8

The display after the connection has been made to ftp.mcom.com.

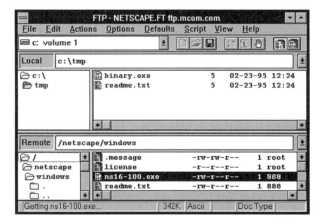

Figure 5.9

The display during the FTP transfer.

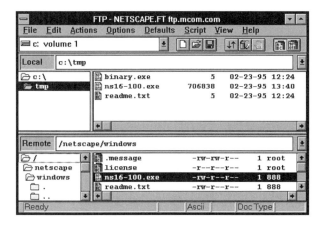

Figure 5.10

The display after the completed transfer.

6. The file transfer is now completed and the user can exit the FTP application. The file ns16-100.exe is a self-extracting zip file. The user can execute ns16-100, which will cause the single file to be unzipped into its various files. The user then follows the now-unzipped instructions to install the Netscape Web browser.

Usenet News

Usenet News—or simply News, Network News, or Netnews—is a term used to describe the world's largest bulletin board. In reality, it is not one, but a collection of over 5,000 bulletin boards called newsgroups. You can find a newsgroup on almost any imaginable topic—from computers to humor to business. No central authority is in charge of the newsgroups. Many of the newsgroups are maintained by individuals on a voluntary basis, even though the content is supplied by individual subscribers. Unlike mailing lists, newsgroup postings don't appear in your mailbox automatically.

For more information on Usenet newsgroups, you can download the following document by using FTP:

rtfm.mit.edu:/pub/usenet-by-group/
news.answers/usenet/faq/part1

Usenet News Software

The Usenet News uses a protocol called *Network News Transport Protocol* (NNTP). Similar to FTP, NNTP is a client-server protocol that offers a version of software for clients, as well as a version of software for servers. Computers with the NNTP server software are called Usenet News servers or news feeds. These servers receive all of the Usenet News traffic in bulk. In turn, users who have computers connected to Usenet News servers can retrieve news by using their favorite newsreader software. Because newsreaders store a file of the users' subscriptions, the newsreader only displays the news from the newsgroups to which the user has subscribed.

For the client, many public domain and commercial newsreaders are available today. Currently, the most popular public domain newsreader is Trumpet. Many of the e-mail packages such as Eudora, however, also offer newsreader functions in the core product. Several Web browsers also offer newsreaders as part of their browsers, thereby reducing the need for a separate newsreader.

Types of Newsgroups

There are two types of newsgroups: *authorized* (mainstream) and *unauthorized* (alternative). The mainstream groups are created by a voting process in which all of the Usenet members worldwide vote on whether or not to create a particular group. The mainstream groups are divided into the following categories:

→ comp—Topics of interest to both computer professionals and hobbyists. Included topics in computer science and software are in source code or binary formats

→ misc—Topics not easily classified under any of the other categories

→ news—Groups concerned with the news network and software

→ rec—Groups oriented toward recreational activities and hobbies

→ sci—Discussions of a technical nature, relating to the established sciences

→ soc—Social issues and socializing

→ talk—Features long discussions, largely debate-oriented without resolution and without appreciable amounts of generally useful information

You can usually determine what a group represents simply by breaking down and examining each component of the group's name. Using the example of a group called comp.novell.sys, you can determine that it is a mainstream group under the computer category that deals with Novell systems. This does not mean that Novell controls the posting on this newsgroup, however, even though some of the questions may be answered by Novell staff. It is a voluntary organization much like the user groups.

The alternate groups are created ad-hoc without the voting process. Most of the alternate groups are classified with "alt" as the initial key word. The group alt.bbs.internet thus is an alternate group that contains a listing of Internet accessible bulletin boards. The alt group contains many of the newsgroups that are less likely to benefit a company; therefore, many organizations filter out alt groups completely so that they are not downloaded from their news feed.

Requirements for Using Newsgroups

Newsreader software, or simply a command-line Telnet interface such as rn, is all that is needed to access newsgroups from the end user site. The end user can have any kind of Internet service for retrieving newsgroups, including shell, PPP/SLIP, or UUCP. *UNIX-to-UNIX Copy Program* (UUCP) is a program initially implemented on UNIX systems and later ported to other systems. It allows systems to send files to other UUCP systems via dial-up telephone lines. It is recommended only for the newsgroup experts that love to use the command-line interfaces.

From the news server standpoint, most sites don't like to host news feeds because it requires a lot of disk space. Therefore, most sites tend to use the news feeds from their IAP. See Chapter 6 for a discussion of NNTP servers.

Common Questions on Newsgroups

As with other Internet topics, new Internet users or system administrators are sure to have questions regarding newsgroups. This section addresses some of the most common questions that arise at new installation sites.

What is a FAQ?

In order to not repeat the same questions and accommodate the new users, most newsgroups have a FAQ, which is a list of frequently asked questions about that newsgroup topic.

Where Can I Get FAQ files?

The newsgroup called news.answers holds all FAQ documents. In addition to being available by way of newsreaders, the FAQ files are kept at MIT and can be obtained by using FTP. To download FAQ files, connect to rtfm.mit.edu and cd into pub/usenet-by-group/news.answers. Here you will find the many FAQ documents. For example, the file novell-faq provides the list of frequently asked questions about the Novell newsgroup.

What Precautions Should I Use in Posting Messages to the News Groups?

Don't print something you wouldn't place in a public letter or speech.

Two newsgroups that may be of specific interest to NetWare networking professionals are the following:

→ comp.sys.novell

→ bit.listserv.novell

The World Wide Web

The World Wide Web is the fastest growing and most dynamic area of the Internet. Originated by CERN (the European Laboratory for Particle Physics), the Web is a gigantic information resource on the Internet that is now widely adapted and used around the world. Almost any type of information imaginable is available on the Web, from corporate and financial documentation, to art galleries and museums, to restaurants and online shopping malls. Even individuals are adding their own personal Web page or home page with text, pictures, sound, video, and more as a way to present themselves and their ideas to the rest of the world.

At the core of the Web are documents that contain information and hyperlinks to other documents. *Hyperlinks* enable you to browse through these documents and follow threads of information by clicking on new topics, pictures, and selections. Essentially, hyperlinks provide a way to navigate through a maze of information on the Web and get back to the original starting point if desired. The hyperlinks you follow may take you from document to document or even from Web server to Web server. Hyperlinks also can automatically start an FTP file download to your computer or initiate an e-mail message to send a comment on something you have read.

Web documents are created by using *HyperText Markup Language* (HTML), the accepted Internet standard for displaying text on Web pages. HTML also defines hyperlinks, graphics, and other information on a Web site. Tools are now available that enable you to create HTML documents from Microsoft Word or Novell's WordPerfect documents. Due to the ease with which a person can create HTML documents with hyperlinks, there has been exponential growth of Web resources.

Much like the FTP, the Web is accessed in a client-server model. There is a server component and a client component. The protocol used to connect to World Wide Web resource is called *HyperText Transport Protocol* (HTTP). Web browsers (the client portion) use HTTP to connect to Web resources on the Internet. See Chapter 6, "Internet Application Servers," for more information on Web servers.

Web Browsers

The key reason for the success of the Web is the development of easy to use, point-and-click client applications called *Web browsers*. A Web browser is the user or client application used to access Web servers anywhere on the Internet. These Web servers maintain their part of the information resources offered on the Internet.

In addition to accessing HTML documents with HTTP, Web browsers can access files by FTP, NNTP (the Internet News protocol), Gopher, and an increasing range of other methods. Also, many Web browsers have added additional search capabilities that enable them to search documents and databases. Many browsers do not stop here, but also implement basic mail and other standard Internet access clients. The next generation of Web browsers are destined to become "the only Internet application most users require." Although some of the added client services may not be as full-featured as the traditional client's applications described earlier in the chapter (i.e., FTP, Usenet, and so on), they will most likely meet the needs of the normal user.

Uniform Resource Locator

The way in which the Web browser addresses all these services is through the *Uniform Resource Locator* (URL)—this is the handle used to retrieve documents that reside somewhere on the Web. URLs look like this:

➜ http://www.whitehouse.gov

➜ ftp://ftp.internetware.com/pub/readme.txt

➜ http://www.ai.mit.edu/stocks/graphs.html

➜ gopher://gopher.internet.com

➜ news:comp.sys.novell

➜ telnet://internetware.com

URL's are made up of two components. The first part of the URL before the colon (":") specifies the access method (i.e., ftp, http, news). The access method defines what protocol will be used to access the specified information. The part of the URL after the colon is interpreted specific to the specified access method. For example, FTP requires a host name and a path to a particular directory, while news requires just the name of a newsgroup. In general, two slashes after the colon are followed by the name of the host machine on the network. If additional information is specified after the host name, it is normally the path to the file or service.

Most browsers let you keep a *hotlist* or *bookmark* of documents or sites you like to visit. By using hotlists or bookmarks, you can save a place or set a marker to the place you are currently visiting that enables you to go directly to it at a later point in time. This is very useful when, after spending an extended period of time browsing the Web, you find a particular site or piece of information that you would like to easily return to at a later time. In addition, Web browsers keep a history of where you have been and enable you to navigate forward and backwards. For greater and more efficient performance, they also cache information in memory and on disk so that the same information does not have to be retrieved over the Internet each time.

Sampling of Web Browsers

In response to the rapid growth of the Web, a tremendous variety of new Web browsers have been developed and are now on the market. The technology is improving with each generation—not only can you get to an unlimited amount of information, but these applications are really fun to use. Three good examples are Mosaic, the original Web browser developed by NCSA and now available from Spyglass, Netscape from Netscape Communications, and InterWorks from Navisoft. The following are some selected screens from a variety of Web browsers.

Most of the Web browsers are initially configured to connect up to a default Web server. In many cases, this is the Web page of the vendor (referred to as the vendor's *home page*). The home page will then have links to other sites and information on the network. In the case of the InternetWorks Web browser, the home page is actually a file stored on the local disk. Figure 5.11 shows the initial screen of the InternetWorks Web browser.

The screen of all Web browsers is broken up into several areas. They all have the same general concepts; however, as you will see in the following screen shots from three different vendors, each one is slightly different. Along the top of the screen, there is the typical Windows drop-down menus such as "File" and "Edit." Below that is a toolbar that provides quick one-click access to different functions. A text window shows the current active URL. There is also a place where you can manually enter a URL. The main section of the screen is the actual display of the HyperText document to which the browser is attached. In addition, each browser

has various areas around the screen that show different status information or activities. For example, all three browsers have an icon in the upper right-hand corner that moves or changes shape when the browser is active.

Figure 5.12 shows the Netscape browser and Netscape's home page. By default, the Netscape browser connects you to their home page As you can see in the URL box (labeled "Location"), the home page URL is:

http://home.mcom.com/home/welcome.html

which indicates that the display you are seeing has been retrieved using the HTTP protocol from the host computer home.mcom.com, and the specific HTML file is /home/welcome.html.

Figure 5.11

The InternetWorks home page.

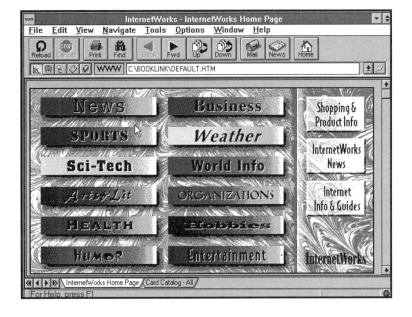

Figure 3.13 shows the NCSA Mosaic browser and the NCSA home page. As you can see by comparing the three different browsers screens, they have many features in common, but again, each has its own style of user interface.

Figure 5.12

The Netscape home page.

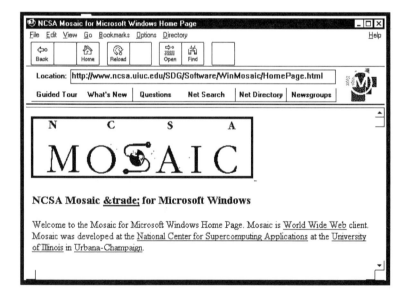

Figure 5.13

The Mosaic home page.

Figure 5.14 is a bitmap graphics picture of a weather map of the United States. In this particular example, the Web browser used is the InternetWorks browser, but any of the three browsers accessing this same picture with a URL of "http://rs560.cl.msu.edu/weather/uscmp.gif" would display the exact same picture.

As stated earlier in this section, Web browsers also have built-in Gopher (see the next section for more information on Gopher) and FTP client capabilities. When browsing through an HTML document that has hotlinks to a document that is to be accessed by Gopher or FTP, the Web browser automatically uses the correct access method. The type of access method is defined by the URL reference that is stored in the document. Figure 5.15 shows how

by using a Web browser, a document can be accessed using Gopher. Note that the URL is:

gopher://gopher.tc.umn.edu

which indicates to use Gopher to connect to the server gopher.tc.umn.edu.

Similarly, all the Web browsers have a built-in FTP client capability. Figure 5.16 show that when connected to a FTP server via the InternetWorks Web browser (in this case, to the host rtfm.mit.edu), as indicated by the URL "ftp://rtfm.mit.edu," you can display the contents of the remote computer's directories that are available through anonymous FTP. Once you find a file you would like to download, all you have to do is double-click on that particular directory entry and the file will be downloaded to your local computer.

Figure 5.14

A picture of a map on the Web.

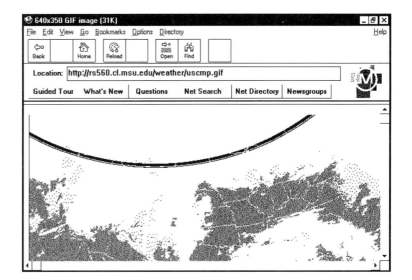

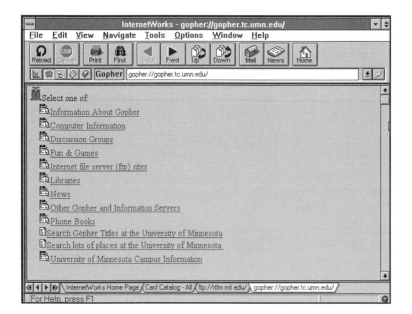

Figure 5.15

The Gopher access screen.

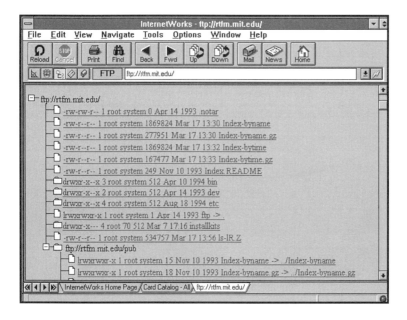

Figure 5.16

Downloading a file using a Web browser.

Communications and Application Software

Gopher

Gopher tools are similar to Web browsers in that they enable you to browse for and retrieve information on the Internet. Conceived at the University of Minnesota, Gopher provides a hierarchical menu system for delivering documents on the Internet. The client-server model is used by Gopher, with Gopher servers being a collection of over 5,000 computers (many of which are IBM mainframes) on the Internet. These Gopher servers keep and exchange information about the location of over 15 million items available on the Internet. Gopher items or documents include files, binary programs, pictures, and more. Unlike Web browsers, Gopher does not require a fancy graphical user interface. Because there is no special graphics requirement, Gopher clients have been developed and are available for almost every operating system. As shown in the proceeding section, Gopher clients are also built into the different Web browsers.

The basic task of a Gopher client is to present a hierarchical menu of documents, and to fetch, display, and retrieve documents. To learn more about Gopher, you can connect to Gopher Central (gopher.tc.umn.edu) by using Gopher client software, as shown in figure 5.15 in the section on Web browsers. One of the features of Gopher is the ability to search Gopher servers for information. As shown on the third line from the bottom in figure 5.15, there is an entry to "Search Gopher Titles at the University of Minnesota." Figure 5.17 shows the result of selecting this entry and requesting a search on the word "gopher." The result is another Gopher list that can be used to find additional information. You can continue this way until you locate the document you want—when you click on that document, it is downloaded to your computer.

Figure 5.17

Using Gopher to search for "gopher."

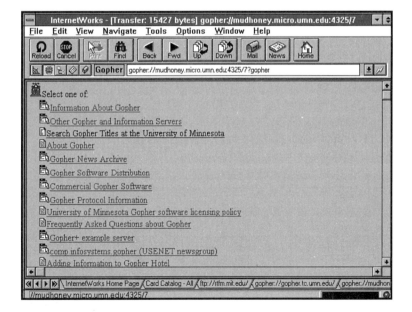

Internet Indexing Tools

The Internet does not have a map showing all of its resources and where they are located, which makes it difficult for even the most experienced user to find information. The task for finding information is getting easier, however, with tools such as Archie, Veronica, and WHOIS, in addition to Gopher, discussed in the previous section. All of these search tools rely on the concept of accessing a server that maintains pointers to various information sources on the Internet. It is similar in concept to a database query from your local database server about "latest inventory of widget A." The big difference is that when you do a search with Internet tools, it is looking for information at tens of thousands of sites and millions of documents. With all of these tools, you only require some knowledge of server locations that may contain the information for which you are looking. This section provides an introduction to these tools and how best to use them.

Archie

A team at McGill University developed Archie, a tool that provides an Internet-wide index facility. *Archie* is an Internet information service for gathering data and indexing widely distributed collections of data. Archie servers provide an archiving search service to help Internet users find directories and files on anonymous FTP hosts. The anonymous FTP hosts contain certain files and directories that are designated for public access. In addition, Archie enables you to receive files (text, graphics, or audio) from anonymous FTP.

Archie clients can contact any one of the Archie servers and search the Archie database for the location (host and path) of files available that matched your search request. Most of the vendors now provide a Windows-based Archie program, which makes it easier to use the Archie tool. The following aspects are important to an Archie search:

→ **Specifying search criteria:** The search criteria can be very loose, such as "pegasus.exe," in which case it provides a list of all anonymous ftp sites that have "pegasus.exe" in its name. The search criteria can also be an exact matching or a regular expression. Figure 5.18 shows screen shots of an Archie program from NetManage.

→ **Specifying Archie servers:** To find the information for which you're searching, you need to specify an Archie server. A current listing of all available Archie servers can be obtained from any of the Archie server sites. Note that all Archie servers contain the same information; therefore, if you don't find the specific information you are looking for on one of the servers, don't keep searching other servers. If one of the servers is busy, however, you should try an alternate server. Some of the Archie sites are listed in table 5.3.

Table 5.3 Archie Sites

Organization Maintaining the Server	Archie Server Name
ANS Network Services, now owned by AOL	archie.ans.net
AT&T	archie.internic.net
Rutgers University	archie.rutgers.edu
SIRAmet, now owned by BBN	archie.sura.net

In addition, many other Archie sites are located in countries outside the USA.

Figure 5.19 shows an example of an Archie search for "eudora.exe." The Archie server is specified as archie.ans.net. The result of the search is a listing of the many ftp site addresses from which you can obtain the eudora.exe file.

You also can reach Archie by using Telnet to access one of the Archie servers. This is useful if you do not have an Archie client available, but do have a Telnet application. Telnet is covered later in this chapter.

WHOIS

WHOIS databases are used for searching information on registered hosts. In these databases, you can find information about particular sites on the Internet, including their IP addresses. You may also get additional information about the sites, such as the administrator and the host connected to the Internet.

Figure 5.18

An Archie search for pegasus.exe.

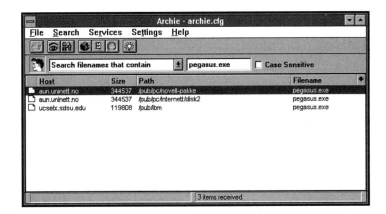

Figure 5.19

An Archie search for eudora.exe.

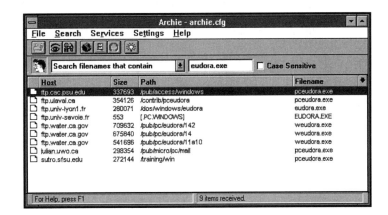

As with any database search, you do need to access the WHOIS servers. The most common use of WHOIS is to search the InterNIC database which is, "rs.internic.net." For example, if your company wants to apply for a domain name called "Internetware," you may want to search the WHOIS servers to see if other similar names have already been registered. In this case, you would find out that it is already in use. An interactive session with whois.internic.net site is shown in figure 5.20.

Veronica

Veronica, like Archie, is a search tool. The main difference between Veronica and Archie is that Veronica searches Gopher space, whereas Archie searches anonymous FTP space. Gopher space represents all documents accessible via Gopher servers, whereas anonymous FTP space would include all documents and files that are available through anonymous FTP. Essentially, Veronica searches a list of document titles for the requested information. You can do more complex searches with Veronica than with Archie. For example, you

can do boolean searches, which look for the occurrence of two words in a document title. Veronica searches are done using Gopher. For more information on Veronica, you can get the veronica-faq by using Gopher to access the following:

gopher://futique.scs.unr.edu/00/veronica/veronica-faq

Telnet

Telnet is the virtual terminal protocol. Telnet allows a workstation to connect to a multiuser host computer, such as a UNIX system, a DEC OpenVMS system, or an IBM Mainframe computer, and act as if it were a locally attached terminal.

In general, if you are a new Internet user, the applications that will prove to be most useful are the Web browsers, FTP, E-mail, and Usenet News. You will probably not have a need for Telnet. On the other hand, if you are part of an enterprise network where you need access to a multiuser system such as UNIX, you will need Telnet to access it.

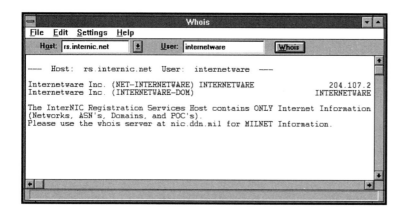

Figure 5.20

Searching the InterNIC with WHOIS.

Telnet Components

Telnet has two main components that are integrated in the Windows environment. These parts include the telnet protocol and a terminal emulator.

The *telnet protocol* defines the way in which the client program contacts the server and the way that the data is sent (for example, how you pass control information to the server along with the data). The telnet protocol does not define the form of the data stream or the way it should be interpreted. The interpretation of the data stream is the job of the terminal emulation component. Most Telnet clients support at least basic DEC VT100 terminal emulation. Many of the commercial Telnet applications also support a variety of additional terminal emulation capabilities such as the DEC terminal line, including VT340, Regis Graphics, and more. If you need specific terminal emulation capabilities to access host computers in your enterprise, you should review the vendors' literature and product to make sure it meets your needs.

In addition to DEC VT terminal emulation, a variety of other ASCII terminal emulations are available from different vendors, including ASCII, WYSE, SCO, HP, and UNISYS.

A completely different class of terminal emulations exist for IBM systems. They are generally referenced as TN3270 for Mainframe running VM or MVS and TN5250 for AS400 systems. Some support graphics options such as 3179.

When you use Telnet to access a host computer, you are providing the same access and user interface that users would see if they were connected to the host computer with a directly connected terminal. For example, figure 5.21 show a Telnet session to a UNIX system. Once connected, you get the standard user interface provided by that UNIX system. The user then needs to know how to use the UNIX system to do any work. If you do not need terminal style access to a host computer, you will not need the Telnet applications. For most Internet users, a Web browser will be the only application they need.

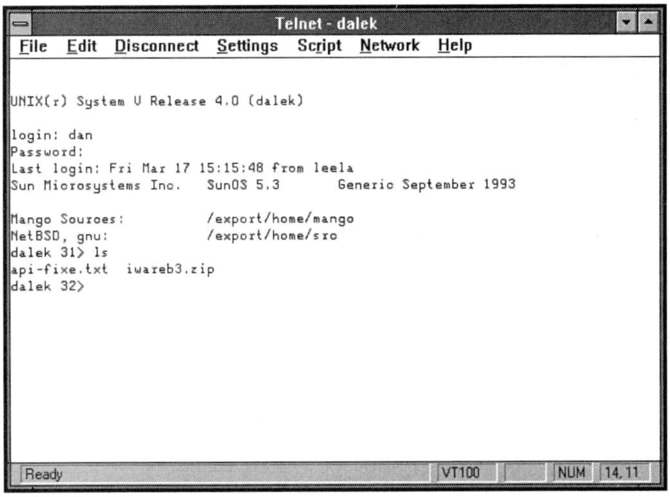

Figure 5.21

A sample Telnet/VT100 terminal emulation connection to a UNIX system.

The following table contains a sample list of the commercial vendors' product offerings. These and additional vendors are continually adding new features to their products. You should check with your vendors for the latest information.

Table 5.4   Software Availability

Vendor	Telnet	FTP Client	E-Mail	Gopher	Newsreader	Web Browser
Beame & Whiteside	Yes	Yes	Yes	N/A	Yes	N/A
Booklink Technologies	N/A	Yes	Yes	Yes	Yes	Yes
Internetware	N/A	Yes	Yes	Yes	Yes	Yes
Distinct Software	Yes	Yes	N/A	N/A	N/A	N/A
Esker Corporation	Yes	Yes	Yes	N/A	N/A	N/A
Firefox	Yes	Yes	Yes	Yes	Yes	Yes
Frontier Software	Yes	Yes	Yes	Yes	Yes	Yes
FTP Software	Yes	Yes	Yes	Yes	Yes	Yes
Novell	Yes	Yes	Yes?	Yes?	Yes?	Yes?
IP Switch	TN3270 only	Yes	Yes	N/A	N/A	N/A
Netscape Communications	N/A	Yes	N/A	Yes	Yes	Yes
NetManage	Yes	Yes	Yes	Yes	Yes	Yes
UB Networks	Yes	Yes	N/A	N/A	N/A	N/A
Wollongong	Yes	Yes	Yes	N/A	N/A	N/A
WRQ	Yes	No	N/A	N/A	N/A	N/A

In addition to the commercial applications shown in the table, the following public domain applications are also available from various sites on the network:

→ Mosaic (Web browser)

→ WS_FTP (FTP)

→ Trumpet (Newsreader)

→ EWAN (Telnet)

→ WinWeb (Web browser)

→ QVT (Telnet and FTP)

→ Archie

→ Pegasus Mail (E-mail client)

→ Eudora (E-mail client)

→ WinGopher

You can use any of the search tools discussed in this chapter to locate copies of these and other freely available software. The following list offers a good starting point. In addition, you can talk to your Internet Access Provider, which normally maintains a mirror site with all of the public domain software.

→ oak.aokland.edu

→ sunsite.unc.edu

→ ftp.cica.indiana.edu

→ ftp.cdrom.com

→ ftp.demon.co.uk

Another location to check for application information is the Web page at the following:

> http://bongo.cc.utexas.edu/~neuroses/
> xcwsa.html

There you will find a Web page called "The Consummate Winsock Apps Page," which provides a short product review and locations for both commercial and non-commercial versions of Internet applications.

Summary

To access the power of the Internet, end users need Internet applications. Most of the applications are now graphical and let you surf the Internet from a Windows workstation with simple point-and-click user interfaces. Web browsers have become the most popular Internet applications, and most browsers now integrate FTP, Gopher, a Newsreader, and an E-mail reader. Finding information on the Internet is also getting easier with indexing tools such as Archie, Veronica, and WHOIS. This chapter covered different Internet client applications that are available commercially or in the public domain, as follows:

→ E-mail

→ FTP

→ Usenet Newsreaders

→ Web browsers

→ Gopher

→ Internet indexing tools, such as Archie, Veronica, and WHOIS

→ Telnet

You should now have a basic understanding of these applications so that you can choose the correct applications for the right purpose. While it was not the intent of this chapter to focus on application usage, you should have a better understanding of how to use the applications from the examples provided. You also have had a glimpse at the vast amount of information that is available on the Internet. It is this information and the ease of access you get with Internet applications that makes the world of Internet access so exciting and valuable.

You now have looked at the Internet applications from the client component of the client-server model. The next chapter, "Internet Application Servers," will focus on the server component of Internet applications.

p a r t
• •

Hardware Components and Issues

Internet Application Servers

As discussed in Chapter 5, Internet applications are useful for outgoing access to the Internet (i.e. surfing the Internet). If you want to establish your company's presence on the Internet with perhaps an e-mail server or a Web server, however, you need to understand application servers and the criteria for choosing the right server based on your needs. Not all application servers have to be located at your site, but an understanding of the options, including equipment and management resources needed, will be very helpful in making this decision. This chapter discusses these and many other issues with different types of servers. The emphasis is placed, however, on the two most important Internet servers, as follows:

→ E-mail servers

→ Web servers

 n o t e This chapter focuses on layer 3 of the Internet connectivity matrix.

7	SECURITY AND MANAGEMENT
6	Internet Access Providers
5	WAN Access Devices
4	WAN Access Services
3	Internet Application Servers
2	Internet Navigation Software
1	Network Communication Protocols

E-Mail Servers and Electronic Mail Solutions

Electronic mail (e-mail) is the number one reason the Internet is used. It is estimated that over 20 million people have e-mail access to the Internet. This number includes anyone who, by using a computer with any type of messaging system or user interface, can address a mail message to info@somehost and receive a reply message. As shown in figure 6.1, the "big picture" for electronic mail is even bigger than the TCP/IP-based Internet. This larger group of mail users will be referred to in this chapter as the Mail Internet. This picture is also complicated by the fact that many LAN systems are already using a local mail system. There is not one easy answer to explain how you provide access to the Mail Internet for your Novell users.

This section covers the following topics:

→ Basic components of e-mail systems

→ Mail system topologies

→ Mail clients

→ Internet mail protocols

→ Mail envelopes

→ Mail content

→ Internet mail routing

→ E-mail gateways

→ Selecting mail solutions

Due to the complexity, the number of variables that may exist in your environment, and your requirements, you still may not have all the answers after you read this chapter, but you will be in a better position to ask more questions.

Basic Components of E-Mail Systems

E-mail systems have many components, depending on a vendor's implementation. At a global level, however, most e-mail systems can be categorized into three main components, as follows:

→ User agents (e-mail readers or clients)

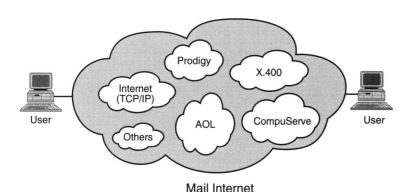

Figure 6.1

*Electronic mail—
the big picture.*

Mail Internet

→ Local servers (mail transfer agents or post offices)

→ Mail gateways

These issues were briefly discussed in Chapter 5, "Internet Applications," from an end-user point of view. This chapter, however, is targeted strictly for network administrators. Some of the points raised in Chapter 5 have been repeated here for completeness.

User Agents

The *user agent* (UA) or client is the software or program that the user utilizes to compose, send, retrieve, and view his or her mail. There are many types of user agents. Different user agents may provide different features. The following list provides a sample of some of the features that may be supported:

→ Message composition

→ Message addressing

→ Message reply

→ Automatic message reply

→ File attachments

→ Address books (local and remote)

→ Spell checking

→ Storage management (filing systems)

→ Mail searching

→ Mail filtering

→ Template documents

Many mail systems are *closed systems*, which means that once the mail server or system is chosen, you must use a particular mail client or user agent. Other systems are built using open standards that allow a wide variety of user agents from different providers. If a company is using cc:Mail servers, for example, almost all users use the mail client that comes with cc:Mail. In a TCP/IP environment, you can use user agents from any vendor to access the mail servers. Novell's MHS system is somewhere in-between these two extremes. A number of companies offer MHS-compatible systems.

Examples of mail user agents include Eudora, Pegasus, and the user interface of Lotus cc:Mail or Microsoft MS Mail. In addition, the mail clients that are included in almost every commercial TCP/IP vendors offerings are also user agents.

Local Servers

The local mail servers (also referred to as *mail transfer agents* (MTAs) or post offices) interact with the user agent to allow mail to be sent between two or more users. Mail servers have two main functions—the storage of mail, and the transfer of mail between servers if there is more that one server involved. The storage of mail includes storing of mail waiting to be delivered to another user or mail server, storage of mail received by the server awaiting delivery for the intended user, and remote storage of mail for a user after the mail has been read.

Examples of local servers include TCP/IP-based SMTP/POP servers, server portion of Lotus cc:Mail or Microsoft MS Mail, and Novell MHS.

Mail Gateways

As you have learned, there are a wide variety of types of user agents and servers, all with different capabilities. Each system has its own unique way of dealing with addressing, file formats, and message attachments. These differences make it impossible to directly attach two different types of mail systems and provide interoperability. In order to attach two dissimilar mail systems, mail gateways are used. Mail gateways take care of address conversions, file format conversions, and data encoding to allow two different mail systems to communicate. Mail gateways to the Internet are responsible for transferring mail to and from the local mail server, doing the necessary conversions and communicating with other mail servers or gateways on the Internet using SMTP.

Mail gateways include cc:Mail Link to SMTP, Internet Exchange for cc:Mail, SMTP for NetWare Global MHS, Mercury (which is also a SMTP/POP server), and a variety of other gateway packages.

Mail System Topologies

The various components of a mail system may be linked in different topologies, depending on your network requirement. Many e-mail systems claim to be client-server based. E-mail is a more complex application, however, especially when more than one server or multiple mail systems are involved. Therefore, a basic understanding of the mail system topologies may be helpful before diving into SMTP protocols.

E-mail topologies can be categorized as the following:

→ Single server topology

→ Multiple homogenous server topology

→ Multiple heterogeneous server topology

Single Server Topology

Most of the smaller size NetWare networks may already be providing an e-mail system for the LAN users with a single server. Figure 6.2 shows the two main components of a single-server e-mail system—the user agent, which is the software or program that the user uses to compose, send, retrieve, and view his or her mail, and the mail server, which is responsible for storing mail and distribution.

This topology can be implemented as an interactive client-server application or as a shared file-based system. In an interactive client-server implementation, the client software (client application) interacts with a program (server application) on the server. In a shared file-based model (used by many LAN e-mail systems such as cc:Mail), the client application retrieves and places files on the server in a known location.

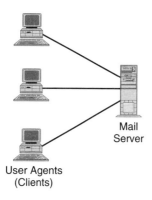

Mail
Server

User Agents
(Clients)

Figure 6.2

A local e-mail system.

In the single-server topology, the same e-mail protocol is used throughout the network, and the configuration is very simple. This topology is generally used for a local LAN e-mail system.

Multiple Homogenous Server Topology

For networks with multiple locations or many LAN segments, more than one e-mail server is needed. Figure 6.3 shows a simple e-mail system with more than one network and mail server. In this case, the user agent or client talks to a local server, which in turn communicates to one or more other servers. This is a typical topology for a homogeneous environment. A *homogeneous* mail environment is one

that uses the same type of mail system throughout the network, such as all cc:Mail-based or all TCP/IP-based mail systems.

Just like the single-server topology, the same e-mail protocol is used throughout the network. The configuration is more complex, however, due to multiple servers.

Multiple Heterogeneous Server Topology

Mail is becoming a universal communication vehicle, but different mail systems use their own proprietary protocols. Thus, for any two mail server systems that use servers that speak different protocols, a mail gateway is needed. Also referred to as the *client-server-gateway model*, the multiple heterogeneous server topology is shown in figure 6.4. This is the configuration that is used when connecting Novell LANs that are already using a LAN-based e-mail system and desire to add access to the Internet using their existing e-mail client software. With this approach, users continue to use the same e-mail software they have been using, but are now able to address mail to users that are not on their local LAN. The mail gateway is responsible for interfacing between the local mail server and other servers on the Internet. The other option in this environment is to use two mail systems—the existing LAN-based mail system with its user

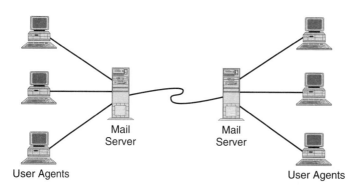

Mail
Server

Mail
Server

User Agents

User Agents

Figure 6.3

The components of a homogeneous e-mail system.

agent, and a TCP/IP-based mail system used in parallel to access the Internet.

Mail Clients

Within the three e-mail topologies discussed previously, different client implementations exist. Some of these client implementations work with other servers, while others are proprietary and only work with the server from the same vendor. Different mail clients can be classified into three broad categories, as follows:

→ TCP/IP-based clients

→ Proprietary LAN-based clients

→ Other mail clients

TCP/IP-Based Clients

As discussed in Chapter 3, "Understanding TCP/IP," one of the basic components of the TCP/IP protocol suite is the *Simple Mail Transfer Protocol* (SMTP), which defines how mail is sent between servers. (SMTP will be covered later in the chapter.) SMTP addresses the issue of mail transfer between systems on a peer basis. SMTP does not specify how the user accesses the messages in a client-server environment. The *Post Office Protocol* (POP) was developed to allow computers that were not always connected to the Internet and those that wanted their messages stored on a larger host computer to communicate with the server. POP was first specified in RFC 918 in 1984, before personal computers were used to access the Internet. POP continued to be refined, and the current version, POP Version 3 (POP3), is described in RFC 1725. Today, POP is widely implemented as the standard way for PC mail clients to retrieve mail residing on a mail server.

A newer protocol, *Internet Message Access Protocol* (IMAP) has been developed. IMAP includes additional capabilities, including operations for creating, deleting, and renaming mailboxes, the capability to check for new messages, and the capability to search and selectively retrieve messages

Figure 6.4

A local LAN e-mail system with a gateway to the Internet.

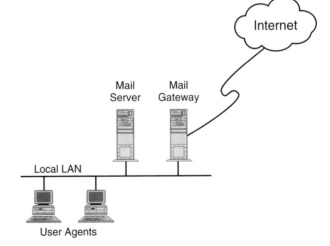

based on specified attributes. The current version, IMAP Version 4, is specified by RFC 1733.

Most clients today implement POP, with a few also implementing IMAP. Figure 6.5 shows a user agent or mail client using POP or IMAP to retrieve mail from the mail server. POP and IMAP only define the retrieving of mail from the server. The SMTP protocol is used to send mail from the user agent to the mail server. When mail arrives over the Internet using SMTP, the mail server stores the user mail on the server. This way, because the mail server is normally always connected to the Internet and always running SMTP, the client can access the mail using POP or IMAP any time it is convenient.

ProprietaryLAN-Based Clients

Proprietary LAN-based systems, such as cc:Mail from Lotus and MS Mail from Microsoft, have their own user agents (client applications) that operate on the local LAN. MHS from Novell, on the other hand, has a large support of third-party user agents/ client applications, such as DaVinci e-mail and BeyondMail.

Other Mail Clients

Before the wide spread use of personal computers with user-friendly, graphical user interface mail clients, the typical computer user used host-based mail systems from character mode terminals. UNIX systems come standard with character-based mail systems that use SMTP to exchange mail between systems. Today, many users using time-sharing systems and users of BBS systems with dial-in accounts still use character-based mail systems.

Users of online services such as CompuServe, Prodigy, and America Online have mail access to the Internet through mail gateways. Most of these services offer their own proprietary mail clients that are part of the sign up services. The same is true for commercial mail service providers such as AT&T Mail, Sprint Mail, MCI Mail, and others. A large number of X.400-based mail systems (the International Standardization Organization's standards) are also connected to the Internet through mail gateways, but they need a different mail client.

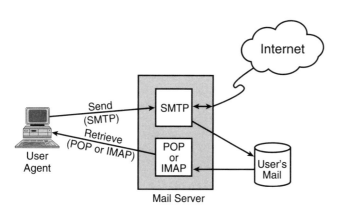

Figure 6.5

TCP/IP-based client-server mail.

Internet Mail Protocols

Because the objective of this chapter is to understand how to set up servers to send and receive e-mail from the Internet, understanding the most common Internet e-mail protocols is essential. The three most common protocols that have been discussed in subsequent sections include the following:

→ Simple Message Transport Protocol (SMTP)

→ Post Office Protocol (POP)

→ Internet Message Access Protocol (IMAP)

SMTP

As discussed earlier and shown in figure 6.5, electronic mail is sent from the user agent to the mail server via SMTP in Internet mail servers. Mail is also exchanged between servers over the Internet using SMTP. SMTP is the standard for transporting electronic mail on the Internet, and is defined in RFC 821. Its companion document, RFC 822, identifies the specific message formats used by SMTP. These formats have been extended by the *Multipurpose Internet Mail Extensions* (MIME), discussed later in the chapter.

Living up to the "simple" part of its name, SMTP uses a simple command-based communication between the sender and receiver. With SMTP, the receiver could be the ultimate destination server for the mail or mail relay, which will take the mail and forward it on to another server. The server or mail relay can also store the mail for later delivery if the destination server is not available. Based on this

capability, SMTP mail is sometimes referred to as a *store-and-forward mail system*. SMTP does, however, work best when all servers in the network are up and always available to receive mail. In many cases, client software tries to communicate directly with the destination mail server; if the server is not accessible, the client has no way of automatically storing the mail for later delivery.

Computers that can receive mail listen for connection requests on TCP port 25. A computer or client that wants to send mail opens a connection to the destination server or mail relay. The interaction between the two is then a simple series of commands and responses. SMTP is called a "lock-step" protocol because after every command is issued, the sender of the command waits for one of limited number of responses before going onto the next command. Commands and data are exchanged using standard 7-bit ASCII text. No line can be longer than 1,000 characters. There also other limits, such as a user name cannot exceed 64 characters and a mail path cannot exceed 256 characters. These limits may be modified or extended by RFC 1425, "SMTP Service Extensions," (referred to as ESMTP), which allows negotiation of additional capabilities, like sending 8-bit data.

The following table lists the commands used by SMTP in transporting mail. Although a user or administrator does not necessarily have to use them, the commands are included here to give a better insight as to how SMTP works.

Table 6.1 SMTP Commands Used in Transporting Mail

Command	Command Summary
HELO <domain>	The host sending the command identifies itself with its domain name.
MAIL FROM:<reverse-path>	Identifies the sender of the message.
RCPT TO:<forward-path>	Identifies the recipients of the message.
DATA	Signifies that the message text follows. The message test portion is terminated by a line with a dot by itself (".").
RSET	Resends the connection and aborts the current transaction.
SEND FROM:<reverse-path>	Delivers mail to a user's terminal.
SOML FROM:<reverse-path>	Delivers mail to or sends mail from a user's terminal.
SAML FROM:<reverse-path>	Delivers mail to or sends mail from a user's terminal.
VRFY <string>	Asks to verify that <string> is a valid user.
EXPN <string>	Expands the address <string> as a local mail alias or mail list.
HELP [<string>]	Requests list of commands or help on a specific command.
NOOP	No operation, but requires acknowledgment.
QUIT	Requests to close the connection.
TURN	Requests that the sender and receiver change roles, so that the previous sender can now receive any mail that was queued on the remote host.

The following is a list of all possible reply codes. For each specific command, there is only a subset of replies allowed:

211   System status, or system help reply

214   Help message

220   <domain> Service ready

221   <domain> Service closing transmission channel

250   Requested mail action okay, completed

251   User not local; will forward to <forward-path>

354   Start mail input; end with <CRLF>.<CRLF>

421   <domain> Service not available, closing transmission channel

450   Requested mail action not taken: mailbox unavailable

451   Requested action aborted: local error in processing

452   Requested action not taken: insufficient system storage

500   Syntax error, command unrecognized

501   Syntax error in parameters or arguments

502   Command not implemented

503   Bad sequence of commands

504   Command parameter not implemented

550   Requested action not taken: mailbox unavailable

551   User not local; please try <forward-path>

552   Requested mail action aborted: exceeded storage allocation

553   Requested action not taken: mailbox name not allowed

554   Transaction failed

POP

As discussed in the previous section, SMTP is used to send mail between servers. As shown earlier in figure 6.5, once the destination mail server receives mail for a user, it stores the mail for retrieval by the user. The standard method for this retrieval is with the POP or IMAP protocols.

Using POP, mail is stored on the server, and the user agent or client, normally a personal computer user, periodically connects to the server and downloads all of the pending mail to the local machine. Thereafter, all mail processing is local to the user agent. You can think of POP as providing the last leg of the store-and-forward service. POP is used to move mail (on demand) from the final staging server (drop point) to a single destination machine. Once delivered, the messages are typically deleted from the POP server. Some client software automatically moves and deletes the mail from the server, while others enable you to control this function.

Two versions of POP exist—POP2 and POP3 (specified in by RFC 1725). Most clients are now POP3-based, and most servers that support POP support both POP2 and POP3. POP3, however, has become the universal standard.

IMAP

IMAP is a client-server mail protocol designed to permit manipulation of remote mailboxes as if they were local. IMAP differs from POP in that POP simply delivers all mail messages and expects the client workstation to manipulate at its end. With IMAP, mail is stored on the server as with POP, but the mail client machine does not normally copy it all at once and then delete it from the server. Unlike POP, IMAP clients can ask the server for headers or the bodies of specified messages, or to search for messages meeting certain criteria. Messages in the mail repository can be marked as deleted and subsequently expunged, but they stay on the repository until the user takes such action. In other words, POP is only a mail retrieval protocol, while IMAP is both a retrieval and a manipulation protocol.

IMAP (Specified by RFC 1730) is a newer protocol and is not as widely implemented as POP. It is expected that over the next several years, IMAP will become more widely implemented based on its enhanced capabilities.

Selecting an SMTP System

Many operating systems can be used for hosting SMTP mail servers. Like with many other Internet servers, however, UNIX is the most prevalent SMTP server environment. The reason for UNIX's popularity with SMTP mail servers is that most UNIX systems come with SMTP servers as a core part of the operating system. POP server support is also needed, however, for enabling PC workstations to communicate with the UNIX-based SMTP mail server. Many of the UNIX system vendors, like Santa Cruz Operations, Sun Microsystems, and Silicon Graphics, are creating Internet servers that include SMTP and POP servers. Today, IMAP is not as widely used and does not come standard with UNIX systems. There are public domain versions of both POP and IMAP available on the Internet, however, that have been ported to UNIX and a variety of other systems. Figure 6.6 shows how a

NetWare LAN with an SMTP mail server with UNIX would be set up.

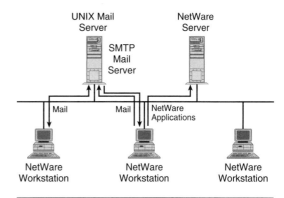

Figure 6.6

A UNIX mail server in a NetWare environment.

For NetWare administrators with limited UNIX expertise, UNIX-based SMTP mail servers are not the best choice because UNIX requires a huge learning curve. NLM-based SMTP mail servers are thus a better alternative for NetWare sites. The most popular NLM-based SMTP mail server, called Mercury, was developed by David Harris, based in New Zealand, and is available on the Internet. Mercury has the unique distinction of being the only mail server that can be a stand-alone SMTP mail server, as well as a gateway between NetWare MHS and SMTP. Firefox, a UK-based company, has also released an SMTP mail server NLM. Few details are available at the time of this writing, however. Figure 6.7 shows the setup for SMTP mail with an NLM-based solution. As shown in the figure, NLM eliminates the need for UNIX server hardware or a dedicated UNIX administrator. If your environment has a centralized mail server for many users (greater than 500), however, UNIX servers might be more advantageous due to their more scalable architecture.

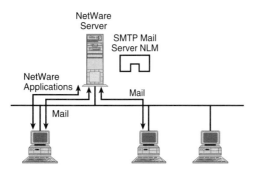

NetWare
Server

SMTP Mail
Server NLM

NetWare
Applications

Mail

Mail

Figure 6.7

An NLM-based SMTP server in a NetWare environment.

n o t e Windows NT may also be another alternative for sites that prefer something other than a UNIX-based server. The choice of products is rather limited at this time however, but will grow in the future.

Mail Envelopes

Electronic mail messages are organized much like a letter or package that would be sent via the U.S. postal service. In the e-mail world, mail sent via U.S. mail is often referred to as "snail mail." A typical U.S. mail package is composed of an envelope and its contents, which may include any number of things (i.e., a letter, pictures, floppy disks, spreadsheet lists, etc.). This is the same with electronic mail. With electronic mail today, users can send any kind of computer data (i.e., a letter, pictures, computer programs from a floppy disk, spreadsheets, etc.) that is stored on their computer.

Just like a postal service envelope contains addresses of senders and receivers, there are similar, though more strict, rules for electronic mail,

discussed in the next section. Some of these issues were discussed in Chapter 5 from an end user's stand-point, but are presented here again from a network administrator's point of view. Certain information is thus repeated for the sake of completeness.

E-Mail Addressing

In Internet mail, RFC 822 (standard for the format of ARPA Internet text messages) defines the format of the messages that are sent over the network. RFC 822 also defines the format and syntax of mail addressing. Because e-mail addresses are read and used by computers, they must follow a standard form, unlike with the U.S. postal service, where humans are involved—everyone has heard stories about U.S. mail being delivered even with an improper or incomplete address.

RFC 822-compliant electronic mail, as with U.S. mail, is enclosed in an "envelope" that is used to route and deliver the message through the network. The content of the message is then divided into 2 parts: the "header" and the "body." In RFC 822, the message is limited to simple ASCII text. As discussed in the next section, a new standard has been developed to allow other types of data to be encoded and sent via e-mail. The header in an RFC 822 message consists of lines of keywords followed by a colon and a text string. As with U.S. mail, where the recipient address and the return address are placed on the envelope, this same type of addressing information is placed in the header of the e-mail message. It is this addressing information that is used to send the mail through the network to one or more recipients on the network. The following table contains the key portions of the RFC 822 header. The complete list and syntax can be found in the RFC. Each keyword is followed by one or more valid e-mail addresses.

Table 6.2   Key Portions of the RFC 822 Header

E-Mail Header Field	Description of Field
FROM: / RESENT-FROM:	This field contains the identity of the person or process who wanted this message to be sent. A forwarded message would be indicated by "Resent-From:" This entry should specify only one mail address.
SENDER: / RESENT-SENDER:	This field contains the authenticated identity of the agent (person, system, or process) that actually sent the message. It is intended for use when the sender is not the author of the message, or to indicate who among a group of authors actually sent the message. If the contents of the "Sender" field are the same as the "From" field, then it is optional.
REPLY-TO: / RESENT-REPLY-TO:	This field provides a general mechanism for indicating any address(es) to which responses are to be sent. This can be used when the sender wants the responses be sent to a person or address other than the sender. If the contents of the field are the same as the "From" field, then it is optional.
TO: / RESENT-TO:	This field contains the identity of the one or more primary recipients of the message.
CC: / RESENT-CC:	This field contains the identity of the secondary (informational) recipients of the message.
BCC: / RESENT-BCC:	This field contains the identity of additional recipients of the message. The contents of this field are not included in copies of the message sent to the primary and secondary recipients.

Just like registered U.S. mail or Federal Express, messages contain a unique "Message ID" that can be used to trace the message. Other fields may be added by the mail systems, such as "Received:," which is placed as a time stamp or postmark each time a mail system processes a message. It is not uncommon to see multiple "Received:" fields on a single mail message that has been processed by a number of mail systems.

E-Mail Addresses

Now that you are familiar with message addressing syntax, the e-mail address itself is the next important thing to understand. E-mail addresses or mailbox addresses are made up of two parts—the *domain part* (on the right side) and the *local part* (on the left). They are connected by the "@" symbol, which is pronounced "at." For example, the e-mail address dan@internetware.com would be pronounced "dan at internetware dot com." The domain part of the address indicates how the message should be routed on the Internet, while the local part is used to specify how it should be delivered when it arrives at its destination. In a simple case, the local part is just the user's name on the local mail host that is specified by the domain part.

 The *Domain Name System* (DNS), discussed earlier in the book, was developed and adopted after RFC 822. As such, much of the information in RFC 822 regarding domain syntax and semantics has been superseded by the DNS standards.

The local part of the address is used by local delivery agents to determine how to handle the message locally, which may include further transporting of the message to another mail system (in the case of some mail gateways). For this reason, the local part may be case-sensitive, and care should be taken to specify it correctly. For example, because many mail servers are UNIX-based and the normal standard in UNIX systems is to use lowercase, it is quite common to spell e-mail names in lowercase. Mail sent to the name *Mike* when the correct user name is *mike* may not get delivered. The domain part, like other host names in the DNS, is not case-sensitive.

In addition to the actual address information, RFC 822 allows additional comments to be placed in the recipient or originator header fields. This is commonly used to identify the actual or full names, the names of mailing lists or mail aliases, or the names or versions of programs that send or receive mail corresponding with the mailbox address. Parentheses around a text string always signify comments.

If the actual mail address is enclosed in angle brackets ("<" and ">"), other arbitrary strings can be enclosed in angle brackets, but are more commonly seen with quotation marks.

The following are a few examples of this:

> To: scottadams@aol.com (The creator of Dilber)
>
> From: "Dan Ladermann" <dan@internetware.com)
>
> To: jack@goodschool.edu (Professor Jack)

which is the same as:

> To: jack@GoodSchool.EDU (Professor Jack)
>
> From: postmaster@computer.net (Mail system zoro gateway server)

Some mail systems allow more than one name to be mapped to a particular user. For example, a user's real name might be used for his or her mail address, such as John_Public@company.com, instead of a more traditional mail address. Traditional mail addresses can often be difficult to remember; allowing a user's real name to be part of or represent his or her mail address provides a much easier way to recall mail address. This, however, is not an accepted standard shared by all mail systems.

Local Delivery Addresses   As stated earlier, the local part of the address is used by local delivery agents to determine how to handle the message. This process may include passing or delivering the message by way of another mail system, which would likely display a more complex address. For example, you may see addresses similar to the following.

Address	Type of Destination
mary%comp@hosta.edu	mail destined for uucp or bitnet network
12345.6789@compuserve.com	CompuServe system
abcde!mike@attmail.com	ATT Mail (EasyLink)
"/C=US/ADMD=mailservr/O=CompanyX/ PN=John.Smith/"@hostb.com	X.400 Mail system

Mail Lists   Mail addresses can also specify mailing lists. Mailing lists may be simple distribution lists that are maintained on the local mail server or mail clients that just forward the mail on to a list of users. This feature is sometimes referred to as a mail reflector. Mailing lists may also be implemented with more powerful systems called list servers. One particular version of list servers is based on a tool called LISTSERV. There is a collection of computers on the Internet that implement LISTSERV. These LISTSERV hosts know about each other and know what mailing lists are maintained where. There are over 10,000 mailing lists maintained in the LISTSERV system. Users can get information from LISTSERV by sending an e-mail message to any of the list servers. For example, send a message to the following address:

> To: listserv@listserv.net
>
> list global /subject

where subject is the topic for which you want to find a list server. In addition, a user can subscribe and unsubscribe to mailing lists by sending mail to the list server.

Mail Content

Having understood the mail envelope, let us now discuss mail content issues. The U.S. postal service has rules and regulations pertaining to the size of the mail, as well as the actual mail contents— e-mail has similar rules. Internet e-mail content rules were very simple when only ASCII text was permitted, but this is changing with the demand for sending other types of files by way of e-mail. Internet mail has two popular standards that specify the mail content rules, as follows:

→ SMTP

→ MIME

SMTP
SMTP is defined by RFC 821 and RFC 822. RFC 822 defines the text message format, which has a number of limits. This is not surprising due to the fact that these standards were developed in 1982, and the main concern was moving text-based messages between different computers, most of which were accessed with character-based terminals. These limits included only sending 7-bit ASCII text with lines shorter than 1,000 characters. Several schemes were developed to encode binary data (for example, uuencoding) so it could be sent

through the mail system. These methods were either nonstandard or required the user to take multiple steps before sending the information. For example, the user would first use an encoding tool, such as uuencode, to encode or convert the binary data to a file that only contained 7-bit ASCII text with short lines. The user would then go in the mail system and send the encoded file. The recipient on the other side would have to do the reverse operation.

Times have changed, however, and today the most common access to mail and other Internet services is from a PC with a graphical user interface. This enables users to attach all types of files or documents to a standard mail message simply by using the point-and-click or drag-and-drop features that are part of these graphical user interfaces. Upon delivery to its destination, the mail message attachment should automatically be stored or displayed with the appropriate application.

MIME

Because of the growing need to send multiple data types and files electronically, a new standard was created called *Multipurpose Internet Mail Extension* (MIME). MIME extends the functionality of the basic Internet mail message format (RFC 822) to allow additional types of message contents to be transported by SMTP. MIME is fully described in RFC 1341.

MIME allows mail message attachments to contain the following:

→ Text having unlimited line length or overall length

→ Character sets other than ASCII

→ Multiple objects in a single message

→ Multifont messages

→ Binary or application specific files

→ Graphical images, audio and video files, and multimedia messages

MIME does this by standardizing additional fields for mail message headers, which describe new types of content and organization for messages.

MIME Header Fields   MIME defines the following new header fields:

→ A MIME-Version header field, which uses a version number to declare that a message conforms to the MIME standard. The current version number is 1.0.

→ A Content-Type header field, which can be used to specify the type of data in the message body.

→ A Content-Transfer-Encoding header field, which specifies how the data is encoded.

→ Content-Description, which is a description of the message body.

→ Content-ID, which is used to identify different message body parts.

MIME Content Types   There are seven top-level content types defined today that are used to specify the type of data in the body of a message, as follows:

→ Text Content-Type value, which can be used to represent textual information in a number of character sets and formatted text description languages in a standardized manner.

→ Multipart Content-Type value, which can be used to combine several body parts, possibly of differing types of data, into a single message.

→ Application Content-Type value, which can be used to transmit application data or binary data.

→ Message Content-Type value, which can be used for encapsulating a mail message.

→ Image Content-Type value, which can be used for transmitting still image (picture) data.

→ Audio Content-Type value, which can be used for transmitting audio or voice data.

→ Video Content-Type value, which can be used for transmitting video or moving image data, possibly with audio as part of the composite video data format.

The Content-Transfer-Encodings   Most of content types listed in the preceding contain 8-bit character or binary data in their native format. Since SMTP in RFC 821 restricts mail messages to 7-bit ASCII data with lines no longer than 1,000 characters, these must be encoded before being transported.

MIME provides two mechanisms for encoding such data into a 7-bit short-line format—BASE64 and QUOTED-PRINTABLE. The Content-Transfer-Encoding header field indicates the mechanism used to perform such an encoding.

The possible values for the Content-Transfer-Encoding field are as follows:

→ BASE64

→ QUOTED-PRINTABLE

→ 8BIT

→ 7BIT

→ BINARY

→ x-EncodingName

Both BASE64 and the QUOTED-PRINTABLE values are encoding systems that convert binary data to data of lines no longer than 76 ASCII characters. The encoding schemes are used very differently.

The BASE64 encoding mechanism is well-suited for representing binary files, whereas QUOTED-PRINTABLE encoding is most appropriate for data that consists primarily of printable ASCII characters. With the QUOTED-PRINTABLE method, printable ASCII characters are represented as themselves. The equal sign (=) serves as an escape character. Any character that is not a printable or white space ASCII character is represented as an equal sign followed by two hexadecimal digits. An equal sign in the message is also represented in this way. Lines that are longer than 76 characters are cut off after the 75th character, and the line ends with an equal sign.

For messages that are mostly printable ASCII characters, few additional characters are required when using QUOTED-PRINTABLE encoding. The message can be read by users who do not have a MIME-aware mail reading program.

The values 8-bit, 7-bit, and binary all infer that no encoding has been performed. An encoding type of 7BIT requires that the body is already in a 7-bit representation suitable for SMTP if it is to be sent out to the network. This is the default value (Content-Transfer-Encoding: 7BIT) if the Content-Transfer-Encoding header field is not present.

While data with 8-bit or binary encoding cannot normally be sent over SMTP, both values are useful because they indicate the kind of data contained in the object, and therefore the kind of encoding that might need to be performed for transmission in a given transport system. *8-bit* means that the lines are short, but there may be non-ASCII characters. *Binary* means that not only may non-ASCII characters be present, but also that the lines are not necessarily short enough for SMTP transport.

The difference between 8-bit and binary is that binary does not require adherence to any limits on line length. 8-bit and binary are intended for compatibility with future Internet e-mail transport standards and with gateways to non-Internet environments. As of this writing, there are no standardized Internet e-mail transports for which it is legitimate to include unencoded 8-bit or binary data in the mail bodies.

The standard permits implementations to support additional Content-Transfer-Encoding values. They must have names that begin with X- to indicate its non-standard status.

MIME is an extensible mechanism—over time, new content-type will be added. In addition, other MIME fields, such as character set names, are likely to have new values defined. As with TCP reserved port numbers, these new values will be managed by the *Internet Assigned Numbers Authority* (IANA). This will ensure that the set of such values will be developed in a public and orderly manner.

With MIME, it is now possible to send arbitrary types of data objects in RFC 822-conformant mail messages and not violate any restrictions imposed by RFC 821 or RFC 822. Multipart and message content types allow mixing and hierarchical structuring of objects of different types in a single message. The content types provide a mechanism for identifying messages or body parts as audio, image, or other kinds of data. With these MIME capabilities, mail user agents have the information they need to identify specific mail content and present it properly and easily to the user.

Internet Mail Routing

Mail client programs (either user agents or mail servers) normally route Internet mail messages based on one of several routing options, which include the following:

➔ Domain Name System (DNS) host name lookup

➔ Host table lookup of destination host

➔ Delivery to default mail relay host

Mail routing via the DNS is the preferred method of mail routing on the Internet. The DNS is an Internet network service that provides for the storage and retrieval of information associated with domain names. In the context of Internet mail, the records that are of interest are *Mail eXchanger* (MX) records and *Address* (A) records. In Chapter 3, "Understanding TCP/IP," the discussion of DNS was limited to host address to IP address mappings.

A-records are used to store Internet address information for hosts, whereas MX-records are used to store mail forwarder information for hosts registered on the Internet. An MX-record will contain the name of the host or domain, a list of one or more mail forwarding hosts, and the preference values associated with these hosts. The preference values are used to determine the order in which to attempt delivery, in the case where more than one mail forwarder has been identified. MX-records are essential for the proper routing of mail, especially in situations where the destination host is not physically connected to the Internet, requiring it to rely upon a mail forwarder for proper mail delivery.

As an example, many organizations rely upon the UUCP communications package supplied with the UNIX operating system to physically exchange mail. Through the use of MX-records, these sites can

Hardware Components and Issues

appear to be connected to the Internet, even though mail is the only Internet service they use. In other cases, MX-records can be used to hide the complexity of internal networks and subnets. The externally visible mail address could use a simple name such as *debbie@companyA. com*, while her real destination could be *debbie@computer3.departmentA.USdivison. companyA.com*.

When configured to use the DNS, mail servers first attempt to obtain an MX-record for the destination host. If an MX-record is found, the list of mail forwarding hosts is used when the SMTP connection is attempted. If no MX-record can be found, the DNS is searched for an A-record. If an A-record is found, then this address is used when the SMTP connection is established. If the SMTP client is configured to use host table lookup, the internal host table, which is usually a text file, is used to determine the Internet IP address of the recipient host. The exact format and path name of the host table depend upon the TCP implementation. Use of a host table is the equivalent of doing an A-record lookup using the DNS. Most internal host tables, however, are far from being as complete a database as what the DNS can provide.

When configured to use a default mail relay host, all messages are sent to a single mail forwarder for further routing. Use of this option will improve gateway throughput as mail forwarding hosts are usually on the same network as the gateway. Because response time and throughput are typically fast in these cases, the result is little to no backlog of messages at the gateway. The use of this option, however, places the burden of routing and retries of blocked messages on the mail forwarding machine, which will add to the existing workload of the mail forwarding machine.

E-Mail Gateways

For LANs with an e-mail standard, gateways may be a better approach to exchange e-mail with the Internet. Most NetWare LANs come with MHS, and many third-party vendors provide client software for MHS-based servers. In addition, there are many MHS to SMTP gateway servers. All e-mail gateways convert envelope contents to correspond to the Internet mail syntax, and also encode the data for transmission across SMTP. Some of the products that implement MHS to SMTP gateway functions include the following:

➜ Novell SMTP for NetWare Global MHS—an optional software package from Novell that is implemented as an NLM, and facilitates communication between MHS and SMTP-based mail systems.

➜ Mercury—an NLM that provides a gateway between MHS and SMTP mail systems.

SMTP Gateway to Other E-Mail Systems

The three most popular LAN based e-mail systems that use their proprietary protocols are cc:Mail from Lotus, MS Mail from Microsoft, and Groupwise from Novell.

Cc:Mail from Lotus is one of the leading mail systems used in Novell networks. If you use cc:Mail internally, you have a number of gateway solutions. The two popular examples are cc:Mail Link to SMTP from Lotus, and Internet Exchange from International Messaging Associates. Both products provide gateways between cc:Mail servers and SMTP. Both solutions run on PCs that are separate from the Novell server. Cc:Mail requires a dedicated DOS machine, while Internet Exchange runs on a Windows computer. Neither product includes a POP server.

Internet Exchange also implements MIME, while a cc:Mail SMTP gateway doesn't support MIME (at the time of this writing). With Internet Exchange, the gateway administrator has full control over how file attachments are encoded for messages originating within cc:Mail. The administrator can set the particular MIME encoding scheme to be used. By implementing standard MIME encoding, Internet Exchange enables cc:Mail users to send mail messages with binary attachments (i.e., spreadsheets, executable programs, and postscript files) to any mail user on the Internet that has a MIME-compatible mail reader. The reverse is also true in that any MIME-compatible mail client can also send binary documents to cc:Mail clients through the gateway.

Similarly, if you are using MS Mail or Groupwise, a number of gateways are available from Microsoft, Novell, and other third parties that can connect you to SMTP.

Selecting Mail Solutions

Now, with all this background, how do you as a NetWare system administrator select the correct solution for your installation? The first thing you must do is evaluate your existing environment and requirements. To do this, you will have to ask questions like the following:

➡ Is there an existing LAN-based mail system?

➡ Must it continue to be used?

➡ Will mail be mostly plain text or also binary?

➡ Will mail be used primarily for internal mail?

➡ Will mail be used primarily for external mail (Internet)?

➡ Do you have a UNIX system that can be the mail server?

➡ Do you have the knowledge or time to manage a local mail server?

➡ What services will your Internet Access Provider supply?

Depending on these answers, your choices may be limited. For example, do you have an existing LAN-based e-mail system such as cc:Mail that you will continue to use? If so, then one option available to you is to provide a gateway so that your users can use their existing e-mail software to send and receive Internet mail. A second option is to have your users run two mail clients—the LAN-based system for internal mail, and an Internet-based client to access the Internet. If you plan to go with a gateway system and your LAN-based users will need to exchange binary data files with other users on the Internet, then you will need to pick a solution that supports MIME encoding. Most of the IAPs are not familiar with the proprietary e-mail systems; therefore, you should be ready to provide support and host gateways at your own site.

If you do not have an existing LAN-based e-mail system or you have the freedom of changing to a new system, then you should look toward an open system based on the Internet standards. This is especially true if the majority of your mail will be exchanged with other users on the Internet.

Once you have decided to implement an Internet-based mail solution, one of the benefits is that you will have a wide variety of mail client software from which to choose. Many commercial and public domain mail clients support TCP/IP-based POP and

Hardware Components and Issues

SMTP standards. Another factor in your favor is that you do not have to choose only one vendor for all users, and you may choose to change client software at any time without impacting the network. This is one of the key advantages of choosing to implement a system based on open standards.

Now that you have an SMTP/POP-based mail client, the next thing that needs to be determined is what and where will your SMTP/POP server will be located. If your Internet traffic is light, one option is to have your IAP provide your SMTP/POP server. This may also be of benefit if many of your users need remote dial up access to their mail. Your IAP may be better set up to provide dial-up access to its server than you can provide into your local network.

For networks with more than 50 mailboxes, hosting an e-mail server at your site is the most economical solution. If you already have a UNIX system or another local system running TCP/IP that supports SMTP and POP, then you can just use that system. If you don't have a UNIX system, you will have to install an SMTP and POP server on an existing or new machine. Your main choices here will be between a UNIX-based system or a Novell server-based system. As stated earlier in this chapter, a number of UNIX hardware and software companies are now promoting turnkey Internet server solutions. The other option is to install a Novell NLM server-based solution. An excellent example of this is the Mercury software, discussed earlier in the chapter. In addition to providing a SMTP and POP server, Mercury can also be a gateway between MHS and SMTP. Windows NT is also emerging as another platform for SMTP/POP3 mail server, but the choices at this time are very limited and immature.

Network News—Usenet, UUCP, and NNTP

Network news is a very important Internet information service that is often grouped with SMTP e-mail. While it does not interact directly with SMTP, it can be considered related based on two major factors. The first is that, by design, the format of the messages resemble the SMTP format. The second factor is that many e-mail clients also support network news and use the same user interface to read and reply to network news as they do for regular e-mail messages. The client portion, or newsreaders, was covered in the previous chapter. This section will cover the server portion of the Network News system. Network news is implemented by a system called Usenet.

Usenet is a system for exchanging information between computer systems. Its growth began in the early 1980s with the increase in popularity of UNIX. Usenet was first implemented on UNIX with *UNIX-to-UNIX Copy Program* (UUCP). UUCP is a program initially implemented on UNIX systems that allow systems to send files to other UUCP systems via dial-up phone lines. UUCP was also heavily used to send e-mail over dial-up connections. UNIX systems come standard with UUCP, but it has also been implemented on many other systems. In addition, there is a standard for running UUCP over TCP/IP. With the growth of the Internet, much of the UUCP dial-up network been replaced with TCP/IP-based communications.

Usenet News is a distributed discussion list system that is carried over both UUCP and the Internet. Usenet News is commonly referred to as Network News, Netnews, Newsgroups, or just as Usenet.

Usenet is made up of tens of thousands of host computers that all exchange among each other messages or articles, the format of which is defined in RFC 1036. Each host in the network receives articles from one or more other hosts in the Usenet network. Each host then forwards the news articles to other hosts in the network. In this manner, articles are propagated quickly throughout the network. Special algorithms are used to make sure articles do not end up in an endless loop between the same hosts. A host computer or site that provides news to another server or client is often referred to as a *news feed*.

In 1986, the *Network News Transfer Protocol* (NNTP) was developed. NNTP is an *elective* protocol, which means that it is not one of the protocols that make up the core TCP/IP suite. Its widespread uses, however, make it one of the most widely implemented adjuncts to TCP/IP implementations. NNTP, as specified in RFC 977, provides for the distribution of news between servers over TCP/IP. The NNTP standard also enables client software to retrieve news from servers. Most TCP/IP client packages provide a newsreader as part of their standard product offering. A newsreader client may be implemented as a stand-alone application, integrated into the mail client software along with POP and SMTP, or integrated into a Web browser. Usenet and NNTP servers are widely implemented in UNIX and other multiuser operation systems. There are no known implementations of NNTP for NetWare servers today.

Because of the sheer volume of information that is distributed daily over the Usenet, most users take advantage of the client-server capabilities of NNTP. Almost all IAPs provide NNTP servers. Some of the larger companies that have many users accessing news servers may choose to host their own local server. Most smaller companies and individuals, however, use client newsreaders at their IAP site. Usenet news is organized by different topics called *newsgroups*. If a site chooses to host a Usenet server at their local site, it is possible to subscribe only to a subset of the newsgroups and have them downloaded to a local server.

 n o t e The information exchanged over the Usenet can exceed over 60,000 articles and 50 megabytes of current news a day!

Chapter 5, "Internet Applications," covered newsreaders from the client application perspective. This section gave a basic overview of the server side. The really good news for most NetWare administrators is the fact that all the issues, including implementation and management of network news servers, will normally be handled by your IAP. Because Usenet network news is an important information source, you will want to make sure your client software supports newsreaders and that your IAP provides your news feed.

World Wide Web

The *World Wide Web* (WWW) has received much media attention recently, but it is still often misunderstood. Quite simply, the World Wide Web is the Internet's world spanning collection of *HyperText Transport Protocol* (HTTP) servers. It is called a web because of the interconnected way in which the many servers reference each other with HyperText links in *HyperText Markup Language* (HTML) documents.

The World Wide Web started as a project to allow high energy physicists to better communicate and share information. In 1989, it found its beginnings as a project proposal at CERN, the European Laboratory for Particle Physics located in Geneva, Switzerland. It has since grown to be the default infrastructure for HyperText and multimedia communication on the global Internet.

The World Wide Web Initiative is now a joint effort between CERN and The Laboratory for Computer Science at the *Massachusetts Institute of Technology* (MIT). Together, these organizations work to define the software, protocols, and conventions used to communicate on the Web. The World Wide Web uses the Internet as its communication backbone. It is comprised of many different servers belonging to many different organizations throughout the world.

Any organization or an individual can put up its own Web server. The components needed to put up your own Web servers include the following:

→ An Internet connection—preferably a dedicated line connection

→ A computer capable of running some version of Web server software

→ Web server software, also called HTTPD, where D stands for daemon or a server

→ A document or documents that need to be put up on the Web server

→ An HTML editor

When you create HTML documents on your Web server, you can include hyperlinks to any other server or document on the World Wide Web. Likewise, other documents on the Web can be set up with hyperlinks to your Web server.

 People are finding an incredible number of uses for the World Wide Web—everything from placing scientific journals online to creating virtual store fronts with online product catalogs.

Web Servers—Operating System Choices

The real foundation of the World Wide Web is the many Web servers that comprise it. The majority of Web servers on the Internet are UNIX systems running either the CERN or NCSA Web server software. This is largely because of the major role that CERN and NCSA have played in developing the networking protocols and software used on the World Wide Web. While these organizations continue to play an important role in the advancement of the Web, many other organizations have begun to develop Web software. Web server software is now available for almost all computer hardware and operating systems, including MS Windows, Macintosh, and even Novell NetWare file servers.

If you are setting up a Web server on a UNIX server, you might want to try out the NCSA Web server software. It can be downloaded from the NCSA anonymous FTP server ftp.ncsa.uiuc.edu. The developers of the NCSA server can be reached at the e-mail address httpd@ncsa.uiuc.edu.

To set up a Web server on a Novell NetWare file server, you can use the GLACI-HTTPD Web server from The Great Lakes Area Commercial Internet. You can learn more about GLACI-HTTPD by connecting to the URL http://www.glaci.com/info/glaci-httpd.html. A copy of the Web server NLM can be downloaded from the anonymous FTP server ftp.glaci.com in the /pub/netware subdirectory. GLACI can also be reached by sending e-mail to httpd-info@glaci.com.

The HTTP Protocol

The most exciting thing about the World Wide Web is the way it makes information on the Internet easier to locate, browse, and retrieve. The software that actually enables you to retrieve and view documents on a Web server is called a *Web browser*, which was discussed in Chapter 5. The first widely used Web client was NCSA Mosaic. Providing a point-and-click interface, Mosaic became the first truly user-friendly, cross-platform interface for browsing the Internet. It has been dubbed the Internet's "First Killer Application" and has spawned a revolution in how the Internet is used and perceived. The fact that NCSA is providing Mosaic for free adds to its incredible popularity.

The communication that occurs between the Web server and the Web browser is made possible by the network protocol HTTP. HTTP is a technical specification of just how the Web browser requests a file from the Web server, and how the Web server then sends that file. HTTP is a *stateless* protocol, meaning that each document or graphic that is downloaded is a completely separate and unrelated connection between browser and server. This lends itself quite well to the distributed nature of the World Wide Web. It means you can have a document stored on one Web server and the embedded graphics within the document stored on another server. For example, the setup in figure 6.8 shows a Web client making a request to both Web servers A and B for different documents using the HTTP protocol; the client portion of HTTP on the workstation and the server portion (also called HTTP daemon) on the Web server are being accessed. Also, contrary to popular belief, Web servers are not restricted to Internet only, but are used by companies for internal document distribution, such as the local Web server shown in the figure. In network hierarchy, HTTP protocol runs on top of the TCP transport layer.

Figure 6.8

An HTTP server can be both local or remote.

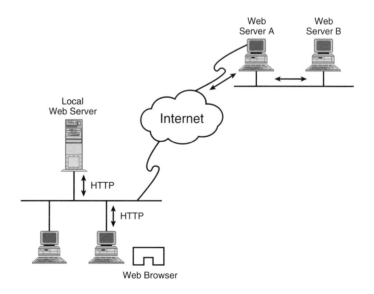

Hardware Components and Issues

Authoring HTML Documents

HTML is used to create multimedia HyperText documents. HTML is the primary document type used on the World Wide Web. There is nothing magic about an HTML document. In fact, it is really only a text file with some special codes and reserved words (called *tags*) to indicate the text layout and font selection. You can use almost any text editor to create an HTML document. The real magic occurs when you load the document in an HTML viewer or Web browser. Reserved words and control codes in HTML documents are always enclosed in angle bracket characters '<' and '>', often referred to as the Greater Than and Less Than symbols. For example, the tag "<br>" is used to indicate a line break in your text. There are numerous tags for selecting a wide variety of fonts and text layouts.

 n o t e   Most HTML viewers enable you to view the source files that generate the formatted documents. For example, if you are viewing a document with Mosaic and want to see the markup used to create it, go to the File menu and select the option View Source. This will display the source text file with all the markup codes. If you are a person who learns well from examples, this is an excellent way to learn HTML.

An even easier way to create HTML documents is to use a specialized HTML editor. Several are available on the market now, including editors from such software as Microsoft and WordPerfect. You might also want to check out the editor HotMetal from SoftQuad. A larger list of HTML editors can be found at the following URL:

http://www10.w3.org/hypertext/WWW/
Tools/Overview.html

Setting Up Your Own Web Server

For setting up your own Web server, you need to estimate the bandwidth needs, choose an appropriate operating system to host it, and also decide on its location. These three issues are discussed in the subsequent sections of this chapter. Initially, however, you must determine why you are setting up a Web server by asking the following questions:

→ Is the Web server being set up for internal use only? If so, then capacity planning becomes easier, and document layout, though important, is not as critical.

→ Is the Web server being set up for external purposes only (i.e., access by customers)? If so, take the same care in building a Web server that you take in developing your brochure and ad copies. Your Web server could be both a brochure *and* an ad copy. Also, you need to keep the content up-to-date and "fresh" so that people have more incentive to come back to your server. The more useful the information available on your Web server, the more traffic it will attract.

→ Is the Web server being set up for selling products over the Internet? If so, make your Web pages more attractive to your potential customers.

Capacity Planning

The first step in setting up your Web server is estimating the scope of its audience and the resulting load on the server. While it is often difficult to derive precise numbers, coming up with your best estimate will help guide your future hardware and software purchases.

Perhaps you want to use a Web server for internal distribution of information within your own organization. In this case, you can come up with a reasonably accurate estimate of the number of users accessing the server. As an example, let's assume you plan to put a company telephone book on your Web server. You estimate that each computer user in the company will access the server an average of five times a day. If you have 1,000 employees with computers, you can estimate approximately 5,000 requests a day, or about 10 connections per minute (assuming an eight-hour business day). If each connection retrieves about 6 kilobytes of information from the server, then the server is transmitting about 60 kilobytes per minute, or 1 kilobyte per second. This is a very small load for any Web server. A desktop PC acting as a Web server or perhaps a shared file server given the added role of a Web server can easily handle such a small load. In this example, installation of Web server software on an existing file server should be sufficient. No additional hardware is needed.

The size of the files being viewed can have a big impact on server utilization. As another example, let's assume you are at university that is developing a Web-based tutorial for biology students. The tutorial contains numerous scanned graphics ranging in size from 20 to 200 kilobytes. This type of Web application could easily put a heavy load on a Web server and might justify a dedicated Web server.

In another scenario, you might want to share information with the millions of users on the global Internet. Estimating the load on the server is more difficult in this case. Often it is not your Web server

that is the bottleneck, but your Internet connection. A 56 kilobit-per-second Internet connection can transfer data at only a tiny fraction of the 10 megabit-per-second transfer rate that is available on a local Ethernet. Even a fast T1 connection of about 1.4 megabits-per-second is still a mere fraction of Ethernet speeds. In setting up your Web server for Internet accessibility, calculate the maximum rate at which data can be transferred over your Internet connection and assume that as the average load on your server.

Choosing the Hardware and Operating System

In the early days of the World Wide Web, Web server software was limited to UNIX platforms—today, it is no longer so limited. Web server software is now available for virtually every operating system and hardware platform. Your decision in choosing a server platform should be guided more by the system administration skills available and the user community who will maintain the documents. If the individuals maintaining documents on your Web server are all engineers using UNIX-based workstations, then it makes sense to stay with a traditional UNIX-based Web server. It will be easier for these people to move files to and from the server and easier for the existing UNIX system administrator to maintain the system. If, however, your organization has a predominately Novell NetWare LAN, then it makes sense to put your Web server on a Novell file server.

Renting Web Space

Many Internet service providers will "rent" space on their Web servers, saving you the trouble of setting up your own Web server. There are advantages and disadvantages to this type of setup.

Advantages

Rented Web space is most useful when you have a low bandwidth Internet connection that you do not want swamped with Web traffic. Your IAP is probably very well connected to the Internet, having T1 or greater capacity. By placing your Web pages on a server at their location, you can receive the benefits of a high capacity Internet connection without paying for such a connection to your own location.

Disadvantages

You will likely be required to pay extra for the rented Web space service. Costs vary considerably depending on location.

It will likely be more difficult for you to maintain the files on the remote Web server. Keeping the files on a local server is much more convenient and easier to manage.

It is unlikely that your IAP can provide you with sophisticated forms processing capabilities. If it does, it will probably charge extra for the service. Forms processing is done more easily on a local server.

Compromise Solution

You might find it useful to have both a local server and space rented on a remote server. You can use the rented space on the remote server to store your large documents and graphics that change infrequently. Information that changes daily and scripts that handle forms processing can be set up on your local server.

Forms Support

One of the more interesting capabilities of a Web server is support for fill-out forms. This enables people to create such useful and interesting things as online surveys and virtual store fronts. The specification that describes how Web servers should handle forms is called the *Common Gateway Interface* (CGI). The CGI specification describes how information is encoded and sent when a form is submitted. When the server receives the information, it passes it on to a specified command script or program. This program can then process the information and send back a customized response in the form of an HTML document created on the fly. The methods for building scripts and programs to handle CGI forms information differs from Web server to Web server.

Network Systems Analyst
Great Lakes Area Commercial Internet

Phone: (414)475-6388
FAX: (414)475-7388

E-mail: tdphette@glaci.com
URL: http://www.glaci.com/

Summary

Sending and receiving e-mail on the Internet requires the use of the SMTP protocol between different mail systems. UNIX-based mail systems use SMTP as their default mail system. For retrieving e-mail from the server, another protocol called POP is used by various PC e-mail clients. For communication between the Internet and non-SMTP mail systems, an e-mail gateway is used.

Web servers are the most common way to establish a presence on the Internet today. Web servers can be hosted at your site, for which server choices vary from UNIX to NetWare. Hosting Web servers at the IAP site is more convenient, but you lose day-to-day control of the environment and may have to pay additional fees for service.

With an understanding of the types of application servers that can be used to establish your company's presence on the Internet, go now to Chapter 9, "Internet Access Providers," which is the next level in the Internet connectivity matrix. Chapter 9 discusses the many issues that you need to consider when selecting an Internet Access Provider for your Internet connection.

7

WAN Access Services

Most network managers say that they can never have enough bandwidth, especially when it comes to *wide area networking* (WAN). Unlike LAN bandwidth, however, WAN bandwidth is not free. Generally, bandwidth price is directly proportional to its size—a 384 Kbps link costs more than a 56 Kbps link, for example. The monthly cost of WAN services is a significant portion of the total monthly cost of Internet access. Selecting the right amount of bandwidth and the right type of WAN access service is critical.

Realistically assess your bandwidth needs, evaluate different services in relation to your needs, and then select an Internet Access Provider (IAP) that offers the best type and WAN bandwidth service.

This chapter provides guidelines for determining the optimum WAN service for your needs, including bandwidth calculations and types of service. The following WAN services are discussed:

→ Analog dial-up services

→ Switched digital services, including ISDN and Switched 56

→ Dedicated WAN services, including Frame Relay and Point-to-Point Leased (or Dedicated) lines

In addition to discussing different services, information is also provided on the types of devices needed at the customer premises to take advantage of different WAN services.

n o t e This chapter focuses on layer 4 of the Internet connectivity matrix.

7	SECURITY AND MANAGEMENT
6	Internet Access Providers
5	WAN Access Devices
4	WAN Access Services
3	Internet Application Servers
2	Internet Navigation Software
1	Network Communication Protocols

Understanding WAN Services

Before delving into a discussion of the different WAN services, it is essential to understand how WAN services function. Traditional data and voice networks connecting any two offices within the U.S. use a local and a long distance provider. The local access provider connects your premises to its nearest central office, where the call is then handed off to the long distance access provider. The same process is mirrored at the receiver's end, where the long distance provider hands off the call to the local access provider. The geographic location of the hand-off points on the long distance network is referred to as *Point of Presence* (POP). Sometimes the same telephone company is both the local and long distance provider. Figure 7.1 illustrates a typical scenario for traditional WAN services.

Local access in the U.S. is generally provided by the seven *regional bell operating companies* (RBOCs)—Ameritech, Bell Atlantic, Bell South, NYNEX, Pacific Bell, Southwestern Bell, and US West. In addition, many smaller local access providers exist. Telephone companies such as AT&T, MCI, and Sprint provide long distance access for WAN services. In most of the European and Asian countries, local and long distance access is provided by one centralized telephone company. There is a recent trend in many European countries (such as the U.K.), however, toward decentralized and multiple telephone carrier systems.

Figure 7.1

An example of typical call routing for traditional WAN services.

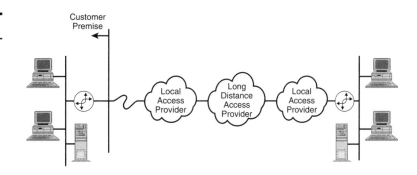

As in a traditional WAN service, you need two types of WAN service providers for Internet access—local and long distance. *Internet Access Providers* (IAPs) are in a sense the long distance carriers for Internet access, while local access is still provided by the RBOCs. Most IAPs lease their lines from long distance carriers, thus acting as distributors for the long distance services. Figure 7.2 shows a typical arrangement of Internet access, with local access being provided by an RBOC going into the POP of the IAP. The IAP then in turn connects to the Internet, using telephone lines leased from the telephone companies.

Telephone companies such as MCI and Sprint have recently entered the Internet access business, while many of the other telephone companies, such as AT&T and the RBOCs, have also announced their intentions to enter the business. Some online services like CompuServe have their own private networks, giving you the choice of using just their network or using their network as an access point to the Internet. Only a few IAPs have their own private network.

Figure 7.2

A typical arrangement of Internet access.

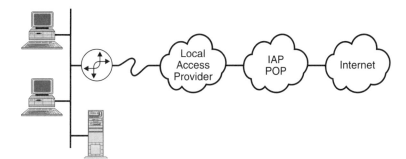

Types of WAN Services

There is no universal way to categorize services offered by telephone companies. For the purpose of this book, WAN services are categorized into the following two areas:

→ Dial-up or switched WAN services

→ Dedicated WAN services

Dial-Up Services versus Dedicated Services

As the name indicates, dial-up services are not always "on," whereas dedicated services are up 24 hours a day whether someone is using them or not. In dial-up, you pay for what you use (the amount of time the connection is up)—the connection times are metered. With dedicated connections, however, you essentially "lease" the line and pay a fee that is independent of the usage level. Your dial-up service can be used in a dedicated line mode, however, if the connection is kept open all the time to a pre-set location. This is very common for Internet access in cases where only a local "unmetered" call is needed from your house or office to the nearest IAP.

From an IAP's standpoint, if the IAP does not have to assign a static IP address and dedicate a port

and a modem specifically for the customer, it is a dial-up service. The IAP will not wake up your host for a dial-up connection—in other words, it won't call your computer if someone on the Internet wants to access your host when you are not connected to the Internet. In figure 7.3, for example, if User X wants to FTP or Telnet into Host A on a LAN that is connected to the Internet using a dial-up service, the user won't be able to complete the connection unless someone from the LAN first dials a connection to the Internet.

When an IAP assigns a static IP address, and dedicates a port and a modem specifically to a customer, it becomes a virtual dedicated link. The type of WAN service can be either a permanent connection or a dial-up connection that is kept on all the time. Most IAPs that provide dedicated analog service (as discussed in the following sections) recommend leaving the dial-up link connected all the time to make it a virtually dedicated link.

Figure 7.4 shows an example of a dial-up service, which appears as a dedicated link to users dialing in from the Internet because the connection is kept on all the time. When User X requests a connection to Host A, the IAP dials into Host A's LAN. The delay caused by setting up the dialed connection is small. From User X's perspective, Host A has a permanent connection to the Internet.

Figure 7.3

The outside user can't initiate a call into the dial-up account.

Hardware Components and Issues

Figure 7.4

A dial-up connection can appear as a permanent connection to outside users.

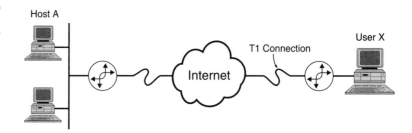

A dial-up service from an IAP's standpoint thus may not always be the same as it is from a WAN access provider's point of view. In the past, all dial-up services were predominately analog, while most of the dedicated link services were digital. That distinction is no longer valid due to new advances in dial-up technology. The next section provides details on different dial-up WAN services from the standpoint of the WAN access provider.

Dial-Up WAN Services

Dial-up WAN services, which enable you to connect any two points in the world, do not provide a permanent connection. The connection is made on an as-needed basis, and you pay only for the time duration of the connection. A device such as a telephone or a modem is required to initiate the connection. Dial-up WAN services can be further categorized into universally available analog dial-up services and dial-up digital or switched digital services, which include ISDN (most popular), Switched 56 Kbps, and others. The discussion that follows first focuses on analog dial-up services, and then progresses into switched digital services.

Analog transmissions follow voice patterns and have voltage levels that vary continuously. Digital transmissions translate all data into 1s and 0s. All of the computer-generated data that is digital in form

is thus converted into analog signal (using modems) before being sent on the telephone wire. The physical telephone wiring for both analog and digital dial-up is the same—it is a copper wire pair that runs into the majority of houses within the U.S. The difference in the analog and digital dial-up, however, comes from the central office switch to which the lines are connected.

Analog Dial-Up Services

Analog dial-up service—also called *Plain Old Telephone Service* (POTS)—is the only service that is available worldwide. Most homes in the U.S. and the rest of the world receive this type of service from their telephone companies. Analog dial-up delivers the most economical service, but it offers the least amount of bandwidth. In most places, selecting an IAP that has a POP in the local calling area is economical—analog dial-up services are not metered within a local calling distance.

Accessing Analog Dial-up Services

Analog dial-up service can be obtained either directly from your local telephone company or by putting an analog line card in a *private branch exchange* (PBX). All data applications, as opposed to voice applications, require a modem. The modem converts the digital data generated by computers into analog signals for sending it over the telephone wire. The maximum theoretical bandwidth from an analog line is 32 Kbps. With the recent advance in modem technology, today's modems can provide 28 Kbps of raw throughput.

Modem Standards

You know that your old modem was rated for 57.6 Kbps, but the maximum theoretically possible bandwidth is only 32 Kbps. How is that possible? Both are correct statements, but the statements refer to different data rates. The following list explains the modem terms that are important to understand before you can make an intelligent modem selection:

→ Raw throughput—This is the maximum throughput in *bits per second* (bps) that you can expect from your modem with no compression. Depending on the line conditions and the modem at the other end, you may make a connection at this speed or drop down to the next fallback speed. A modem with raw throughput of 14.4 Kbps may not be able to connect with another modem at 14.4 Kbps, for example, and therefore may only make an actual connection at 9600 bps, due to either line conditions or the receiving modem. Some of the standards such as V.32, V.32bis, and V.34, set by CCITT, specify the maximum throughput.

→ Error correction—V.42 and MNP4 are the most common standards; most modems come with the V.42 error correction protocol. The error correction protocols were developed to counter some of the errors introduced by line quality and distortion. MNP10 is another standard used in cellular systems for error correction.

→ Compression—Most modems today use the V.42bis as the default compression standard. Under the ideal condition for compression (generally a blank file), V.42bis will yield a 4:1 compression, which is how a 14.4 Kbps modem was marketed as 57.6 Kbps modem; the reality, however, is a compression rate of 2:1. V.42bis only provides compression for text files, and not for binary files. Most binary files available for download on the Internet are compressed with PKZIP or some other compression scheme.

→ Fallback—Before the V.34 standard came into existence, most modems dropped to the next lower speed standard if they could not make a connection at their rated speed. With the V.34 standard, modems fall back in decrements of less than 100 bps. Because V.34 is still a new standard, the same vendor's modem should be used at both ends of the connection to get the full performance benefit.

Table 7.1 provides a list of the most commonly available modems and their specifications.

note Contrary to popular opinion, you can have your own domain name even if you have a dial-up account. You can have domain name of mycompany.com, for example, even if you have an analog dial-up service.

Table 7.1 Modem Specifications

Modem Modulation Standard	Maximum or Advertised Throughput	Raw Throughput	Average Throughput	Fallback
V.32	38.4 Kbps	9600 bps	19.2 Kbps	4800 bps, 2400 bps
V.32bis	57.6 Kbps	14.4 Kbps	28.8 Kbps	12, 9.6, 7.2 Kbps
V.34	115.2 Kbps	28.8 Kbps	57.6 Kbps	<100 bps increments

* Advertised throughput is 4 times the raw throughput and assumes that the modem has V.42bis compression.
** Average throughput is generally twice that of the raw throughput.

Choosing Analog Dial-Up for Your Internet Connection

For a single user Internet connection, many people choose the analog dial-up service because it provides an easy platform for connecting to the Internet. For a LAN connection to the Internet, the decision to select analog dial-up services depends on your current and estimated future usage of the Internet.

The following criteria can be used to help determine if analog dial-up is the appropriate choice for your LAN-based Internet connection:

➜ Do you need both inbound and outbound Internet access? If you only need outbound Internet access, analog dial-up is sufficient. Outbound access enables users on your LAN to access the Internet, but customers could not access your servers unless you initiate the connection to the Internet. Inbound access permits

outside users to access your Internet servers that are made available for their use, thus making your Web server available for your customers to access product information. For inbound access to servers like FTP, Gopher, and Web, analog dial-up is insufficient.

➜ How many users on your network have access to the Internet? The general rule of thumb is that analog dial-up access may suffice for a network of up to five users.

➜ What are the most common applications used? Each application has a different Internet bandwidth requirement. If the application does not require a large bandwidth, an analog dial-up service is usually an acceptable option.

➜ On most networks, e-mail is the number one Internet application. If e-mail is your only Internet application, analog dial-up service is sufficient for large numbers of users; however, if you need to receive your e-mail instantly, analog dial-up service is inadequate because you have to dial your IAP's host to check mail. Also, dial-up service is inadequate if your users send files frequently with their e-mail.

→ FTP access is generally not very bandwidth-intensive except when a file is being transferred. In average settings, not many people are transferring files with FTP simultaneously, so an analog service should be adequate.

→ Web access requires more bandwidth than any other Internet applications. Even for a single user, analog access at V.34 speeds is inadequate. If your users want Web access, analog dial-up access is not recommended for LANs.

→ What about my budget? There are two types of monthly charges—one for the local telephone access into the nearest location of the IAP, and one for the services provided by the IAP, such as access into the Internet. Analog access is the cheapest of all WAN access services, costing between $25 and $100 for unlimited usage depending on your local phone company's tariff structure. Most IAPs charge anywhere from $20 to $150 for unlimited analog access.

In some states, like California, ISDN access is very competitive with analog access. Therefore, you must compare access prices before making a decision.

Switched Digital Services

Switched digital (or dial-up digital) services have become popular in the last few years. The most commonly available switched digital service in the U.S. is Switched 56 Kbps. ISDN, however, is quickly becoming the universal standard for switched digital access in today's environment. ISDN is now readily available in most metropolitan areas within the U.S. and in most industrial countries such as Japan, Germany, U.K., and France.

Integrated Services Digital Network

Integrated Services Digital Network (ISDN) is a set of digital transmission protocols defined by CCITT, the international standards organization for telephony and telegraphy. The protocols are accepted as standard by virtually all the world's telecommunications carriers. ISDN provides end-to-end digital connectivity. Unlike dial-up analog service, data travels in digital form all the way from the sender's computer or telephone, to the central office of the telephone company, to the long distance provider, to the central office, and then to the computer or telephone of the receiver. Unlike dial-up analog services, ISDN also offers the ability to carry both data and voice simultaneously over the same connection. In addition to providing an integrated voice and data service on a digital network (hence its name), ISDN also offers higher bandwidth than dial-up analog services.

There are different types of ISDN services, with *Basic Rate Interface* (BRI) being the most common. The other type of ISDN is called *Primary Rate Interface* (PRI), which is equivalent to T1 services. PRI is discussed later in this chapter. BRI consists of two 64 Kbps B channels and one 16 Kbps D channel (see fig. 7.5). The two B channels carry the actual customer data; whereas, the D channel carries the signaling information that is needed by the telephone company. The D channel is therefore a separate out-of-band signaling channel for ISDN services.

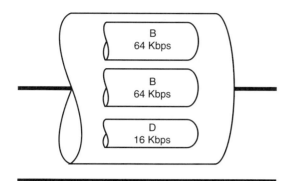

Figure 7.5

BRI is comprised of two B channels and one D channel.

 n o t e ISDN can be thought of as a collection of independent channels—you can reserve specific channels for certain applications, or you can combine channels together for higher throughput.

In the first case, one of the B channels is used for voice, and the other B channel is used for data application, such as Internet access. In the second case, both B channels are used for data, but are going to different locations within the network. Two B channels can also be connected to the same location, with each B channel's bandwidth combined for data applications to generate a higher throughput.

The process of combining two B channels to give a higher resultant throughput is called *inverse multiplexing*. In an ideal situation, inverse multiplexing of two B channels will result in a bandwidth of 128 Kbps (64*2). The telephone system within North America has not been completely upgraded to accommodate ISDN signaling. Therefore, you may not get more than 56 Kbps from each B channel or 112 Kbps from the two B channels.

One of the other benefits of ISDN, besides the higher throughput, is having a very fast call set-up. Analog call set-up takes as long as 30 seconds; whereas, the call set-up on ISDN is less than five seconds. Users with their LANs connected to the Internet with ISDN will thus be able to make the connection much more quickly than users connected with analog dial-up lines.

Also, the pricing of ISDN ranges from $25–$100 depending on the region. In some areas, the price directly correlates with the amount of usage, whereas other areas simply charge a flat rate. Table 7.2 lists the typical pricing structures available through the telephone companies.

Table 7.2   ISDN Pricing Structure

Carrier	Monthly Rate	Usage Charges
Ameritech	$34.15	Voice and data: 1–16 cents per minute (depending on time of day)
Bell Atlantic	$23.00	Voice: 2.9 cents per minute Data: 5 cents per minute
		continues

Table 7.2, Continued

Carrier	Monthly Rate	Usage Charges
BellSouth Telecommunications	$99.50	Circuit-switched voice and data: no charge Packet-switched data: 0.000214 to 0.000257 cents per minute
GTE Telephone Operations	$69.37	Voice: no charge Data: 3–5 cents first minute; 2–3 cents each additional
NYNEX	$28.23	Voice: 8 cents first minute; 1.3 cents each additional Data: 9 cents first minute; 2.3 cents each additional
Pacific Bell	$26.85	Voice and data: 4 cents first minute; 1 cent each additional
Southwestern Bell Telecommunications	$46.00	No usage charges
U.S. West Communications	$35.00	Voice and data: 4–4.5 cents first minute; 1.5–2 cents each additional

Depending on the tariff structure and your usage, ISDN may turn out to be cheaper than Point-to-Point Dedicated lines for the same bandwidth. For areas where there are no usage charges, an ISDN line can be left connected all the time, thus getting a virtual leased line connection for the price of ISDN. Generally, the installation charges for ISDN are also less than the Point-to-Point Dedicated lines.

Accessing ISDN Services

ISDN service, like analog dial-up service, can be ordered either directly from your local telephone company or by putting an ISDN line card in a *private branch exchange* (PBX). ISDN utilizes the same pair of copper wiring that is used by analog dial-up lines. Therefore, if you wanted to get an ISDN service at home, no additional wiring will be needed in most cases. ISDN is now available in all major metropolitan areas—Bell Atlantic, Pacific Bell, and Ameritech are leaders in providing ISDN access within their respective service areas.

Connecting ISDN to Your Network

Just as connecting to the Internet using analog services requires a modem, ISDN requires a terminal adapter. The terminal adapter connects the computer with the telephone company network. Figure 7.6 shows how to connect your network to

Hardware Components and Issues

the ISDN network. The terminal adapter doesn't connect directly into the telephone jack. A network termination unit (NT1) is needed, in addition to the terminal adapter. The NT1 device provides the power for the network, as well as the proper signaling protocol. More and more terminal adapter vendors are incorporating the NT1 into the terminal adapter. With an integrated NT1/terminal adapter, you can connect directly to your telephone jack. Most of the time, it is preferable to have an integrated NT1 because it is one less external device to manage.

Because terminal adapters are all different, it is important to understand your requirements. If you are getting ISDN specifically for an Internet connection, you will need a terminal adapter that supports two data channels and the capability to inverse multiplex the two channels for a higher throughput. The standard on the Internet for inverse multiplexing is called *multilink point-to-point control* (an extension of the PPP protocol). Currently, no products conform to that standard. This situation is likely to change very quickly; at this time, however, most of the terminal adapters have their own proprietary method of inverse multiplexing, which means you must use the same terminal adapter on both ends of the ISDN connection. This is why many IAPs insist you use a particular brand of terminal adapter for ISDN service.

The raw throughput you can expect from a BRI connection is 64 Kbps or 128 Kbps. You would expect that you could increase the throughput with some compression scheme, as is the case with modems. Unfortunately, there is no standard compression scheme for ISDN terminal adapters yet; however, an effort is under way to come up with a compression standard. You will start to see standard-based compression in all the ISDN terminal adapters in the near future. As is the case with inverse multiplexing, standards for compression don't exist, leading to incompatibilities between different terminal adapters. For now, keep in mind that the equipment at your end must be compatible with the equipment at the service provider's end.

Switched 56 Kbps

Switched 56 Kbps is another switched data service that is similar to ISDN. In the same manner as ISDN, you can call up bandwidth when needed. Unlike ISDN, however, Switched 56 Kbps is a single channel service that can only carry data. Switched 56 Kbps is only available in the North American circuits—no equivalent exists in Europe and Asia. Switched 56 Kbps, unlike ISDN, has no separate signaling channel, has only in-band signaling, but is available in most places. When you compare it to either ISDN or to analog services, it is relatively expensive. Switched 56 Kbps probably won't be a

Figure 7.6

BRI ISDN connections require a terminal adapter and NT1 device.

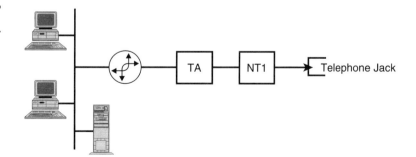

very desirable service beyond the next few years because of the advent of ISDN and *Frame Relay*, a packet switched service discussed later in this chapter.

In order to connect to a Switched 56 Kbps service, you need a *data service unit/channel service unit* (DSU/CSU). A DSU/CSU connects any external Switched 56 Kbps connection to your network. The DSU part of the system converts data into the correct format, and the CSU part of the system terminates the line condition, conditions the signal, and participates in the testing of the connection.

Choosing a Switched Digital Service for Your Internet Connection

For a LAN connection to the Internet, the decision to select a switched digital service depends on your current and estimated future usage of the Internet. The same criteria discussed previously under "Choosing Analog Dial-Up for Your Internet Connection" can also be used to help determine if a switched digital service is the appropriate choice for your LAN-based Internet connection.

Outbound Internet Access? For outbound access, switched digital services offer two benefits over analog connections—faster call setup time and more bandwidth. For inbound access, ISDN can be used in place of Point-to-Point Dedicated lines if it is economical to leave the line connected all the time.

Internet Usage The following rule of thumb may help you estimate your company's Internet usage amount. ISDN access with two B channels inverse multiplexed is sufficient for between 25–50 users; whereas, for 25 users or less, ISDN single B or Switched 56 Kbps is appropriate.

Internet Application Usage What are the most common applications used? Each of the applications, along with its usage pattern, require a different bandwidth. Some applications, such as e-mail and Telnet, take up less bandwidth, while applications such as Web access require large bandwidth.

E-Mail and FTP Bandwidth Requirements E-mail does not require much bandwidth because it is a store-and-forward system. Users do not expect mail they send to arrive instantly, and their computer is not tied up while the mail is making its way through the Internet to its recipient. ISDN or analog access are both appropriate for traditional e-mail users, but as users begin using more MIME-based e-mail (which tends to have many file attachments, such as Microsoft Word document or Lotus spreadsheets), the e-mail application will require a high bandwidth connection such as ISDN.

File transfer with FTP will benefit by higher bandwidth provided by ISDN. If your users download many files from the Internet, they will save significant time with an ISDN connection.

Web Access The application that benefits the most from an ISDN connection is the World Wide Web. Most Web browsers are not optimized for slower speed modems, so any amount of high bandwidth provided to a Web application will make a noticeable difference. The increase in ISDN bandwidth by four times over the analog connection delivers dramatic improvements when it comes to Web access.

The following is a guideline for calculating bandwidth requirements for a LAN:

- ➜ E-mail (ASCII-based)—2 Kbps/user

- ➜ E-mail (MIME-based)—5 Kbps/user

- ➜ Web access—10 Kbps/user

For a five-user LAN with two active e-mail users and three active Web users, you thus need a bandwidth of 50 Kbps for optimum access.

Budget In some parts of the country, such as the area served by Pacific Bell, a small monthly price difference exists between analog access and ISDN access. ISDN gives you substantially more bandwidth than analog—therefore, choosing between the two is an easy decision. Most of the IAPs charge more for ISDN access than for analog access, however. Some IAPs offer a fixed price ISDN service, where the IAP actually pays for the cost of the ISDN access and usage. These access and usage charges are budgeted, however, into the fixed price that is actually offered, so it may or may not be a less expensive option. If you are accessing the Internet 4–6 hours per day or more, a Point-to-Point Dedicated line or Frame Relay (both discussed later in this chapter) may be more economical than using switched digital services. Carefully consider your usage pattern before choosing ISDN or Switched 56 Kbps.

Dedicated WAN Services

Dedicated services are the second most used services after analog access because they are available everywhere and can be configured for

different speeds. The most common speed for dedicated lines is 56 Kbps in the U.S., and 64 Kbps in Europe and Asia. Dedicated services can be further categorized into Packet Switched services and Point-to-Point Dedicated services.

Packet Switched Services —Frame Relay

One of the newest technologies to emerge in the last few years in the area of wide area networking is called Frame Relay. Frame Relay is a packet switching protocol with speed ranges from 56 Kbps to 45 Mbps. Frame Relay delivers a low delay, high throughput connection. Frame Relay is similar to the X.25 protocol, but it does not correct errors or request retransmission. Instead, Frame Relay relies on availability of superior quality lines, such as fiber optics, that are common in today's telephone networks. Frame Relay expects clear, high-quality lines to guarantee virtually error-free transmissions. If errors do occur, it is the responsibility of intelligent end devices to request retransmission.

Frame Relay is yet another wide area service that provides high-speed connections. Frame Relay is more of a substitute for dedicated connections rather than for an analog dial-up or switched digital connection. One of the big benefits Frame Relay offers is that the price is *distance-insensitive*—the distance the call travels does not affect the hourly rate for the call. That is why Frame Relay is being used extensively in the wide area networking environments of different companies. If Frame Relay is already a standard for your wide area communications, use it to connect to the Internet. Frame Relay standards already guarantee interpretability with the Internet protocol, and are set by the Frame Relay Forum.

Frame Relay is a lower layer service—there are implementations available for both IPX and IP over Frame Relay. In the OSI model hierarchy shown in figure 7.7, Frame Relay is at the data link layer. If you are using Frame Relay to connect to the Internet, you need to run IP over your Frame Relay connection. Standard RFC 1274 exists to ensure the interoperability of different vendors' implementation of IP over Frame Relay, which is suitable for all the bursty applications. Because the traffic on the Internet is not constant but goes up and down, Internet access can be classified as a bursty application.

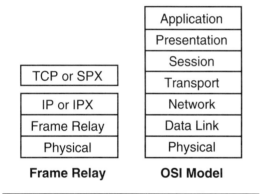

	Application
TCP or SPX	Presentation
	Session
	Transport
IP or IPX	Network
Frame Relay	Data Link
Physical	Physical
Frame Relay	**OSI Model**

Figure 7.7

Frame Relay protocols versus the OSI model.

Permanent Virtual Circuits

A Frame Relay connection is made up of one or more *permanent virtual circuits* (PVCs). A PVC is a dedicated, end-to-end, logical connection that is used for data transfer. Unlike Point-to-Point Dedicated lines, PVCs are not connection-oriented. They get set up like a dedicated line and remain active until the service is terminated, creating virtual dedicated connections as opposed to real permanent connections.

Committed Information Rate

Committed information rate (CIR) is defined as a minimum average data rate that the network guarantees to carry over a given PVC for a specified period. The data rate is chosen at the time of subscription, but it can be modified if users find that their transmission needs have changed. CIR is important because a Frame Relay network may specify a throughput of 64 Kbps or 56 Kbps and a CIR of zero. A CIR is a guarantee that whenever you connect, your throughput will not fall below the threshold specified. In order to provide a CIR above zero, the phone company or access provider must reserve a physical line for your connection. If you purchase a PVC with 56 Kbps of throughput and a CIR of zero, you are not guaranteed any bandwidth. Today, the current state of the Frame Relay infrastructure is such that most users are able to get the full extent of the bandwidth. Frame Relay offers some interesting possibilities when it comes to looking at Internet connections.

Some IAPs, such as PSI, have their own private networks, enabling them to offer multiple PVCs into your network—one PVC is dedicated to one application while the other PVC is designated for a different application. One of the PVCs might be dedicated to newsgroups, for example, guaranteeing newsgroups bandwidth regardless of the level of user activity in other Internet applications. A PVC dedicated to outside users dialing in to a network prevents the network from getting bogged down for inside users. This is one benefit Frame Relay offers over T1 leased lines or other dedicated lines. This advantage may also apply when comparing Frame Relay and switched digital services (i.e., ISDN, Switched 56 Kbps, etc.), depending on the customer usage of the Internet.

Figure 7.8 provides a visual example of the PVCs going to different locations.

Reserving PVCs for particular applications is one way to effectively manage your Internet bandwidth.

Procuring Access Lines for the Frame Relay

Your local access provider can deliver Frame Relay, but if you already have a data multiplexer within your company and you subscribe to the Frame Relay service, use one of the PVCs to access the Internet. Most IAPs that offer a Frame Relay service assist with all the procurement of the local access services. To connect your network to the Internet using Frame Relay, a DSU/CSU is needed. In addition, you will need a router that supports routing of IP over Frame Relay protocol.

Frame Relay Pricing

Frame Relay pricing, like all other services, involves installation charges and monthly usage charges. The monthly usage charge for 56 Kbps Frame Relay is around $200 to $300. The Frame Relay pricing appears more attractive than a 56 Kbps dedicated line until you read the fine print and see that these prices

are for 0 CIR. The installation charges for Frame Relay can sometimes be quite costly—as high as $1,000. Most of the IAPs offer Frame Relay access either at the same or lower pricing than an equivalent Point-to-Point Dedicated line.

Point-to-Point Dedicated Services

Previously, the T1 trunk was the high-end option for Point-to-Point Dedicated lines, and is the one that is still most frequently used. A T1 trunk supports transfer speeds up to 1.544 megabits per second. In Europe, E1 is the equivalent service, offering bandwidth of up to 2.048 Mbps. For companies that don't require this much throughput, telephone companies have begun offering *Fractional T1* (FT1) services. FT1 services are configured as a number of 56 Kbps channels. In spite of the popularity of the T1 service, the emerging high end option for a Point-to-Point Dedicated connection is the T3 line, which supports a 45 Mbps connection. Today, very few sites in the country require a T3 line as their Internet connection, and this will most likely continue to be the case for the immediate future. Only when you start using much higher bandwidth applications, or start to use the Internet as a wide area backbone, is this likely to change.

Figure 7.8

Frame Relay PVCs can be set to guarantee bandwidth for different applications.

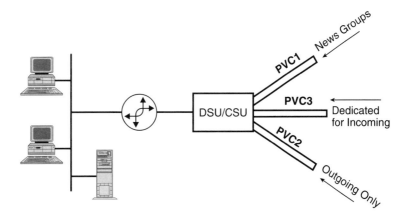

An important difference between Point-to-Point Dedicated lines and Frame Relay is that with the latter, you are not guaranteed any bandwidth above your CIR. At first glance, Point-to-Point Dedicated line prices may look expensive for long distances (they are priced based on bandwidth and the distance between two points). Because you only need the dedicated line from your LAN to the nearest point of presence of your IAP, however, the actual cost for a dedicated line can be very reasonable. Of course, this depends on finding a suitable Internet Access Provider close to your network. Actual costs of Point-to-Point Dedicated lines range from $200–$300 within a 20-mile radius. These numbers vary between different telephone companies. Many sites connect to the Internet using Point-to-Point Dedicated lines because of the numerous benefits this type of service offers.

Accessing Point-to-Point Dedicated Services

First, check with your telecommunications manager. You may already have leased a full T1 line for voice and other services. In this case, your company may have spare channels that can be used for your Internet connection. This happens frequently when the cost of a full T1 is less than the cost of buying exactly the needed amount of FT1 services. If your company does not already have a dedicated line, contact your telephone company or Internet Access Provider.

Choosing a Dedicated Service for Your Internet Connection

Frame Relay and Point-to-Point Dedicated lines are both recommended services if you need to support both inbound and outbound Internet connections, or if you intend to host your own Web server. If you are using Frame Relay for 56 Kbps connections, your actual bandwidth will be identical to a Switched 56 Kbps or ISDN connection.

The actual throughput your applications see does not vary significantly between Frame Relay and Point-to-Point Dedicated lines. The primary economic benefit of Frame Relay—distance-insensitive pricing—is inconsequential when connecting to the Internet since most companies can find an Internet Access Provider located relatively nearby. For this reason, Point-to-Point Dedicated lines are a popular alternative for companies requiring a high-speed permanent Internet connection.

Summary

Table 7.3 summarizes the types of connections you should consider for your Internet connection.

	Analog	ISDN	Switched 56 Kbps	Frame Relay	Point to Point Dedicated
Bandwidth	14.4 or 28.8 Kbps	56/64 or 112/128 Kbps	56 Kbps	56 Kbps to 1.5 Mbps	56 Kbps to 1.5 Mbps
Call Setup Time	30 seconds and up	Less than 5 seconds	Less than 20 seconds	Negligible	None
Tariff Structure	Fixed or Per Minute	Fixed or Per Minute	Fixed or Per Minute	Fixed	Fixed
Availability	High	Medium	High	Medium	High
Suitable for Inbound Access	Only if line is kept on all the time	Only if line is kept on all the time	Only if line is kept on all the time	Yes	Yes

Table 7.3

Comparison of WAN Access Services

Hardware Components and Issues

Dial-up analog access is appropriate for single users or small LANs with up to five users. If ISDN is
available in your area, its pricing may be very competitive with the dial-up analog, especially when you
consider the extra bandwidth provided. For a LAN
of up to 50 users, ISDN is a good alternative. For
more than 50 users, or to set up your own Web
servers, use either Frame Relay or a Point-to-Point
Dedicated line, depending on which is cheaper in
your area. Choosing the right connection up front
is important because of the specialized hardware
and installation charges involved.

Once you've made the critical decision concerning
which WAN service type to use for your Internet
connection, the next step is to select the appropriate equipment you will need to complete the
connection. Chapter 8, "WAN Access Devices,"
provides information on the various alternatives to
help you make the correct decisions for your environment.

8

WAN Access Devices

Having determined your wide area bandwidth and service needs, you are now ready to examine the alternatives for connecting your NetWare network to the Internet. The equipment required for enabling this connection is termed *wide area network* (WAN) *access devices*. The choice of WAN access devices is dependent on the wide area networking service, LAN environment, existing equipment, and support from your *Internet Access Provider* (IAP).

For the purpose of this chapter, WAN access devices include routers, modems, and other devices that make the actual wide area connection. In many cases, your Internet Access Provider may recommend or even resell WAN access devices. This chapter provides details on the various choices for WAN access devices so that you can evaluate and decide on the best option for your environment.

This chapter is divided into four sections based on the types of WAN services available, as follows:

→ Dial-up analog service

→ ISDN service

→ Leased-line and Switched 56 services

→ Combined access

 note This chapter focuses on layer 5 of the Internet connectivity matrix.

7 SECURITY AND MANAGEMENT
6 Internet Access Providers
5 WAN Access Devices
4 WAN Access Services
3 Internet Application Servers
2 Internet Navigation Software
1 Network Communication Protocols

Connecting LANs to the Internet

Before delving into the details of each of the services, it is important to understand the different software and hardware components needed to connect a NetWare LAN to the Internet. The equipment needed is very similar to that needed to connect to another LAN over a private or public wide area network. The WAN access devices for Internet access can, however, be much simpler because there is only one protocol (IP) required. Also, the routing information, in most cases, is very simple— there is only one network to connect to. The WAN access device (or router, in this case) at your premise is connected to the router at the *Point of Presence* (POP) of the Internet Access Provider. The router at the POP, on the other hand, needs very complex routing information tables. This situation is analogous to the private corporate networks where the central site routers, like the routers in the POP, need very complex routing tables and configuration; the branch office router, like the router at your premise for Internet access, can have a much simpler configuration.

As discussed in Chapter 4, "Adding TCP/IP to NetWare LANs," each of the NetWare workstations on a LAN—whether it is Ethernet, Token Ring, or FDDI—can either run a TCP/IP stack in parallel to the IPX protocol stack, or can use the NetWare server's TCP/IP stack and run all Internet applications on top of IPX at every workstation. Whenever a workstation uses any Internet application such as e-mail, FTP, or Mosaic, it effectively generates a TCP/IP packet destined for router B, located in the Internet Access Provider's POP (see fig. 8.1).

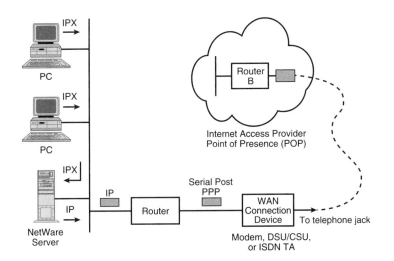

Figure 8.1

*Taking IP packets
from NetWare to
the Internet.*

For the packet to reach router B, however, it has to go through a telephone network. For the telephone network connectivity, a wide area access device such as a modem, a DSU/CSU, or an ISDN *terminal adapter* (TA) is needed. These devices are connected physically to a serial port on the router, which is in turn connected to the network. In addition, an IP router is needed to route the packets appropriately. Therefore, a router with a LAN connection and a serial port for the WAN access device connection is needed.

In order for the packet transmission to occur on a serial link connection, the IP protocol has to be encapsulated in a layer 2 WAN protocol, such as SLIP, PPP, or Frame Relay. Most routers encapsulate the IP received over their LAN into an appropriate WAN protocol, such as PPP, over their WAN ports. The WAN protocol in the router at the customer's premises must be understood by the router at the IAP's POP—this is why most IAPs insist on customers using a router that they have tested for compatibility with their POP equipment. As IP over PPP and Frame Relay are becoming universal standards, however, the issues of incompatibility are becoming less important.

 note *Point-to-Point Protocol* (PPP) is the serial line protocol that is a predecessor to SLIP and is universally used for data encapsulation over the wide area network. Unlike SLIP, however, PPP has implementations of IP, IPX, and other protocols running over it. RFCs 1548, 1332, and 1334 define IP over PPP implementation—the only PPP implementation needed to connect to the Internet.

For connecting to the Internet, a router that supports IP is sufficient—this is the protocol of choice for the Internet. The router has to be attached to a wide area networking device, which connects a corporate network to the wide area network. The following software and hardware is thus needed to provide Internet access for the NetWare LAN:

→ An IP router with serial ports for connecting WAN devices

→ WAN encapsulation software such as SLIP, PPP, or Frame Relay, one of which is generally provided with the router software

→ A WAN connection device such as a modem, DSU/CSU, or ISDN TA

→ A WAN connection from the telephone company

The different equipment possibilities are discussed in subsequent sections, and are based on the chosen WAN service.

Dial-Up Analog Service

If you have determined that dial-up analog service is the best alternative for your needs today, based on the WAN service discussions in Chapter 7, "WAN Access Services," it may be appropriate to review the WAN access device choices. With dial-up analog, you are restricted to a maximum raw throughput of 28.8 *Kilobits per second* (Kbps)—most areas average 14.4 Kbps. The types of devices that can be used to provide dial-up analog connectivity are as follows:

→ Direct attached modem

→ Remote access servers

→ Internal routers

→ External router

Direct Attached Modem

The most common start-up connection is a modem directly attached to a user's PC with SLIP or PPP, and a dialer software to dial the IAP POP (see fig. 8.2). In this particular case, the user's PC needs a TCP/IP protocol stack in addition to the NetWare IPX protocol. In order to take full advantage of modem speed, the user's PC must also have a high-speed serial card. These types of connections don't work well for LAN-connected environments, however—only one user can connect to the Internet at any time with the company's domain name. Furthermore, it requires a modem at each user's workstation to dial the Internet.

Most IAPs don't permit LAN connections with direct attached modems. This alternative, therefore, is not recommended unless only one or two users in the organization need slow and occasional Internet access.

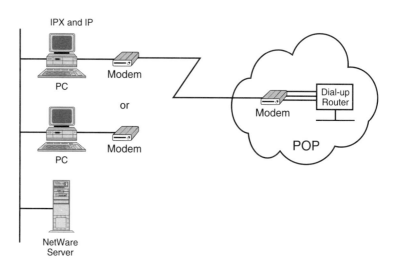

Figure 8.2

Direct attached modem connection—not ideal for LAN environments.

IPX and IP

PC

Modem

or

PC

Modem

NetWare Server

Modem

Dial-up Router

POP

Remote Access Servers

Many organizations are using remote access servers to provide network access to their telecommuters and mobile workers. The majority of remote access servers provide remote node access, whereby the remote user appears as another LAN node that is directly attached to the network. In addition, most of the remote access servers also provide routing capabilities and support IP and IPX protocols. For companies that have been exploring Internet access options and have determined that dial-up access is adequate for their current needs, the existing remote access servers could be used to connect to the Internet in the manner shown in figure 8.3. In this case, you need a spare WAN port, which can be connected via a modem to the IAP POP from where the connection to the Internet is made.

Before using a remote access server, you must ensure that it meets the following criteria:

→ Availability of an extra WAN port—this alternative is only recommended when remote access server is already available and is being used for another purpose.

→ Dial-on-demand routing capability—any packet sent to the remote access server automatically initiates the modem dialing.

→ Routing of IP protocol—must be able to route IP protocol.

→ SLIP or PPP support—make sure that PPP implementation is compliant with the latest standard and supported by your IAP.

Most remote access servers are available in 4-port, 8-port, or 16-port configurations—4-port units are in the $1500 to $2500 price range, 8-port units in the $2500 to $4000 price range, and 16-port units in the $4500 to $7000 price range. None of these prices include modems, which are also required. Therefore, it does not make sense to buy a remote access server just for Internet access.

Some of the well-known remote access servers include LAN Rover from Shiva Corporation, RLA from DCA Corporation, NetBlazer from Telebit, Portmaster from Livingston, LANA from LAN Access Corporation, Access Builder from 3Com Corporation, and NetHopper from Rockwell Information Systems. Novell sells a software version of its remote

Figure 8.3

Remote access servers—a low-cost WAN access device.

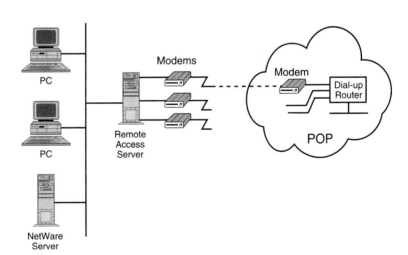

access server called NetConnect. It does not support PPP and dial-on-demand routing at this time, however. Funk Software and Stampede Technology also offer a software version of their remote access servers, which supports PPP access.

Internal Routers

The term *internal router* refers to the routers that are installed on the NetWare server itself, and includes a software/hardware combination that enables a NetWare server to connect directly to the Internet. The most common router in this category is Novell's multiprotocol software—MPR. It is a software-only router that supports PPP and can be installed as a *NetWare Loadable Module* (NLM) on the NetWare server, or on a dedicated PC running NetWare Runtime software that comes with MPR. You can attach a modem directly to the computer running MPR, provided the computer supports a high-speed serial card. It is recommended, however, that a third-party WAN card compatible with MPR be used for performance reasons. It should be noted that you must use MPR version 3.0 or higher for dial-on-demand support. As shown in figure 8.4, this alternative eliminates external routers or remote access servers, but puts additional load on the NetWare server.

 NetWare Runtime is a limited version of NetWare. It enables you to run NetWare NLM Applications—such as MPR and NetWare LANalyzer—on a dedicated machine that can't be used as a file or print server.

This alternative is quite expensive, with MPR priced at about $1,000, plus the add-on cost of $1000 to $1500 for the WAN card and an additional modem. Most WAN cards come with two ports, however. This alternative is thus recommended only if one of the WAN ports on the existing MPR is not being utilized. In this case, it would not be cost-effective to make a new purchase just for Internet connectivity.

Microdyne and Eagle Technology (now owned by Microdyne) sell WAN cards for Novell's MPR. Most of these cards are designed for high-speed networks, but could easily support low-speed analog dial-up service at 14.4/28.8 Kbps. There are also other card vendors, such as Newport/Cisco and Eicon Technology, that include routing software integrated with their cards and WAN ports.

External Dial-Up Routers

The term *external router* refers to a router that is a stand-alone device connected to the LAN on one side and to a WAN/WAN port on the other side.

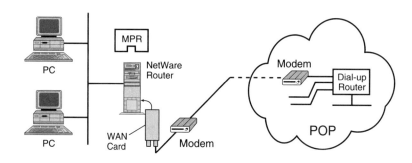

Figure 8.4

An internal router uses the NetWare server as the router.

Even though it is not directly connected or mounted inside the NetWare server, it takes all the traffic destined for a WAN away from the LAN and redirects it to the WAN. For Internet access over dial-up lines, an external dial-up router is recommended. Dial-up routers are designed to support LAN interfaces, such as Ethernet or Token Ring, and they provide asynchronous and synchronous serial ports. These routers provide dial-on-demand capability and support PPP. Many of these routers now come with integrated modems, as shown in figure 8.5.

Dial-up routers range in prices from $1000 to $2000, including the modem. The following criteria may be used in choosing a dial-up router:

→ Support of WAN protocols—SLIP, PPP.

→ Upgradability of modem—if not compliant with the V.34 standard.

→ Availability of additional sync (serial) port—if a sync port is available, the same dial-up router could later be used to support higher speed digital services, such as leased-lines or ISDN.

→ Ease of set-up—for most smaller sites where a dial-up router is adequate, a dedicated network administrator is not provided.

Some of the dial-up routers include NetBlazer PN from Telebit, NetHopper from Rockwell, and Dr. BonD from NEC America.

Table 8.1 summarizes the four devices discussed in this section that can be used to provide dial-up analog connectivity. The price range, connectivity to LANs, protocols, expandability, and pros and cons of each device are included in the table.

 note The "expandability" line in table 8.1 refers to the flexibility of upgrading the WAN device to support other services besides dial-up analog.

ISDN Service

Where readily available, ISDN may be the best WAN service for Internet access because it offers the cheapest price per Kbps. ISDN offers a

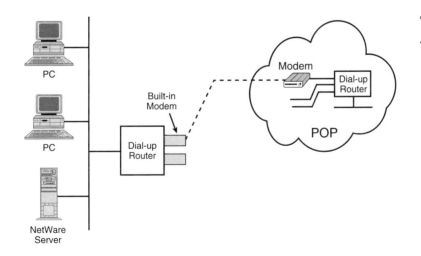

Figure 8.5

A dial-up router for Internet access.

Table 8.1

Comparison of
Dial-up Analog
WAN Devices

	Direct Attached Modem	Remote Access Server	Internal Router	External Router
Price Range	$300 to $500 per user	$2000 to $3000	$2500 to $3000	$1000 to $2000
LAN Connectivity	No	Yes	Yes	Yes
Protocols	Needs TCP/IP at every workstation	Can work with both workstation or server TCP/IP solutions	Can work with both workstation or server TCP/IP solutions	Can work with both workstation or server TCP/IP solutions
Expandability	None	None	Can be used to support higher speed services	Can be used to support higher speed services
Pros	Low initial investment	Can use existing remote access server	Expandable; can be integrated with the NetWare server	Expandable; lowest price per unit
Cons	Need separate modem for every user	Expensive if used only for Internet access	Expensive for slow speed access; increases risk for failure	More expensive than direct modem

maximum throughput of 128 Kbps, however, with normal throughput restricted to 112 Kbps in the United States. Most sites may only be using one B channel in the ISDN service, limiting throughput to 64/56 Kbps.

To provide ISDN access to NetWare LANs, the available WAN devices can be categorized into the following areas:

→ Internal routers

→ External routers

→ Integrated ISDN routers

A terminal adapter that is directly attached to a PC serial port is not considered a viable alternative in this case—it only offers single user access and still does not offer many cost advantages over the other alternatives. Also excluded from consideration are remote access servers—most do not support ISDN to its full potential because the serial port speed is limited and most support TAs in the asynchronous mode. Once remote access servers start supporting ISDN to its full potential, however, they will also

be a viable alternative, involving the same type of issues as found for analog dial-up access.

Internal Routers

As discussed in the "Dial-Up Analog Service" section of this chapter, the term *internal router* refers to the routers that are installed on the NetWare server itself. Internal routers include a combination of hardware and software that allows for connecting a NetWare server directly to the Internet. The most common router in this category is Novell's multiprotocol software—MPR. Until recently, MPR didn't support ISDN services. ISDN support is now available with MPR version 3.0 and higher. There are three alternatives available for achieving ISDN connectivity (see fig. 8.6):

→ Novell's MPR software, in combination with a WAN card and an external ISDN TA

→ Novell's MPR software, in combination with an ISDN TA card

→ Integrated ISDN TA and router on a card

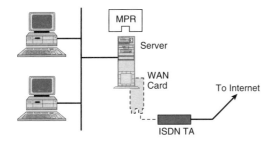

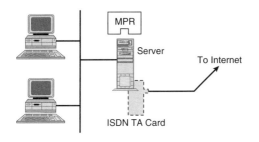

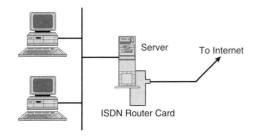

Figure 8.6

The three alternatives for achieving ISDN connectivity with MPR.

The first alternative of using MPR in conjunction with a WAN card and a TA is expensive, with prices ranging from $2500 to $3500. This alternative is only desirable when a WAN card and an MPR are already in place, and a second WAN port is available for connecting ISDN TA. Most ISDN TAs now come with an optional NT1 interface, which is needed to provide power and connect to the public telephone network. If your TA does not have integrated NT1, you must also purchase a separate NT1 in all cases.

The second alternative, using MPR and MPR-compatible ISDN TA, is more attractive than the previous alternative. Any ISDN TA, such as from ADC Kentrox and Motorola UDS, that supports V.25bis dialing protocol can be connected to the WAN card for supporting ISDN. Alternatively, a PC card TA that does not require a separate WAN card is preferable. At the time of writing this book, however, no U.S.-certified, MPR-compatible ISDN cards are available. That will likely change soon, though, because there are many vendors that make ISDN TAs, such as Digiboard and IBM. Some of the vendors who have TAs available include the following:

→ Australia (ITEC Manufacturing)

→ France and Belgium (OST and SCii Telecom)

→ Germany (AVM GmbH, Diehl Electronics, ITK GmbH, and Loewe ISCOM)

→ United Kingdom (Dataflex Design Ltd, First Source Limited, and KNX Limited)

The most economical alternative in this category is the Integrated ISDN TA and router on a card. Unfortunately, at the time of writing this book, no vendor is shipping such a product. Digiboard and Combinet provide an integrated ISDN TA and a bridge on a PC card, but those products are focused on single user access, rather than for a LAN, and don't route IP protocols. Eicon Technology and Newport/Cisco also supply router cards, but their products don't have an integrated TA at this time.

External Routers

Any router that has a LAN and a WAN port can be used for this purpose with an external ISDN TA if it supports the following features:

→ Support of PPP protocols and routing of IP

→ Dial-on-demand software with support of dialing commands such as AT, V.25bis, or X.21

→ Sync port with port speeds of a minimum of 128 Kbps

Some of the dial-up routers discussed in a previous section for analog dial-up access also offer a sync port for ISDN connectivity. In addition, all major router manufacturers, such as ACC, Bay Networks, Cisco, and 3Com, provide routers with one LAN and one WAN port that can be used with an external TA.

These routers range in price from $1500 to $3000. For sites intending to migrate to leased-line connections, these routers may be a good choice. The stand-alone ISDN TA are made by many manufacturers, with Motorola UDS and ADC Kentrox lead-ing the pack. As pointed out earlier, most of these TAs come with a built-in NT1 or will work with external NT1, as shown in figure 8.7. The ISDN TAs range in price from $500 to $1000.

Integrated ISDN Routers

Unlike the previous alternative, integrated ISDN routers provide a LAN and an ISDN interface, thereby combining a router, ISDN TA, and NT1 (generally an optional device) in one device. On one end, these devices connect to the Ethernet or Token Ring LAN interface; on the other end, they provide a direct connection to the telephone jack for ISDN service, as displayed in figure 8.8.

Most integrated ISDN routers provide two B interfaces. One of the B interfaces can be used for connection to the Internet, while the other B channel can be used to dial another destination, such as another branch office. It is also possible to combine two B channels to get up to 128 Kbps of raw throughput. Most of the routers use proprietary *inverse multiplexing* schemes (combining of

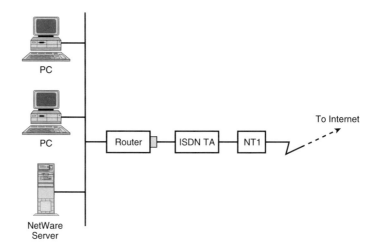

Figure 8.7

External routers with ISDN connectivity.

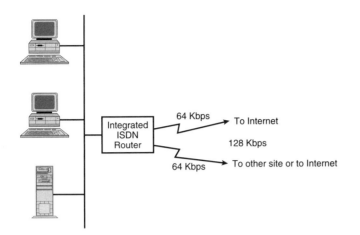

Figure 8.8

An integrated ISDN router combines many components.

64 Kbps → To Internet

128 Kbps

64 Kbps → To other site or to Internet

Integrated ISDN Router

different B channels)—however, the standard for inverse multiplexing of two B channels, called *multilink PPP*, is just emerging. You thus need the same vendor's routers at both ends for getting 128 Kbps connections. If you intend to use ISDN for 128 Kbps connection, you must check with your Internet Access Provider to find out if it supports the same equipment as you intend to use at your end.

ACC, Ascend, Cisco, Telebit, and many other vendors provide integrated ISDN routers ranging in price from $1500 to $3000. Some of the other router vendors like Cisco also provide additional WAN ports

for upgrading to higher speed, leased-line services in addition to built-in ISDN ports, but this comes at a price premium over other vendors. In addition, there are many vendors that sell integrated ISDN bridges, such as Combinet, Digiboard, Intel, and Gandalf. In theory, all of these products can also be used for Internet connectivity. Because these products do not route IP or provide IP over PPP, however, most IAPs do not support these devices.

Table 8.2 summarizes the three WAN devices discussed in this section. The price range, LAN connectivity, protocols, expandability, and pros and cons of each device are included in the table.

	Internal Router	**External Router**	**Integrated ISDN Router**
Price Range	$2500 to $3000	$2000 to $4000	$1500 to $3000
LAN Connectivity	Yes	Yes	Yes
Protocols	Can work with both workstation or server TCP/IP solutions	Can work with both workstation or server TCP/IP solutions	Can work with both workstation or server TCP/IP solutions
Expandability	Can be used to support higher speed services	Can be used to support higher speed services	Can be used to support higher speed services
Pros	Can use familiar NetWare environment	Offers more flexibility and expandability	Most integrated solution; reduces installation and maintenance costs
Cons	Expensive; needs extensive integration	Expensive; needs extensive integration	Least flexible; can't be used for other services

Table 8.2

Comparison of ISDN WAN Devices

Leased-Line and Switched 56 Services

The most common leased-line connections used for Internet access start out in the 64/56 Kbps bandwidth. These could be obtained either from DDS56 type of service or from Frame Relay type of service. Like ISDN, Switched 56 is a switched service, but it requires a DSU/CSU like other leased-line services. The other most common type of leased-line connection is T1, having a bandwidth of 1.544 Mbps. In addition, there are many fractional T1 services, called *FT1*, which could vary from 56/64 Kbps to N* 64 Kbps where N=24.

In Europe, E1 is the predominant standard instead of T1. While T1 offers a maximum speed of 1.54 Mbps, E1 offers a speed of 2.04 Mbps. A T1 service can be thought of as a combination of 24 pipes, each delivering 64 Kbps, while E1 is a combination of 30 pipes, each delivering 64 Kbps.

For the leased-line connections, a DSU/CSU is needed to connect to the telephone network. The DSU/CSU is connected in turn to the WAN serial port on the IP router. Most of the routers support Frame Relay encapsulation, in addition to the PPP encapsulation. There are two possible categories of solutions for leased-line connectivity, as follows:

→ Internal routers

→ External routers

In addition, there are some routers, such as those from Imatec and Ascend, that integrate DSU/CSU within the router itself for Switched 56, Leased 56, and Frame Relay services. These routers are limited to 56 Kbps connections, however, and are therefore not suitable for customers with FT1 and T1 needs.

Internal Routers

This alternative assumes Novell's MPR in conjunction with the integrated DSU/CSU WAN card, as shown in figure 8.9. There are many vendors that provide integrated DSU/CSU WAN cards for Novell's MPR router, including ADC Kentrox, Arnet Corporation, Eicon Technology, Microdyne Corporation, and Newbridge Microsystems. The total cost of this solution is in the range of $2500 to $3500, unless you have to dedicate a PC for this operation. If this is the case, the cost would increase by the value of the dedicated PC.

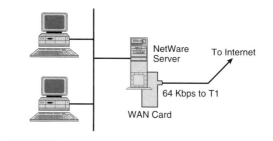

Figure 8.9

MPR integrated with WAN cards for Internet access.

Alternatively, there are many other vendors, such as Newport/Cisco and Eicon Technology, that provide a router and a WAN device on a card for use in the NetWare server.

External Routers

This alternative assumes an external router that, when connected to a DSU/CSU, provides Internet access (see fig. 8.10). These types of routers are provided by all major router vendors, including ACC, Bay Networks, Cisco, and 3Com. The DSU/CSU for leased lines can be obtained from ADC Kentrox, Digital Link, Larsecom, Motorola UDS, and others.

The total cost of this solution ranges between $2500 to $3500.

This alternative of using external routers is similar to the previous alternative of using internal routers. The selection of one alternative over the other is controlled by your comfort with a particular vendor and your company's philosophy on external versus internal routers.

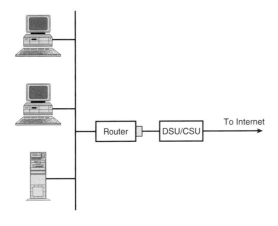

Figure 8.10

External routers and DSU/CSU for Internet access.

Combined Access

The Internet offers many other possibilities, some of which are useful today, while others will become more practical over time. This section provides discussion on some unconventional scenarios of Internet access, including the following:

→ Providing Internet access to remote offices

→ Providing Internet access to telecommuters

→ Using the Internet as a private virtual WAN

Providing Internet Access to Remote Offices

Depending on the size of the remote office and the company structure, it may be more desirable to provide Internet connectivity to the remote office using the corporate office's Internet connection. Consider the example of a company with a remote office in San Jose linked to the corporate office in Boston with a dedicated 56 Kbps link, as shown in figure 8.11.

The corporate office is linked to the Internet over a T1 line. The router in the remote office and the corporate office could be configured in such a way that all of the remote office users can also transparently access the Internet, just as users in the corporate office do. Therefore, both the remote office and the corporate office users benefit from the Internet connectivity.

Providing Internet Access to Telecommuters

With growth in telecommuting, many organizations use remote access servers to enable their telecommuting users to access the corporate LAN resources. With the Internet becoming another corporate LAN resource, it is possible to provide Internet access to telecommuters using the company's Internet connection. The remote users could be dialing in directly with a TCP/IP package, or they may be dialing with an IPX remote node software and using server-based TCP/IP access on the LAN to get to the Internet. Figure 8.12 displays a graphical representation of this scenario.

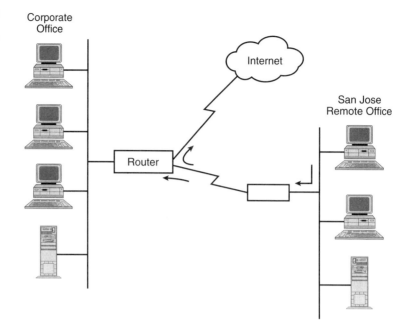

Figure 8.11

Connecting remote offices to the Internet using the corporate Internet link.

Corporate Office

Internet

San Jose Remote Office

Router

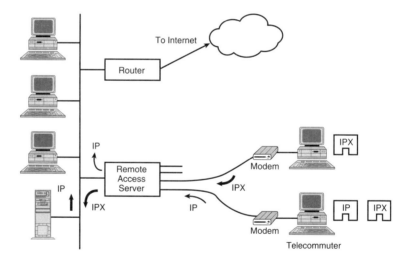

Figure 8.12

Providing Internet access to telecommuters.

To Internet

Router

IP

IP

IPX

Remote Access Server

IP

Modem

IPX

IPX

IP

Modem

IP

IPX

Telecommuter

Using the Internet as a Private Virtual WAN

It is possible to use the Internet as a wide area network, connecting a company's multiple offices over the Internet. For this to be an effective and viable alternative, however, an utmost level of security must be established. The security devices at both ends should not only authenticate the users, but should also encrypt all conversations traveling through the Internet (see fig. 8.13).

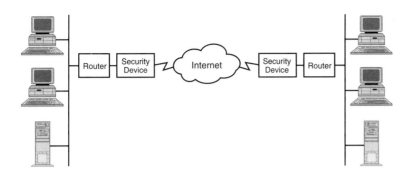

Figure 8.13

*The Internet as a
private virtual
WAN.*

At this time, these security devices are very expensive. It is expected that within a couple of years, however, these devices will become more affordable and will help to make the Internet more suitable for use as a private virtual WAN.

Summary

In order to connect to the Internet from your LAN, you need a router that provides a LAN interface, a WAN port, and support for WAN protocols such as SLIP, PPP, and Frame Relay. In addition, you need a WAN connection device to complete the LAN-to-Internet connection. This device might be a modem for analog access, an ISDN TA for ISDN services, or a DSU/CSU for Switched 56, Leased 56/64 Kbps, Frame Relay, FT1/E1, or T1/E1 services.

For analog access, dial-up routers are the preferred alternative because they incorporate integrated modems with the option to upgrade to higher-speed line services. Overall, dial-up routers offer an economical solution for a network's analog access to the Internet. For ISDN access, integrated ISDN routers are the best alternative because they incorporate integrated ISDN TA and are priced aggressively. For leased-line access, both Novell's MPR with WAN cards from third parties or external routers with external WAN devices are equally attractive, depending on a site's needs and policies.

There are many choices available for WAN access devices, but the objective of all WAN devices is to provide a connection to the POP of the Internet Access Provider. Furthermore, your IAP may recommend or sell a WAN access device that best meets your needs, as discussed in Chapter 9, "Internet Access Providers."

Internet Access Providers

The use of the Internet continues to grow at an unbelievable rate. We are constantly reminded of the Internet—tomorrow's information superhighway—through the evening news, daily media publications, and even in the cartoon section of the Sunday newspaper. While the Internet was once considered something strictly used by the highly technical users from the research and university communities, it is rapidly becoming a facet of the lives of the general populace. The Internet is commonly used today in many commercial companies, government offices, libraries, local school systems, and even our homes.

This chapter sets out to assist in the process of procuring the services of an *Internet Access Provider* (IAP). As discussed in Chapter 2, "The Internet: Yesterday, Today, and Tomorrow," the first step in this process is justifying the Internet connection. At this point, it is vital to have in hand a clear listing of the needs and a definition of the benefits that must be gained. The monetary implications, both in terms of cost and financial benefits, must be considered in detail. Then, by reviewing your requirements in light of the offerings from several IAPs, a sound decision can be made.

Frequently, the IAP may be the first company that most people contact while seeking an Internet connection. Recognizing that fact, many of the IAPs have extended the scope of their product offerings to include all seven layers of the Internet connectivity matrix, discussed in Chapter 1, "Components for Connecting to the Internet."

This chapter covers the following areas:

→ Understanding the Internet Access Provider

→ Determining your Internet requirements

→ Determining the suitability of the IAP with your requirements

→ Obtaining the correct information from prospective IAPs

note This chapter focuses on layer 6 of the Internet connectivity matrix.

7	SECURITY AND MANAGEMENT
6	Internet Access Providers
5	WAN Access Devices
4	WAN Access Services
3	Internet Application Servers
2	Internet Navigation Software
1	Network Communication Protocols

Understanding the Internet Access Provider

There are many models available to describe the role of an Internet Access Provider. In a way, the IAP is like your long distance carrier for data services. In some ways, it is similar to a local system's integrator whose vertical focus is Internet access. For some, the IAP is a gateway into an online service. All of these are valid descriptions of the Internet Access Provider because its role is evolving.

This section is divided into three main sections, as follows:

→ Types of IAPs

→ Point of Presence

→ Services offered by IAPs

In order to appreciate the role of the Internet Access Provider, an introduction to the history of the business, along with categorization by service offerings, might be helpful. This subject is discussed in the section entitled, "Types of IAPs."

What is a *Point of Presence* (POP), and what kind of equipment exists at the POP? From the POP, how does Internet connection get established to the rest of the world? Answers to these questions are provided in the section entitled, "Point of Presence," later in this chapter.

Before deciding on the services you need and establishing a comparative matrix, it may be desirable to understand the different services offered by various service providers and what they mean to your business needs. This chapter's section on "Services Offered by IAPs" covers details on this topic.

Types of IAPs

The Internet Access Provider business began as a cottage industry, but it has now become a business generating over $300 million annually, and is still growing at a phenomenal rate. The Internet access business has not gone unnoticed by major telephone companies such as MCI, Sprint, and AT&T, all of which are offering access to the Internet in some way. Many of the larger IAPs offer their services on a wholesale basis—selling their services to smaller IAPs, who in turn resell their services directly to the consumer.

Consolidation among Internet Access Providers is becoming very common today as customer needs become greater and customer service requirements are heightened to new levels. Many of the smaller service providers are being bought or merged with larger service providers to meet these increased industry demands. Even though consolidation will result in a limited number of large nationwide providers, there will continue to be a market for the well-focused niche player in the various regional

markets. Furthermore, these niche players may be more suited to more unique situations that may be part of your requirements.

The various commercial Internet Access Providers can be combined under two general categories:

→ National IAPs

→ Regional IAPs

National IAPs

At this time, no IAP offers Point of Presence and support within every local community worldwide. For the purpose of this text, therefore, *national IAPs* are those that have a significant number of access points or POPs, offer LAN services, and have extended their presence to more than a few states. PSI, SprintLink, UUnet, and ANS (now owned by America Online) are some of the national IAPs that focus on the LAN users. MCI has also announced its Internet service offering, which is nationwide in scope. BBN, with its recent acquisition of BarrNet, Suranet, and NYSERnet, is also assuming a national status for business users. In addition, some of the service providers that had traditionally focused on end users like NETCOM are adding programs and services to address the needs of customers who require access for a large number of LAN users.

Regional IAPs

The demarcation of regional and national IAPs is somewhat of a blur. The Internet Access Providers that have chosen to focus their services within certain regions, however, are called *regional IAPs*. The regional IAPs could be as small as serving one city, or they could be serving a particular state or some neighboring states. Colorado SuperNet and CERFnet are two of the regional providers that focus on LAN connectivity, and are also among the top ten providers based on the revenue. There are more than 100 providers that can be categorized as regional and also offer LAN-based access. A list of national and regional IAPs that offer LAN-based access is provided in Appendix A, "Examining Internet Access Providers." This list contains the most current information available at the time this book was written; however, due to the changing nature of the industry, all service providers may not appear.

A current listing of both regional and national IAPs can be obtained from one of the following sources:

→ http://www.internic.net/ds/dspg0intdoc.html—This resource includes InterNIC documentation, as well as a listing of IAPs.

→ http://www.umd.umich.edu/~clp/iaccess.html—Maintained by Ritesh Patel, this list provides a list of all IAPs sorted by area code.

→ gopher://nic.merit.edu:7043/00/internet/providers/pdial—This is a list of access providers that offers dial-up access, and is maintained by Peter Kaminski.

→ http://www.tagsys.com/Provider/List OfLists.html—This list provides *HyperText Markup Language* (HTML) links to other sites that maintain lists.

→ http://www.netusa.net/ISP—This is a list of service providers by country and by the area code within the U.S.

→ http://www.teleport.com/~cci/directories/pocia—This is a comprehensive list of all providers that lets you find out information by area codes.

One of the significant issues in selecting an IAP is determining its closest access location or POP. This will have a considerable effect on both the cost and the services available from the IAP. Therefore, it may be appropriate to understand POP from the technical and business point of view.

Point of Presence

Point of Presence (POP) is a term used in the telecommunications industry to represent a central office switch in a local area from which a telephone company routes calls within or outside of that area. In the Internet business, POP can be thought of as a regional hub through which end user nodes have to go in order to connect to the Internet. The POP of a service provider looks similar to a corporate network except that most of the networks in the former case are joined by a wide area connection, and there are very few LAN nodes. Ideally, a POP should be an office containing all of the necessary LAN and WAN equipment, as well as local staff available to support customers in the area. Many IAPs, however, use the term POP in loose terms to mean any place from where they can offer a local access number without toll charges for the customer. The local access numbers could be offered by IAPs with special arrangements with their long distance telephone company without a local POP. In strict technical terms, the use of POP in the Internet community is incorrect.

Figure 9.1 shows the set up of a POP with a T1 input of 24 channels and an aggregate throughput of 1.544 Mbps. Some POPs may have more capacity than a single T1 and may even go up to T3 speeds of 45 Mbps. Using a data multiplexer, T1 is split into separate channels and fed into the router ports at the POP. Each of those router ports may be dedicated to a 56 Kbps leased connection coming from a customer site. For providing dial-up connections, an IAP may use a remote access server wherein the asynchronous ports are attached to the modems. The modem lines at the POP may be coming separately from the telephone company, or a T1 pipe may be feeding directly into modem racks that accept T1 input and allow analog modems to connect directly. In addition, POP contains many computers used as servers for hosting different applications. Once you are connected to the POP, your data packets are delivered to their destination. The following section clarifies how this process takes place.

End-to-End Connectivity

Figure 9.2 shows a simplified version of an end-to-end connectivity scenario from a customer network A to a customer network C. Customer A's LAN is connected with a router and a WAN connection device to a port on a router at the POP of customer A's service provider. The Internet service provider A may have leased a connection from one of the *network service points* (NSP) that provides connection to the *network access points* (NAP). NAP is a hub for most of the NSPs. The same type of infrastructure exists at the intending receiver's end (i.e., customer C's network, as shown in fig. 9.2).

Figure 9.1

Typical POP equipment.

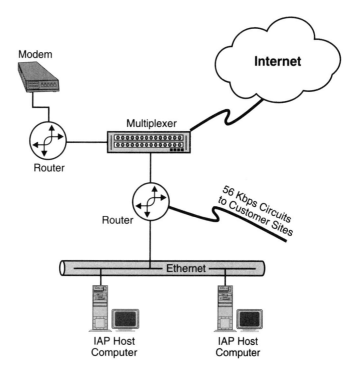

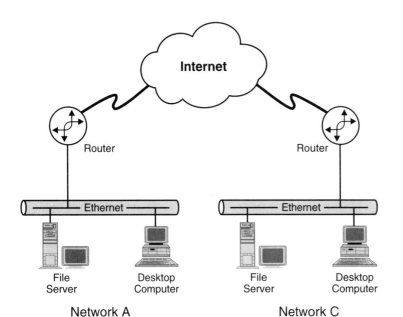

Figure 9.2

End-to-end Internet connectivity.

Router

Router

Ethernet

Ethernet

File
Server

Desktop
Computer

File
Server

Desktop
Computer

Network A

Network C

A POP at the service provider end generally services many customers. Various customer LANs may be coming to the POP at different bandwidths, such as 56 Kbps, 128 Kbps, or T1 (1.544 Mbps). Some of the large providers have their own backbones, which tap directly into the NAP. ANS, PSI, MCI, NETCOM, SPRINT, and UUNET have their own backbone networks. Some of the service providers like UUNET and SPRINT, besides servicing direct end users, also sell access to their network to regional Internet access providers.

The Internet hierarchy for interconnection is undergoing major changes with the expiration of government subsidies for the NSF backbone. Figure 9.3 shows a simplified version of this hierarchy, and does not represent the actual connection. As shown in figure 9.3, the lowest level in the hierarchy is the Internet Access Provider, from whom most Internet connection services are bought by end users. The next level up consists of the network service points.

NSPs are generally owned and operated by different telephone companies because they already have the wiring structure in place, but need to add the routing infrastructure anyway in order to offer these services. Some of the NSPs include MCI, SPRINT, and WILTEL. In addition, UUNET serves the same role because it services small IAPs. The next level from the NSP is the network access points. All of the NSPs must connect to every NAP for increasing network reliability. There are four major access points for NAPs—one in New York, another in Chicago, a third in San Ramon, California, and the fourth in Washington D.C.

Commercial Internet Exchange (CIX) was established to enable exchange of commercial traffic among different providers on a peer basis. In a logical sense, it is like another NAP. CIX is also a membership organization, consisting of various IAPs and having over 100 members. CIX has an access point located in Santa Clara, California. Some of the IAPs

Figure 9.3

The Internet hierarchy.

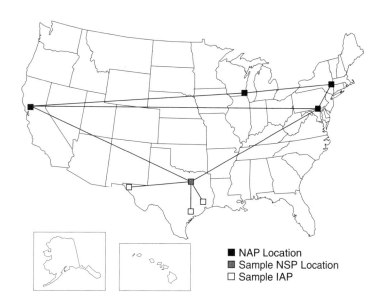

■ NAP Location
■ Sample NSP Location
□ Sample IAP

have signed up with NSPs that are CIX members, like UUNET, and have therefore opted to not sign up directly with CIX. Even though CIX has the potential of filtering out non-member traffic, thereby forcing everyone to become its member, it has opted to not do so at this time.

 n o t e The Internet business can be compared to the distribution model used for the Novell products. NAPs can be likened to a manufacturer such as Novell, which in turn sells its products and services to national distributors such as Tech Data, Ingram, and Merisel. Mid-level networks are like the national distributors in the Internet business. Many of the *value added resellers* (VARs) buy it from the distributors and sell to the end user. Similarly, an IAP is similar to a VAR of the mid-level networks. Just like VARs, IAPs sell to the end users. IAP services, like VARs, differ from one IAP to the other. Some of the IAPs use price as their main differentiation, while others differentiate with complete solution or better service.

Bandwidth Issues If you subscribe your Internet connection at T1 speed, it does not mean that you will be able to get a T1 speed connection to the receiver's end. Many bottlenecks exist that will prevent you from getting full bandwidth. Also, the receiver's Internet connection may in fact be a communications link with less bandwidth. If this is the case, your end-to-end bandwidth will be less than the bandwidth of your connection to the Internet. As with any network, communications are only as fast as the slowest portion of the network.

At any time, there may be more than one user sharing the Internet connection, and therefore no single user on the customer LAN will get the full bandwidth to themselves. Your Internet service provider may have overloaded the system by signing up more customers than its infrastructure allows. If your IAP's connection to the mid-level network is 56 Kbps and many customers have all subscribed with a 56 Kbps link there will be bandwidth bottlenecks at your IAP. This will especially be true when all of the IAP's customers increase the utilization of their Internet connections. If you are looking for a 56 Kbps or higher speed connection to the Internet, make sure that your IAP has adequate bandwidth to the mid-level network to ensure that your access to this level is not limited in a bandwidth. Generally, mid-level networks have a bandwidth of T3 (45 Mbps), which may become the bottleneck if many of their IAP customers are all running at full load.

Services Offered by IAPs

Just like a VAR offers you many more services than merely delivering the equipment ordered, Internet Access Providers also offer many services. Some of the services are offered by most providers, while others offer many more value added services. In addition, the pricing models offered for different services vary from one provider to the other. Generally, for most LAN connections, the pricing model is a flat monthly fee rather than usage-based. For single-user connections, some providers offer both flat fee-based pricing as well as usage-based programs. Different services offered by the IAPs can be classified into the following areas:

→ Basic connectivity services

→ Basic support services

→ Value added services

Basic Connectivity Services

This is the main reason for subscribing to any Internet access provider. The basic connectivity services include both single user and LAN services. Generally, most IAPs charge more money for the LAN connection than for a single-user connection,

even though both may be at the same speed. For example, single-user ISDN access is being offered by some IAPs at $29/month with 30 hours of usage cap. The same IAP charges over $200 per month for a LAN connection with no usage cap. Besides being identified as single-user versus LAN connection, the basic connectivity is also identified by the available bandwidth. The most common basic connectivity services offered include the following:

→ Dial-up analog or leased analog circuits up to 28.8 Kbps

→ Switched 56 or ISDN with 64 Kbps or 128 Kbps

→ Dedicated 56 Kbps line with DDS56 type of service or Frame Relay

→ T1 (1.544 Mbps) or Fractional T1 (N* 64 Kbps)

Needless to say, all IAPs provide some level of basic connectivity, which may include only dial-up or a combination of dial-up and dedicated services. In fact, there are more providers that offer dial-up only services than the ones that can offer dedicated line services. Generally, IAPs that provide leased line services also offer LAN-based services.

Basic Support Services

Most of the IAPs include some level of support in helping their customers get started. The level of support can vary all the way from a busy-sounding network technician to an on-site installation and support from a professional technical person. Depending on your needs and the level of expertise at your site, you may want to decide the most important services from your perspective. Following is a list of the most common support services offered by many IAPs:

→ Domain naming services

→ Assigning IP addresses

→ Resale and installation of hardware and software

→ Support and monitoring services

→ Archive/mirror site

Domain Naming Services   In this case, the IAP merely acts as your agent with the InterNIC in registering the domain name of your choice. Some providers charge you a nominal fee for domain name registration service while others will provide this service for free. Whether you apply for the domain name or your IAP applies for a domain name, the process takes the same amount of time (about 6 to 8 weeks, at the time this book was written). If you already have a domain name registered, all providers will be able to use it and advertise it on their hosts. The domain name you receive is granted to your organization, not to the IAP. Once your company has a domain name, your organization can change service providers without impacting anything on the outside (i.e., all e-mail addresses and Web server addresses will stay the same).

Most of the service providers host your primary and secondary domain name server, and advertise their hosts to be the one knowing the location of your DNS servers. Unless you have a very large network with DNS servers already established at your site, it is advisable to use the IAP servers as your DNS server.

Acquiring IP Addresses   Before you connect to the Internet, it is imperative that any devices that will communicate on the Internet use NIC registered addresses. A registered IP address can be obtained from the InterNIC or from your Internet Access Provider. In most cases, you will be able to get IP addresses faster from your IAP than from the InterNIC. As in the case of your domain name, the ownership of these registered IP addresses is important. It should be confirmed whether or not your organization can continue to use this same addressing scheme in the event that your organization switches to a new IAP.

Resale and Installation of Hardware and Software   Many of the service providers have assumed the role of a systems integrator, and therefore will be willing to supply all components needed to implement the connection to the Internet. Most IAPs that resell equipment concentrate on selling the router and the WAN connection device because that is their area of expertise. In addition, some of the IAPs resell not just the hardware, but all of the software components, such as Internet applications and communication software. Some IAPs like UUNET have developed their own security software, while others prefer to resell third-party solutions.

Generally, IAPs that resell equipment also provide an installation service as part of their offering. In many cases, you may find the equipment price charged by the IAPs to be very competitive with other sources. If you have a router in place or prefer to buy from your reseller, however, you should be able to use it to connect to the IAP. In cases where you may use your own router or buy from a reseller, you may have to take care of the installation issues yourself.

Support and Monitoring Services   As Internet connectivity assumes the role of mission critical within an organization, any outages in your Internet connection are undesirable. Just as the local area network environment might be expected to be functional at least 95 percent of business hours, so too the Internet connection is required to provide the same consistent level of service.

Therefore, many of the service providers offer 24 hour, 7 days a week (24*7) monitoring services, whereby your connection is constantly polled by the IAP. For monitoring, most of the IAPs use *Simple Network Management Protocol* (SNMP) to poll your connection.

This monitoring service can provide online statistics of daily, weekly, and monthly use of the Internet connection with detailed information on individual workstations, servers, and applications. The devices and connections involved in your Internet connection are frequently displayed on a *network management station* (NMS). A failure of any component of this network will immediately generate an alert, which is displayed visually on a NMS display console and may even dial a pager number of technical support personnel. This is why most service providers insist on a router at your end that supports SNMP.

Mirror Sites   The Internet is a vast resource of public domain software. In fact, most of the commercial Internet applications are now also offered on the public domain in their beta/lite versions. For example, most Web browsers like Netscape, NCSA Mosaic, Booklink Internetworks, and browser from Quarterdeck were all put in the public domain before being released commercially. There are many sites from which the public domain software can be downloaded for a trail, but finding those sites—and once found, connecting to them—is very difficult—especially during the day, which is peak

usage time. Therefore, many of the IAPs offer a mirror site with a copy of the most popular public domain software for their customers. Therefore, customers can download the software from a known site of the IAP, rather than surfing the Internet.

Value Added Services

There are many value added services, above and beyond the basic services, that are offered by the Internet Access Providers. Some of the value added services are part of the core pricing, while others may be an extra charge item. It is difficult to list all possible combinations of value added services. Based on a survey of several different IAPs, however, the following category represents some of the more common value added services:

→ Consulting and turnkey services

→ Server hosting services

→ Security services

→ Training services

Consulting and Turnkey Services   Some of the IAPs offer a complete turnkey solution—from inception to connection to servicing and support. This is similar to the outsourcing services offered by many companies for your LANs and WANs. Obviously, these type of services have a premium for the pricing, and may suit some companies with an ample budget and lack of internal resources to implement the Internet connectivity projects.

Some IAPs also offer consulting services to evaluate and recommend your Internet connectivity needs. There are many Internet consultants in the market, however, who may be less biased and provide a more objective evaluation of your Internet connectivity needs.

Server Hosting Services   In addition to domain name servers, which were discussed earlier, there are other servers that an organization may want to implement, such as e-mail servers, Web servers, and FTP servers. Some IAPs do offer mail hosting services, whereby all of the user post offices and mailboxes are hosted on the IAP's computers. This will reduce your initial cost and management overhead. This option may limit the amount of control that your organization may be seeking, however, by being forced to depend on the service provider for changing, adding, or deleting user names and user lists.

Most of the IAPs offer you a certain amount of disk space on their host for free and charge more for disk space above the specified amount. The disk space required will be the total of all your files, including e-mail and other files you may keep on the IAP host. Therefore, disk space on an IAP server must be used judiciously.

One of the most common services being added by most service providers is a facility to host Web servers and FTP servers for their customers. If a company wants to host its Web server at its IAP's POP, the IAP may provide the disk space, the HTTP server, and the advertisement of the server on company's behalf. The same is true of FTP and other servers. The alternative of hosting these servers at your own site provides more control, but adds additional management overhead. Because no user accounts need to be maintained in hosting Web servers, however, it is more efficient to host Web servers at the IAP site if the price is reasonable.

In addition to hosting Web servers, most IAPs will recommend or provide the services of setting up your home pages for an extra price. These home pages provide for a highly graphical interface for

users accessing these Web servers. See Chapter 6, "Internet Application Servers," for more details on Web servers.

Security Services   The most common security service offered by the IAPs is to recommend and install security software at customer premises and help in configuring and designing security policies for the company. Some of the IAPs also provide 24-hour security monitoring whereby IAP will generate security alert whenever it observes a suspicious activity on your network. This is like having a security company monitor your house all the time. Many of the IAPs also offer security consulting services or can recommend the services of a security consultant in your area. In addition, IAPs focused on security services will also keep you abreast of the new changes and alerts issued for the security.

Training Services   Some of the IAPs have training centers where they conduct classes on different topics, including using the Internet, managing the Internet connection, Internet security, and a host of other topics. Some of the training services are included as part of their services, while others are extra price items. In many cases, you may have to develop your own Internet end user training courses customized to your needs.

Now that you have a good idea of the types of services offered by the Internet Access Providers, it is time to examine your needs and determine your Internet requirements.

Determining Your Internet Requirements

Planning for your Internet requirement is no different than planning for your LAN and WAN connectivity. Therefore, understanding your current and future needs, as well as taking stock of skill levels and the availability of network administration resources, is the first step in planning your Internet connection. The first issue that should be addressed initially is your need for Internet connectivity. In order to establish your requirement, you need to answer the following questions:

→ What level of connectivity do you need?

→ How do you establish your presence on the Internet?

→ What support resources are available within the organization?

→ Is Internet connectivity a mission-critical application?

→ What is your budget for Internet connectivity?

→ How do you deal with decentralized organizations?

What Level of Connectivity Do You Need?

No single type of service is suitable for everyone. Many of the Internet providers have numerous levels of offerings specifically tailored to the needs and budget of nearly everyone, from the individual wanting to access the Internet from their home computer to the large corporation needing Internet connectivity for thousands of employees. The ideal solution for your needs may actually span more than one type of Internet connectivity. For example, a dedicated leased line might be used for LAN access and a PPP dial-up service for users while they are traveling.

There are four levels of Internet connectivity, depending on your needs, as follows:

→ E-mail-only access

→ Dial-up time-sharing accounts

→ Dial-up SLIP/PPP

→ Dedicated connections

 n o t e This book is not intended for single-user access to the Internet. Most corporations that have a LAN should obtain a LAN access account, even if only a few users on the LAN are permitted to connect to the Internet. Do you let your employees use a business card with the logo and name of your answering service? If the answer is no, why would you want your employees to give out their e-mail addresses with the domain of an Internet service provider, such as john@ix.netcom.com instead of john@abccompany.com?

E-Mail-Only Access

At the lowest level of Internet connectivity, you will find electronic mail and/or Usenet access. E-mail access enables you to send and receive electronic mail messages from other individuals who have access to the Internet. Access to Usenet enables you to read and post messages to some of the many Usenet news groups. This level of service does not allow for access to Internet resources using applications such as FTP, Web browsers, or Gopher, however.

This level of service is available from many organizations whose primary function is granting Internet access. It is also available from several of the online service providers, such as America Online, CompuServe, or Prodigy.

The primary benefit of this level of service is cost. Limiting access to electronic mail and Usenet provides the cheapest way to communicate on the Internet. It also provides an easy transition for the novice Internet user since this option presents a limited scope of new applications to learn. This level often presents the user with the most choices because there are many organizations providing e-mail and Usenet services.

The access to the Internet is quite limited, however. The wealth of information that can be accessed using Web browsers, Telnet, FTP, and many of the Internet search tools is not accessible with this level of service. It should be noted that several of the online service providers charge additional fees for access to the Internet.

While this option presents some considerable limitations, it enables you to explore the Internet and establish some familiarity without the higher cost of other services available.

For e-mail-only access, the most important service needed from the IAP is a reliable connection, followed by installation and support services. If you don't want to manage user accounts and are just starting with e-mail, you might want to consider an IAP that will host your e-mail server at its POP.

Depending on the number of users, you may be able to determine the bandwidth requirement. The rule of thumb as stated in Chapter 7, "WAN Access Services," is to allocate 2 Kbps per user to determine the total bandwidth need. If your users use MIME e-mail and transfer large attachments, however, you might want to allocate 5 Kbps for those users. If you want your e-mail to be delivered to you instantly, you are better off with a dedi- cated line. Even for e-mail-only connectivity, it is highly recommended that you get your own domain name from the InterNIC.

Most of the e-mail-only accounts have already chosen a LAN e-mail standard like cc:Mail, and tend to use SMTP gateways from their mail servers into the Internet. See Chapter 6, "Internet Application Servers," for details on e-mail servers.

Setting up an e-mail-only account still needs all of the other components, as stated in the seven layer connectivity matrix, including routers, WAN connection, and devices. Since e-mail-only accounts are not intended to provide access for other Internet applications such as FTP and Web, there is no need to set up TCP/IP at every workstation. TCP/IP, in this case, is only needed in the SMTP Mail gateway server. If you are using a UNIX server as your e-mail server, you must review your security procedures and put in appropriate safeguards, as discussed in Chapter 10, "Network Security."

Dial-Up Time-Sharing Accounts

Many Internet providers grant access to the Internet by renting electronic space on their computers. The provider can assign a user account to you on one of its internal computers, which can be accessed by dialing into the provider's computer. By dialing into the provider's computer, you will function very much like an individual using a terminal directly connected to the computer.

The most significant benefit of using a time-sharing account is access to the entire Internet and its applications. Applications such as FTP, Web browsers, Telnet, and numerous Internet search tools are available.

This is also a very simple means of access. All that is required is a simple communications software package on the user's computer and a modem. All of the responsibility for IP addressing, troubleshooting, and maintenance of the actual Internet connection is handled by the provider.

This option presents the user with full access to the Internet with minimal complexity and responsibility. It does present some issues, however. First of all, a time-sharing account potentially presents some significant limitations for the user. The applications that will actually be used for accessing Internet resources, such as FTP and Web browsers, are chosen by the Internet provider. Frequently, there is little flexibility in the selection and use of these applications. If a time-sharing account seems like the correct solution, ensure that the provider has applications that will meet your needs.

Another significant limitation is if files will be transferred frequently. Using a time-sharing account will often require double file transfers—files will be transferred to the provider's computer using FTP, and then transferred from there to the user's computer using a modem communications software. If your users will be downloading files frequently, the two steps required to download files may in fact make a time-sharing account impractical.

Dial-Up SLIP/PPP

Like the use of a time-sharing account, this option involves the use of a dial-up or switched digital connection to the Internet provider. The difference is that rather than dialing into the provider's computer and functioning the same as an asynchronously attached terminal, this connection is established by dialing into a communications server using SLIP or PPP communications software.

A dial-up SLIP or PPP connection enables users to select applications that are best suited to their needs. All applications, such as Web browsers, FTP client software, or electronic mail programs, are loaded locally on your computer. This enables you to select applications that you find easy to use and have the features that are required. File transfers are also considerably easier. Files that are downloaded from the Internet are transferred directly to your computer.

Using a SLIP or PPP connection provides the user with the highest level of functionality without the higher cost of dedicated line Internet access. Like a time-sharing account or limited electronic mail access, dial-up SLIP or PPP connections are best suited to individual users. Many Internet providers, however, are providing a higher level of dial-up SLIP/PPP access by providing a dedicated connection. A port, modem, and communications line is dedicated for each customer. This makes the use of a dial-up router using standard telephone lines, ISDN, or switched 56 Kbps services viable.

Dedicated Connections

If your users will be accessing the network throughout the day, a dedication connection using a Point-to-Point Dedicated or Leased line or perhaps Frame Relay will be the appropriate selection. Using a dedicated line provides users with a permanent connection to the Internet. By attaching a router to your local network with a connection to the communications circuit from the IAP, you will have constant and permanent access to the Internet. Whether a Point-to-Point Dedicated line or a Frame Relay circuit is available largely depends on the services offered by the IAP.

One of the significant advantages of a dedicated connection to the Internet is that the connection will provide a higher bandwidth connection than dial-up or switched digital connections. These connections offer bandwidth options that typically range from 56 Kbps to T1 circuits at 1.544 Mbps. Several service providers such as PSI offer connections as high as 45 Mbps. But how much bandwidth is actually required?

It is hard to determine the bandwidth requirement for LAN access unless you have decided on the applications and have a fair idea of its usage. FTP is a very bursty application since it consumes bandwidth only when a file transfer is occurring. Web browsers are very bandwidth-intensive because many of the Web servers offer extensive graphics that consume bandwidth. The general rule of thumb is to account for 10 Kbps per user for Web and FTP access. One of the ways to get control on the bandwidth is by restricting access to certain groups, users, or applications at certain times during the day. Several communication software products and routers enable system administrators to control the access by user, group, application, or time of the day.

If you want to offer outgoing Internet access to all of your LAN users, the requirements of a reliable connection, installation, and support are as important as they are for e-mail-only access. The equipment needs are also very similar to that of e-mail-only access. In addition to the e-mail reader and server, you will require Internet application software, such as FTP and Web browser.

How Do You Establish Your Presence on the Internet?

Having your own Web server on the Internet has become synonymous with establishing your presence on the Internet due to the large-scale popularity of Web servers and Web browsers. Web servers, discussed in detail in Chapter 6, are being used for external use to provide services to customers, and even to provide sales and marketing information to prospective customers. Before the advent of Web servers, FTP servers used to be a hallmark of having presence on the Internet. However, the highly graphical interfaces made possible by HTTP-based Web servers have made Web server access one of the fastest growing uses of the Internet. Gopher servers are another popular vehicle for establishing your presence on the Internet.

As explained in Chapter 6, setting up a Web server involves the design of a usable and eye-catching home page, along with the loading of files containing useful information. This is a process that will likely be a new task for your organization. As mentioned earlier in the discussion of IAP services, many service providers can assist in the design and implementation of a Web server. The Web server can be located at your site or at the IAP site. If you want to locate the Web server at your site, you need to have resources at your end to maintain the server. Even when the Web server is located at the IAP site, someone at your site should be trained to modify the content files. It is also possible for an organization to set up its Web presence, but have no Internet access for its LAN users.

What Support Resources are Available in the Organization?

Internet connectivity is similar to the management of both LAN and WAN connectivity. Initial installation and ongoing support of the Internet connection is needed in all types of connectivity options. Therefore, if you don't have installation and a support staff trained in internetworking, you must ensure that your IAP provides those services. For e-mail-only connectivity, ongoing maintenance of user mailboxes is needed, which requires the expertise of a network administrator. LAN access increases network administration resources as all user workstations have to be configured. For NetWare networks, server-based TCP/IP solutions like Novix from Firefox and IWare from Internetware can reduce the network administration when compared to the client-based TCP/IP solutions. Hosting your own servers requires the services of a full-time person to continue to enhance and maintain the server. If your Web server is just few pages, however, it will need less resources.

Is Internet Connectivity a Mission-Critical Application?

This question is important to answer in order to decide the emphasis you may place on reliability of your IAP's network. Your connection to the Internet becomes mission critical when users in your company communicate with their customers, vendors, and distribution partners over the Internet using e-mail or other means. Another example indicating that your connection is mission critical is if your company has put up its own Web server on site and uses it as a selling tool for existing and potential customers. As Internet connectivity becomes more and more important to the organization, the reliability of the IAP network becomes crucial.

In light of this issue, you should ask your prospective Internet Access Provider for information and statistics that show the reliability of its network and the consistency of its service to their customers. Clearly, the needs of your organization will not be met if an IAP has a history of frequent downtime

and your Internet connection becomes a mission critical part of your overall network.

What is Your Budget for Internet Connectivity?

The answer to this question is an overriding factor. If your budget is less than $100 per month, a dial-up LAN connection is likely to be an appropriate solution. There are three types of budget items that must be accounted for, as follows:

→ Up front capital cost of the hardware and software needed for Internet connection

→ Monthly WAN access fees

→ Monthly Internet access fees

See Chapter 2, "The Internet: Yesterday, Today, and Tomorrow," for details on how to sell the Internet connectivity within your organization, along with details on calculating costs of connection.

How Do You Deal with Decentralized Organizations?

Some companies are totally decentralized, where each department has its own budget and manages its own network, which may or may not be connected with other departments' networks. If your organization structure is closer to this decentralized organization model, each individual department may want to obtain an Internet connection of their own, depending on their needs. Providing multiple connections to the Internet for various departments, however, will likely present problems in terms of addressing and domain naming. These issues will likely be manifested by problems in communications, such as e-mail within the organization, since data between departments would have to cross the Internet.

The other organization model may consist of decentralized departmental nets that are all well-connected to each other. In this kind of a structure, it is possible to share one high-speed Internet connection for all of the departmental LANs. For example, one of the ports on a router at LAN A is used to connect to the Internet. Therefore, all LAN users—whether they are on LAN A, LAN B, or LAN C—can be configured to connect to the Internet. In this case, the decision to locate the Internet connection (i.e., on which network segment) will determine which service providers may better serve your needs.

For organizations that use e-mail as their principal means of communication, have many traveling employees, or have many telecommuters who work from home, the requirements from an IAP may be an availability of local POPs or a toll-free 800 number to give access to e-mail and other resources from anywhere in the county.

Determining the Suitability of IAPs For Your Requirements

Having decided on your requirements, you are now ready to evaluate different IAP's offerings. There are no clear-cut answers as to what kind of IAP is best for your needs—it all depends on your requirements. The various questions could be categorized under the following general headings:

→ National versus regional IAPs

→ Network reliability

→ Orientation

→ Understanding your needs

→ Services offered

→ Cost

National versus Regional IAPs

The decision of whether to choose a national provider versus a regional provider is similar to whether you chose a national or regional systems integrator for your network needs. If you have offices located throughout the country and want to sign up with one provider for the whole company, national service providers may be a better choice. If your business is concentrated in few states, however, your choice of provider will also include regional providers. You may get more personal attention from the regional provider, and that may change the scales in its favor. In addition, if your organization is decentralized and each of the divisions make its own decisions, the choice of national versus regional may be a moot point. The bottom line is that you should evaluate the services offered by the provider in relation to your needs, and not make a decision based solely on whether it is a national or a regional provider.

Network Reliability

Network reliability is an important issue that should be evaluated in relation to your needs. If Internet connectivity is the most critical component of your business, you should pay more attention to how IAP maintains a reliable connection. There are many failures that impact the reliability, with the most common ones being the following:

- → Telecommunication line failure—This is the most common reason for failure. Therefore, you must ask the IAP about its network structure and backup plan if the main line fails.

- → Power failures—Guarding against short-term power outages is crucial to maintain reliability. Therefore, ask if the IAP's POP has any power backup system, such as a *uninterrupted power supply* (UPS), to feed the major equipment in case of a power failure.

- → Equipment failure—It is hard to determine whether equipment used by IAP is reliable or not. Therefore, ask for references and history of equipment failures.

Problems occur in the best of the networks. It is thus important to understand the problem resolution procedures within the IAP organization. Asking for references of who may have personal experiences is a useful check. You must ask the IAP of the escalation and problem resolution procedures.

Orientation

Many Internet providers are targeting their services toward consumers and individual users rather than businesses. Most providers with a single user target may not have an understanding of the services and reliability needed by businesses. Therefore, ask your IAP as to what percentage of its business comprises single user dial-up accounts versus business accounts. The lower this percentage is for the dial-up account, the better equipped the IAP will be to meet your needs.

Understanding Your Network Needs

Most IAPs start with a background in UNIX. Many of them thus assume TCP/IP and UNIX expertise at your site, and recommend solutions based on their experience. If your network is predominantly NetWare and you don't have much UNIX expertise, however, find out if your IAP has any experience with the NetWare networks and can recommend an appropriate solution. Some of the IAPs work with NetWare-savvy systems integrators in the area to meet the needs of their NetWare customers.

Services Offered

Based on your requirements and list of services provided in the section, "Services Offered by IAPs," in this chapter, evaluate different services offered by IAPs before choosing a provider.

Cost

Just like your telephone service, you likewise pay a setup fee and a monthly fee to your IAP. Most of the services are priced based on the chosen bandwidth (i.e., T1 bandwidth costs more than 56 Kbps, and 56 Kbps costs more than a 28 Kbps connection). Some IAPs include all of the value added services as part of their basic costs, while others charge extra for each service. Some IAPs even charge for domain name registration, while others include that as part of their service. In relation to your requirements, therefore, you should ask which of the services are included in the quoted prices and which ones will cost you extra.

The following table provides a range of prices based on a survey of some national and regional IAPs.

Table 9.1 The Price Range for IAP Services

Services	One Time Setup Fees	Monthly Fees
Leased dial-up of up to 28.8 Kbps	From $50 to $150	From $100 to $300
ISDN—1 B channel to 64 Kbps	From $100 to $400	From $200 to $400
ISDN—2 B channels to 128 Kbps	From $200 to $500	From $400 to $600
56 Kbps leased line	From $300 to $500	From $300 to $500
T1 leased line to 1.544 Mbps	From $2000 to $5000	From $1000 to $2000

Developing an RFP for Internet Access

Based on an assessment of your needs, you may develop a *request for proposal* (RFP) to get information from different access providers. Using a standard set of criteria will assist in making an objective decision as to which IAP will best meet your needs at an acceptable cost. Table 9.2 provides a quick checklist for developing the RFP.

Table 9.2 A Checklist for Developing an RFP for Internet Access

Feature	Possibilities	Requirement
Domain name registration	Already done	IAP to host DNS if not at site.
	Not done	IAP to provide domain name registration and host DNS server.
Obtaining IP addresses	Already done	
	Not done	IAP to provide IP addresses—must be transferable .

continues

Table 9.2, Continued

Feature	Possibilities	Requirement
Bandwidth needs	Look at today's needs and future needs	IAP must provide services for today's bandwidth needs and have provision for increased bandwidth.
Number of hours of connectivity per week	Less than 20 hours	IAP must provide high speed switched access like ISDN. Prefer usage-based pricing, if available.
	More than 20 hours or don't know	Must ask for a fixed pricing with no usage charges.
Hardware—router and WAN	Already have	Check if IAP supports your WAN access device and router.
	Doesn't have	Compare IAP pricing to your reseller pricing.
Software—TCP/IP and applications	Already have	Check if your application will work. If not, ask for IAP's recommendation. Also check if there is any expertise within IAP's technical staff on your applications.
	TCP/IP available, need to buy applications—public domain OK	Check if IAP has a local mirror site for public domain software.
	TCP/IP available, need to buy	Check if IAP sells the applications you like

Feature	Possibilities	Requirement
	applications— public domain not OK	or can recommend some products that you may like.
Installation of hardware and software	Already done	
	Have staff, need training	Check what kind of support and training help is available.
	No dedicated staff	Make sure IAP does a turnkey installation and support at site leased.
WAN services	Already have (Analog line, 56 Kbps leased line, ISDN, or Frame Relay)	Make sure that IAP supports the services you intend to use.
	Have staff—will order	Check the services supported by IAP and decide based on your needs.
	No dedicated staff	Ask IAP to order the line. Many people prefer single billing, which is offered by some IAPs for high-speed services.
Servicing and maintenance	Tools available for remote monitoring, such as SNMP	Check what kind of remote monitoring tools are deployed by the IAP.
	Service center hours	Ask if 24*7 service is available and ask for number of hours of guaranteed response.

continues

Table 9.2, Continued

Feature	Possibilities	Requirement
Reliability	Important	Ask IAP to furnish reports of failures.
		Ask IAP to furnish time taken to fix the problems when they occurred.
	Critical	In addition to preceding, get details of IAP networks, including backup services such as alternate circuits, UPS at each site, and redundant equipment at POP.
E-mail-only access	Have LAN e-mail standard—also have SMTP gateway installed	
	Have LAN e-mail standard—need help with the SMTP gateway	Ask IAP if expertise on supporting your LAN e-mail standard and SMTP gateway is available.
	No LAN e-mail/ready to change LAN e-mail —will set up and host e-mail at site	Ask IAP for recommendation.
	No LAN e-mail—don't want to host and manage e-mail at site	Ask if IAP provides mailboxes for your users and will host their mail.
Outgoing LAN access	Need to restrict user access—already have software	

Feature	Possibilities	Requirement
	Need to restrict user access—doesn't have software	Ask IAP/your LAN reseller for recommendations.
	Need to train users	Ask IAP if they offer a training programs for users.
	Need access to FTP, Gopher, News, and Web	Ask for news feed and supported newsgroups. Ask if any service is not fully supported.
Establishing your presence	Need to host FTP, Gopher, and Web servers at your site—need help	Ask IAP about what kind of help it provides.
	Need to host FTP, Gopher, and Web servers at the IAP site	Ask about IAP's programs for hosting these application servers.
Security services	Need security devices at your site—already have a solution	Ask if IAP is familiar with your your chosen solution.
	Need security devices at your site—need a solution	Ask for IAP recommendation.

Summary

Choosing an Internet Access Provider is similar to choosing a systems integrator for your network. IAPs offer a wide range of services—from a basic Internet connection to a complete turnkey service that offers installation, selling, and support of all seven layer components needed for Internet access. Determining your requirements, and then evaluating IAP services in relation to those require-

ments, are necessary and critical steps in selecting an IAP. Developing a cost comparison matrix that lists IAP services and respective prices will also prove to be extremely helpful in making your IAP selection.

One of the most frequently asked question regarding Internet access is one that pertains to security. Security is often thought of a balancing act of a number of issues. As an administrator, how do you balance access for your users with the protection of company information? How do you balance the manageability of a secure environment with the complexity that often comes with security? How do you balance the cost of maintaining a secure network with the benefits that it provides? In Chapter 10, "Network Security," the answers to these and many other questions are discussed in detail.

Hardware Components and Issues

10

Network Security

Many companies are abstaining from connecting to

the Internet because of growing security concerns.

The media is fueling these security concerns with

stories about Internet hackers and network secu-

rity. People have not stopped driving their cars for

fear of accidents or thefts, so why would the same

fears keep companies from driving on the Informa-

tion Superhighway? The benefits from connecting

to the Internet are real, and therefore companies

should not deprive their employees of these

benefits. Instead, you should learn about Internet security issues, ways to reduce the risks involved, and implement systems that monitor, control, and reduce security risks of connecting to the Internet.

The objective of this chapter is to discuss some of the most common solutions for Internet security for pure IPX networks, as well as mixed IP and IPX networks. After providing basic information on security, including how some break-ins occur, as well as designing a security policy, this chapter discusses the following security solutions:

→ Packet filtering with routers

→ Firewall software

→ Application relays

→ Security for emerging uses of the Internet

 note This chapter focuses on layer 7 of the Internet connectivity matrix.

7 SECURITY AND MANAGEMENT
6 Internet Access Providers
5 WAN Access Devices
4 WAN Access Services
3 Internet Application Servers
2 Internet Navigation Software
1 Network Communication Protocols

Network Security Fundamentals

To most people, network security seems so complex, and this lack of understanding feeds the growing security paranoia. With the lack of information, paranoia grows. What are the real threats? How can you protect yourself? Some companies react to these concerns by refusing to consider connecting their LANs to the Internet. Many of their users, however, are allowed to dial into the Internet directly from their desktop with a modem and a single-user account, which is just as risky as connecting your whole network to the Internet. Only by dealing with security head-on, developing rational policies, and communicating these policies to all employees can a company really protect itself.

Security concerns are universal. Whether it is for a home, car, or network, all security systems share some of the same basic qualities, as follows:

→ Security comes in varying degrees or levels.

→ No security system is totally crack-proof.

→ The more secure a system, the harder and more expensive it is to use, and the more costly it is to purchase and maintain.

For most homes, a simple lock and a deadbolt may be sufficient. Other homes have more elaborate security systems, such as alarm systems, 24-hour security monitoring, or even a full-time security guard. Each additional level of security is more expensive and can lead to its own difficulties. All levels of security, however, can be broken by some vandal or thief.

Similar concerns arise when planning a network security system. Nothing can be totally secure, but you can minimize the cost of any damage. The security risks can be minimized by restricting and monitoring the information that flows in and out of your network. As with a home security system, you can add many levels of security to your network from a simple password access, to firewalls, to encryption systems, and ultimately to 24-hour monitoring by your IAP. You should try to reach a realistic balance between security costs and benefits, however.

Planning for Network Security

UNIX systems, which make up a large part of the Internet, were designed for open and easy interconnectivity. This open architecture has enabled Internet connectivity for many people, and has also created the Information Highway's bandits and thieves, who are commonly referred to as "computer hackers." The majority of the computer attacks to this date have been the harmless pranks of computer hackers rather than serious espionage.

Hackers and espionage certainly make good press, but when planning security for your network, securing your network from the inside should be considered as important as securing from the outside. The majority of security breaches occur from within the company, rather than from outside the company, and some are intentional while others are accidental. Therefore, any security system should secure the network from accidental or intentional security breaches from the insiders—people who work inside your company: employees and contractors.

How Security Break-Ins Occur

Most of the computer hackers are knowledgeable about UNIX and TCP/IP, and thus use that knowledge to break into computer systems. There are many ways of breaking into your network via the Internet. For most break-ins to occur, a hacker requires the presence of a daemon on your network. A *daemon* is the equivalent of a server, such as an Anonymous FTP daemon. If you have ever downloaded any information off the Internet from a host with anonymous FTP, you have communicated with a host that has an anonymous FTP daemon loaded on it. UNIX systems come with many daemons—some optional and some standard—which provides for many different ways for hackers to break into systems.

NetWare, on the other hand, was designed to be a proprietary system focused at solving the LAN connectivity issues rather than building large internetworks. NetWare's lack of TCP/IP services has become an advantage from an Internet security point of view. For example, NetWare doesn't contain any daemons by default, even though all NetWare servers include the TCP/IP protocol. Daemons such as FTP, however, are an option that can be loaded on the NetWare server, in which case some of the same security issues as with UNIX need to be addressed in the NetWare environment.

IP spoofing is a common technique for break-ins where hackers create packets with spoofed source IP addresses that make the internal systems "trust" the hacker's IP packets. This enables hackers to break into the systems and use many other tools at their disposal. Some of the well-known ways hackers have broken into the computer systems include the following:

→ Using Finger daemon on a host—Finger is a protocol that lets you find information about users on a specified host, including the last time they logged on, their home directory, and their login names.

→ Using the .rhosts file—The .rhosts file enables a user to specify from which remote machines the account can be logged into without a password. Needless to say, it is a dangerous file.

→ Anonymous FTP daemon on a host—This is the way to enable outsiders access to files on your system using anonymous FTP. Therefore, care must be taken so that it can't be used to break into the system.

→ Sendmail daemon—Sendmail, in combination with Telnet, has been used to break into the systems as well.

For details on these and various other daemons and their related security impacts, please consult a text on UNIX security. Many of the well-known problems with the commercial UNIX systems have been addressed by the vendors of the systems. Many companies that use UNIX systems with public domain versions should pay closer attention to the security on those systems. *Computer Emergency Response Team* (CERT) points out well-known security holes, and offers advice on fixing them from time to time. You can get CERT advisory by sending an e-mail message to the following:

cert-advisory-request@cert.org

For more detailed information on Internet security and firewalls, you may consult New Riders Publishing's *Internet Firewalls and Network Security*, written by Karanjit Siyan and Chris Hare.

Before you evaluate any security system for your organization, it is best to develop a security policy. This policy could be described in as little as a few lines or may be as elaborate as hundreds of pages. Whatever the length, it is a critical step to take in implementing a security system for your network. The next section discusses some of the issues involved with designing an appropriate security policy.

Establishing a Security Policy

Begin planning for your security with a security audit. This will save you considerable expense and headaches, and enable you to end up with a more secure network. Here are just a few of the questions you should consider. Make sure to answer the who, what, and why questions before deciding on the how question.

What are You Protecting?

Protecting every resource costs money. You should consider each resource on your network, including data, programs, and machines, and you should also decide the level of protection. The temptation is to protect all resources at the same level, but that is not practical from a cost standpoint. To protect your personal valuables, you only deposit jewelry and other important material in a bank locker—not all the contents of your house. For each resource, ask the following questions: Are you trying to prevent unauthorized access to the resources? Are you trying to protect information from being destroyed? Are you trying to stop people from using information for free for which there is really a charge? Are you trying to prevent unauthorized disclosure of confidential information?

From Whom are You Protecting Your Network?

No network is more secure than the people who run it and use it. Do you really want to protect against professional hackers? Do you just want to discourage curious net surfers? Do you only need to protect against accidental destruction of data by employees? No network can be completely secure, but if you are willing to spend the money, you can protect against all but a small pool of dedicated hackers.

Why are You Protecting Your Network?

What is the real cost to your business if this information is discovered? How much would you lose if certain systems were unavailable for a period of time? How much would it cost to re-create lost information? Are there corporate policies to which you must adhere? For each resource, you should attempt to balance the cost and benefits of your security system.

What Access Restrictions Should be in Place?

Just like you have access restrictions to enter into your office building, the same type of restrictions may be imposed on Internet access. For example, one policy might state the following: "Unauthorized access to the Internet by attaching a modem to your desktop and connecting directly to the Internet using SLIP/PPP is not permitted." Or the guideline might be a simple statement such as "Internet access is only allowed between the hours of 7 a.m. and 6 p.m." The guideline also might state that weekend access to the Internet is not permitted.

Therefore, you may want to restrict Internet access to certain hours or certain applications to ensure that your MIS/security personnel are on sight monitoring systems while your network is connected to the Internet.

How Much are You Willing to Spend?

Implementing the highest level of security is not cheap. It can run you from as low as $1,000 to as high as $100,000.

Once the company security policy is in place, it becomes easier to pick the right security solution that meets your needs. The subsequent sections describe different security solutions, the implementation and cost issues for each solution, and the advantages and disadvantages of each alternative.

Security Solutions

Good security systems are a blend of policy, education, and technology. In dealing with any security issue, you have to balance the ease of use and access versus the level of security and the cost of the system. Except for a password (or similar technique), security should be transparent to the end user.

Understanding the capabilities and limitations of security technologies is fundamental to planning a secure network. Although hackers get the attention of the press and should not be ignored, the threat from inside your network should not be taken lightly. Make sure your security system can protect against both inside and outside threats.

The security systems needed to protect a NetWare LAN may be different from the systems needed to protect a TCP/IP-based LAN. There are many security solutions in the market—each of them catering to different needs. These different solutions can be categorized under the following headings:

→ Packet filtering with routers

→ Firewall software

→ Application relays

→ Security for emerging uses of the Internet

Packet Filtering with Routers

All routers implement some kind of packet filtering mechanism. *Packet filtering* is the process of barring specified network packets from entering or leaving your network. Packet filtering is achieved by designating a set of rules specifying which packets are allowed to pass through the filter. The process of setting packet filtering on most routers is very complex. If you are not an expert on router technology, get help from an expert when implementing packet filtering.

A *router* is a basic security requirement for every network that connects to the Internet—they are the most popular form of firewall. Even if you are using dial-up connection to the Internet, it is advisable to use a dial-up router with IP packet filtering to enhance security on your network.

Since the packet filtering router (also called a screening router) is the cornerstone of your network's security, it is important to find one that supports extensive packet filtering. The packet filtering is actually a set of rules stored on the router. Each packet that enters the router is tested against the rules, and a decision is made either to block the packet or let it pass. These rules describe *Transmission Control Protocol* (TCP) and *User Datagram Protocol* (UDP) packets in terms of their destination and source addresses and the application port numbers. The rules are set to permit or deny access to certain packets flowing through the router.

Tips from the CERT advisory suggested that routers with sophisticated packet filtering can thwart the IP spoofing attack described earlier. It listed many vendors who have support for IP Spoofing features in their routers, including Bay Networks, Cabletron, Cisco, and Livingston. Therefore, you must check with your router vendors in terms of their support of packet filtering for dealing with Internet connections before making a decision. Figure 10.1 shows the data flow through a router that provides packet filtering/screening for incoming and outgoing packets. The packet screens shown in figure 10.1 are not a separate component, but just a representation of the screening capabilities.

Most routers with packet filtering capabilities, one LAN port, and one WAN port can be bought for under $2,000. Packet filtering routers provide sufficient security for small and midsize networks—especially the ones with a small number of UNIX systems. If your network environment is NetWare, adopting one of the server-based IP solutions discussed in the "Firewall Software" section of this chapter will increase the level of protection.

Packet filtering is fast and transparent to the end users in most cases. Packet filtering with routers is not the best solution for all sites, however, because it has the following limitations:

→ For a connectionless protocol like UDP, most routers don't maintain any state information. Each packet that arrives at the packet filter is assessed individually without regard to packets that have come before. If a packet arrives indicating that it is in response to a request, the packet filter has no way of knowing if the request was ever actually made.

→ Most routers don't log the attacks that may be made on your network. They either accept or reject a request.

→ For most UDP-based applications like *Domain Name Server* (DNS) requests, many routers don't provide the desired filtering for UDP packets.

→ Packet filtering is difficult to configure.

→ Packet filtering does not support per-user or time-of-day restrictions.

The next level of protection after a router is a *dedicated firewall*, whose main function is routing with a subsidiary function of packet filtering.

Firewall Software

The next step up from packet filtering routers, both in terms of protection and cost, is the use of dedicated firewalls. Most of the dedicated firewalls are software packages running on a dedicated UNIX machine. Most firewall software packages offer a lot of flexibility in implementing security policies. Like packet filtering routers, a dedicated firewall includes the address-based filtering rules. The rules for firewalls can be more flexible than for routers, however, such as in setting time of day restrictions. In addition, dedicated firewalls also provide filtering capabilities on connectionless protocols like UDP.

Figure 10.1

The data flow through a router providing packet screening/filtering.

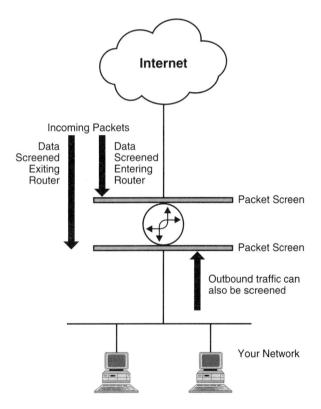

All network traffic between your network and the Internet should flow through a firewall. This controlled information flow enables you to use the firewall as a single "choke point" to impose security and perform audits. Figure 10.2 shows the typical network configuration with a dedicated firewall. It creates a total barrier between the internal and the external network. Therefore, all publicly accessible servers should be located in the external insecure zone in the network.

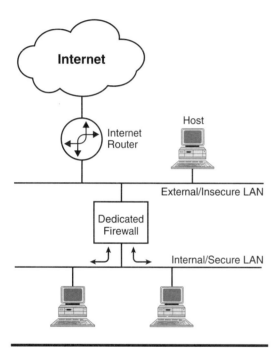

Figure 10.2

Network architecture with a dedicated firewall.

The dedicated firewall is very expensive. It requires a dedicated computer generally running UNIX and firewall software, which ranges in price from $5,000 to $50,000. Therefore, most dedicated firewalls are affordable only by organizations with huge budgets.

Dedicated firewalls provide an excellent security system for networks, but it comes at a hefty price. There are certain applications, such as X Windows and NFS, however, for which firewalls do not offer as much protection. Firewalls cannot protect against viruses. Firewalls are no more secure than the equipment on which they run. Therefore, make sure that you run firewall software on an operating system that you trust, and you carefully control access to the firewall equipment.

For most NetWare-only networks, a dedicated firewall may be an overkill. A server-based IP solution in combination with a packet filtering router may be sufficient for even large NetWare networks.

Firewall for NetWare-Only Networks

NetWare servers include a TCP/IP protocol stack for free, but they don't have any of the daemons or IP server applications, such as FTP, Telnet, or Sendmail. Therefore, the lack of IP server applications on a NetWare server is an advantage because it provides for greater Internet security. NetWare environments that use server-based IP solutions (see Chapter 4, "Adding TCP/IP to NetWare LANs," for details on different server-based IP solutions) have essentially made a provision for a security firewall. Because the clients on a NetWare network are running IPX, they have no identity outside of the local network. When server-based IP solutions are used in conjunction with packet filtering routers, they provide a robust security solution for NetWare LANs. For networks with mixed IP and IPX networks and a dedicated firewall, using server-based IP will serve as a second defense against intruders.

Figure 10.3 shows the network diagram for the preceding configuration. The screening/packet filtering

Hardware Components and Issues

router filters packets based on a source and destination address. Because all of the workstations access the Internet through the server, extensive controls can be placed on the access security and audit trails.

Some of the features offered by server-based IP solutions include the following:

→ NetWare bindery integration

→ Controlling access by time of day

→ Controlling access by application

→ Access reporting

NetWare Bindery Integration   An added advantage of the server-based TCP/IP approach is that it allows integration with the bindery (the name service used in NetWare 3.x) and NDS (the name service used in NetWare 4.x). This integration enables the administrator to build on pre-existing groups and restrictions. Internet access restrictions can be the same as, a subset of, or a superset of the restrictions allowed for NetWare servers. This

advantage offers administrators the benefit of a single place to track all rights and restrictions for the network.

To give you an example of how access may be controlled by the user type, refer to figure 10.4—an example of a screen shot from Internetware's IWare product. The system holds the information about users and groups, enabling the network administrator with supervisory rights to control access by user or group.

In this example, the access control is being applied to user DAN. DAN is restricted to using the Internet during the week day from 07:00 hours to 18:00 hours. Also shown are his restrictions for both incoming and outgoing access by applications. In this example, DAN is denied access to FTP and NNTP applications (see Chapter 5, "Internet Applications," and Chapter 6, "Internet Application Servers," for further details). Instead of totally restricting access by user or group, different amounts of granularity are provided, enabling the network administrator to restrict access to all or part of the Internet.

Figure 10.3

A NetWare environment using server-based IP with a router—this set-up can provide an effective firewall.

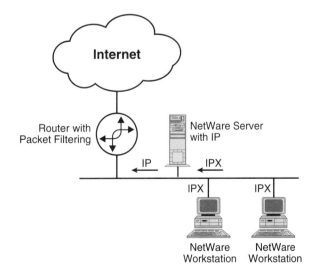

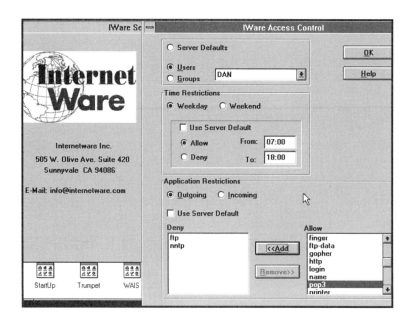

Figure 10.4

Managing access control with a server-based IP solution for NetWare LANs.

Controlling Access by Time of Day Companies often want to restrict access to the Internet by time of day. For example, you may want to minimize the load on gateway machines by screening out low priority applications and groups, whereby guaranteeing Internet access to high priority applications and groups. For example, assume your engineering or marketing departments need to use the Internet as a market research tool, which essentially requires that both groups have access to the Internet all day. Because the accounting department has virtually no need for Internet access, this department is given access only after 4:00 p.m. when the peak activity has subsided. This is one method of restricting access using the server-based TCP/IP approach in a NetWare environment.

Controlling Access by Application NetWare administrators can also restrict Internet access by types of applications. For example, an administrator can prevent a user from accessing a specific application such as FTP. Doing so prevents the user from using FTP to access outside hosts. Similar restrictions can be set up for Telnet, Web, Mail, and other applications. These restrictions can be set up for both incoming and outgoing connections. By default, you should deny incoming access completely to most users so that they can't inadvertently execute the FTP server, for example, and in doing so compromise the whole network.

Access Reporting *Access reporting* is an important tool that enables a NetWare administrator to track the activities of the host main access, the activities of the types of applications being accessed, and even the time during which the access is occurring. Armed with this type of information, the NetWare administrator gets substantially more information about security breaches from within the organization. Most of the server-based IP solutions provide information on Internet access. Figure 10.5 provides an example of one of the Internet access reports. For example, user PAULS did a POP3 query to a server called "dalek" at 15:11 hours on March

17 for 1 second. Similarly, an HTTP request was made to a server "Farstar.secapl.com" at 15:20 hours that lasted for 18 seconds.

Therefore, for networks that are predominately IPX, server-based IP solutions in combination with a router that does extensive packet filtering provides a good level of Internet security. The dedicated firewall solution may not be sufficient for predominantly IP networks, however, which require a high level of granularity in their security policy. If these sites can afford and are willing to pay the extra costs, application relays or gateways may be a better solution.

Application Relays

Application relays—also known as proxy servers, bastion hosts, and application gateways—are applications that control traffic between your network and the Internet. Application relays prevent traffic from passing directly from the Internet to your network. They are application specific (i.e., FTP, Web, etc.) and use the knowledge of applications to provide an extra level of security. For example, an FTP application relay can be set up to allow inbound FTP traffic, but block outbound FTP traffic. Many application relays also come with advanced logging functions and support for user authentication. Application relays may be used instead of or in addition to the router-based packet filtering or software firewall.

Figure 10.6 shows network configuration with an application relay. Two routers are used in this network. The first router knows of the corporate network topology, but directs all traffic to the application relay. The second router that is connected to the Internet only knows of the application relay address. It delivers all packets to the application relay, which then decides whether or not to forward the packets to the router on the company backbone.

Figure 10.5

Internet access reporting for a network using a server-based IP solution.

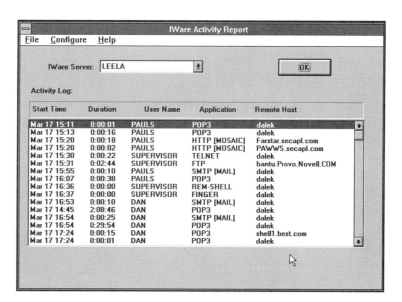

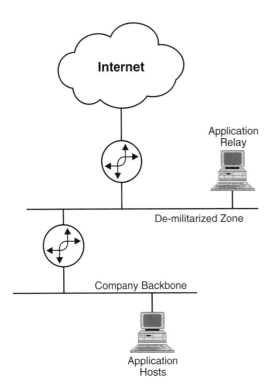

Figure 10.6

An application relay configuration with multiple routers.

 n o t e Routers and bastion hosts are configured to create an area called a *de-militarized zone* (DMZ). A DMZ is a network, visible to the Internet, on which a company places all of its network applications and public information.

All users on the corporate network have to go through the application relay for access to the Internet resources. In some of the application relays, reference to the internal network numbers is completely removed before a packet is sent out. Application relays offer the utmost in sophistica-

tion and enable control by user, by time of day, by application, and by destination.

Advantages and Disadvantages of Application Relay

An advantage of having an application relay is that it gives you the capability to monitor the usage of both inbound access and outbound access by application and user. Most application relays, like dedicated firewall software, also run on UNIX systems but cost between $10,000 to $100,000.

The disadvantage with application relays is that many of the standard client packages may not work. You may need to upgrade or replace the software running on your client machines so that they can work with these new secure application hosts in the network. Also, the user transparency is significantly comprised with this alternative.

IAP-Provided Security Monitoring

Another alternative to consider is having an IAP provide you a security monitor 24 hours per day. Many companies such as ANS, UUnet, and BBN are offering security patrol services for a fee. The IAP monitors all security systems and responds to any security alerts coming into the network. Of course, these services are expensive, and a proper needs analysis will help in determining if this service is appropriate for you.

Security for Emerging Uses of the Internet

All of the security issues discussed thus far in this chapter concern protecting your internal network.

For companies that only want to browse and retrieve information from the Internet, the security systems described previously may be adequate. If your company wants to transfer confidential data between sites using the Internet, or if your company hopes to conduct business transactions over the Internet, you need to provide some form of privacy and authentication.

Privacy is a technique that ensures that the intended receiver is the one who actually gets the information. In this case, even if someone on the Internet can get access to the information, it can't be read by the intruder. *Authentication,* or ensuring and validating the identity of individuals attempting to use one of the computers on your network, is a basic security technique with which you are most likely already familiar. Authentication usually consists of a simple password, although other forms such as thumb print scans and written signature verifications are available. Encryption is a common technique used to provide privacy and authentication. Two of the emerging uses of the Internet include the following:

→ Private virtual WAN

→ Electronic commerce

Private Virtual WAN

Someday, the Internet will be used as a private virtual WAN. Corporations will use the various highways and by-ways on the Internet to connect two branch offices together. Before that can happen, however, some form of privacy software is needed. The most popular privacy product on the Internet today is a product called *Pretty Good Privacy* (PGP). It was developed by Philip Zimmermann, and it provides a confidentiality and authentication service

that is used for e-mail and file storage applications. Available in the public domain, PGP can be obtained in DOS, Windows, UNIX, and Macintosh versions. PGP is not transparent for your end users as it is not yet integrated into common office applications. If you want more information on it, you can point your Web browser at the following Web site:

http://www.mantis.co.uk/pgp/pgp.html

There are many other encryption products available that encrypt the messages for safe transmission across the Internet. At this time, the prices of these solutions are high, but will likely come down rapidly with increased competition and more demand.

Electronic Commerce

Shopping malls that you can visit using a Web browser are now available on the Internet. From these cyber-malls, you can buy goods and services much like you do on the Home Shopping Network. No standards currently exist, however, for verifying identity and securing your credit card information from potential hackers, the result of which has slowed the growth of true Internet commerce. The industry is feverishly working to find an acceptable solution for verifying and securing confidential information—standards may likely emerge in the near future. Most of these standards will likely be dependent on public key cryptography.

In *public key cryptography*, two keys are used, with both keys generated at the same time. One key is private, which is unique among all users; the other key is public, can be shared, and is generally published with a key management agency. Data encrypted using one of the keys can only be decrypted using its partner. For privacy, the sender uses the public key of the recipient, because only the recipient has the corresponding private key; therefore, only the recipient can decrypt the message. For authentication, the sender encrypts a message using his private key. The recipient decrypts the message using the public key of the sender. If the message decrypts correctly, the recipient knows that the message must have been encrypted using the private key of the sender, which in turn indicates that the recipient is indeed the true, intended recipient of the sender's message. By decrypting the message, the recipient authenticates the identity of the sender.

In addition to general purpose security solutions, many other application specific security solutions are emerging, one example of which is the secure HTTP protocol. For most corporate networks, the reality of using the Internet for secure electronic commerce is at least few years away.

Obtaining Additional Information on Security

The Internet offers a wealth of information on Internet security. Generally, a Web site will also point to many other destinations, thereby expanding your search considerably. For more information on security, you can point your Web browser at the following Web site, which is linked to a multitude of other sites:

> http://www.cs.cmu.edu:8001/afs/
> cs.cmu.edu/user/bsy/www/sec.html.

A good source of information on security alerts as well as up-to-date information on potential security problems is the *Computer Emergency Response Team* (CERT). CERT puts out security warnings and advisories. Most of the alerts concern the UNIX operating system. An alert will point out a security hole in the UNIX system and suggest procedures to fix it. CERT advisories can be found by utilizing the FTP application to view and/or download files from the following FTP server:

> ftp.cert.org
>
> cd /pub/cert_

You should first read file 01_README for a summary, and then you can refer to other documents in that directory for additional information. You can also join the Usenet newsgroup called comp.security.announce to get all CERT advisories. CERT can also be reached via phone at (412)268-7090.

Summary

This chapter has provided only a glimpse into the world of Internet security. With a little background, the issues are not difficult to understand. Still, actually implementing and monitoring a security system is a challenge. Keep in mind that a more complex security system may create its own security problems simply because no one understands it; however, don't let concerns about security paralyze your organization. Because it is getting easier to connect to the Internet, and no corporation can completely control all employees, ignoring the Internet will not make the security issues go away.

For NetWare environments, a server-based TCP/IP approach in conjunction with a packet filtering router provides a good level of security. NetWare, by default, does not contain any daemons. This provides a much more secure environment for Internet connectivity than a UNIX system, which has many more daemons and security loopholes available for Internet hackers. Dedicated firewalls are also an effective means of increasing network security, especially in a TCP/IP network, but are very expensive. Application gateways are the most sophisticated security solution; however, they compromise a user's transparency and are also very costly.

Electronic commerce is the next frontier for the Internet. Many companies in the industry are working on the development of encryption techniques to make electronic commerce on the Internet a reality. As the market evolves, standards will develop, after which the general purpose market for electronic commerce will emerge.

Up to this point, each chapter of this book has been dedicated to a specific level of the Internet connectivity matrix. All of the layers in the Internet connectivity matrix build upon one another, making it essential for you to understand the current level before proceeding up the hierarchy to the next level. Since all layers of the Internet connectivity matrix have now been covered in detail, you should have an excellent understanding upon which to base your decisions for connecting to the Internet. For a conclusive summarization of all that you have learned thus far in this book, continue on to Chapter 11, "Case Studies." This particular chapter provides detailed accounts of two companies faced with an Internet connection, why each wanted or needed to get connected, the issues each confronted within the process, and how each arrived at its final decisions. Chapter 11 will put the many pieces of the Internet connectivity puzzle together to ensure that all relevant issues have been considered in connecting your NetWare network to the Internet.

part IV

Administrative Issues

11

Case Studies

The objective of this chapter is to take many of the

concepts of the preceding chapters and illustrate

how they are actually implemented in the connect-

ing of a NetWare network to the Internet. Two

separate case studies are examined with the inten-

tion of providing a guideline to your implementa-

tion. Keep in mind, however, that no case study will

match your environment completely. The concepts

discussed here are simply intended to be represen-

tative.

Each case study specifically addresses the following areas and issues:

→ A description of the current environment.

→ The whys, the needs, the wants, and the benefits. In other words, what are the factors that have necessitated the Internet connection?

→ Selecting the method of connecting to the Internet. Issues to consider and evaluate are examined here. Aspects of the local environment, the business requirements, and so on need to be considered to provide the basis for decisions such as selecting an *Internet Access Provider* (IAP), determining the type of connection to the Internet, what hardware and software will need to be procured, and what aspects of the network will affect the actual configuration and setup of the connection.

→ The actual Internet connection. Topics reviewed here include the following:

> Equipment requirements
>
> Software requirements
>
> IP addressing configuration and implementation
>
> Security and administration

→ Case study review.

Case Study #1

The Current Environment

This case study consists of an organization whose core business is the publication of a newsletter that discusses global events, financial information, and political issues that are pertinent to organizations involved in commerce in third-world countries.

The current network environment, as shown in figure 11.1, is comprised of a single site with approximately 100 users. Topologically, this network uses 10BaseT and contains a single Ethernet segment. At this point, five NetWare servers have been installed. Of the 100 users using this network, 75 of them are using Intel-based personal computers. The remaining users are using Apple Macintosh computers providing graphics design, page layout, and the production of the newsletter.

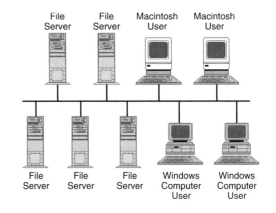

Figure 11.1

Case Study #1—the current environment.

Factors Necessitating the Internet Connection

Information is the strategic commodity of this organization in that it must be immediately available, it must be accurate, and it must be cost-effective to obtain. Previously, this organization has obtained their information from sources that were costly and frequently not up-to-date. Information that is not current is relatively useless—the timeliness of this information thus is critical. Furthermore, the availability of free information on the Internet reduces the overall cost of the newsletter production.

Selecting the Method of Connecting to the Internet

Upon evaluating the business requirements for the Internet connection, it has been determined that the connection to the Internet must be a permanent connection. Dial-up or Switched access, such as analog services, ISDN, or Switched 56 Kbps, would not provide the access to the vital information that the business factors demand. Also, by using the cost analysis provided by the IAP, it has been shown that a leased line service will in fact cost less than a switched service, such as ISDN, simply because the Internet connection will be active for approximately eight hours per day.

This organization, therefore, has selected an IAP that is able to provide them with a 56 Kbps leased line connection, with the opportunity to upgrade to *fractional T1* (FT1) services as the bandwidth requirements increase.

The Internet Connection

Equipment Requirements

Two pieces of primary equipment must be selected in order to establish the connection to the IAP—a router and the equipment connecting the router to the communications circuit provided by the IAP. While both of these items may well be provided by the IAP, it is important nonetheless that the customer establish criteria to ensure that the services and products from the IAP meet both current and future requirements. Figure 11.2 graphically depicts the equipment needed to connect to the Internet.

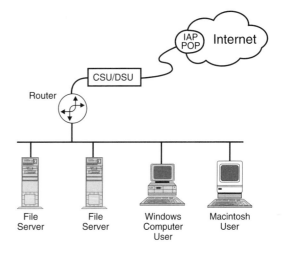

Figure 11.2

Connecting to the Internet.

In many situations, the IAP will either provide the router or indicate the specific routers that it will enable the customer to provide. The primary reason for these specifications is compatibility—the router at the customer site must encapsulate the network traffic in a format that is compatible with devices within the IAP's point of presence. Furthermore, the customer's router must utilize a routing protocol that can communicate with routers within the IAP's network. With the rapid growth of standard-based WAN protocols such as PPP, the customer may have several options in the selection of the router.

Initially, the router must support the transport of TCP/IP traffic to the IAP POP and provide adequate performance to utilize the communications circuit. The future, however, should also be considered. Will this router perform adequately on higher speed circuits, such as FT1? If this router cannot fully take advantage of higher speed circuits, what are the options for upgrading to a router that can? Again, it is critical that the equipment selected not only meet current requirements, but also future requirements.

Another issue that must be considered here is filtering or security. For this organization, information is a strategic item. The router, therefore, must provide appropriate access for the organization's users to obtain information, but it must not allow unauthorized users access to its hosts and information.

In this case, a CSU/DSU will be required to connect the router to the 56 Kbps communications circuit. These devices were discussed earlier in Chapter 8, "WAN Access Devices." Clearly, the current requirement is that this device provide the physical connection and framing functions between the router and the 56 Kbps circuit. The future should also be considered—if the organization chooses to upgrade to a higher bandwidth circuit such as fractional T1, can this device be used on the new circuit, or will it require replacement? If a replacement is required, what is the cost for this replacement?

Software Requirements

Essentially, two issues need to be considered from a software perspective. First, a package must be selected to implement TCP/IP on the individual workstations. This application is often referred to as the *protocol stack* for TCP/IP. Its function is to provide support for the TCP/IP protocol suite on the user workstation.

Second, a package must be selected to provide the applications that will be used to procure the information from the Internet. In this case, software must be implemented to provide SMTP-based e-mail, FTP client access, a newssreader to access Usenet groups, and Web browsers to access the World Wide Web. Given the mixed environment of Intel-based personal computers and Apple Macintosh computers, at least two software packages must be selected.

For the Windows-based personal computers, Microsoft's Windows for Workgroups provides support for TCP/IP, and could therefore be used to provide the protocol stack. Other packages that could be selected include NetManage's Chameleon, FTP Software's PC/TCP, or even Trumpet Winsock, which is available in the public domain.

Macintosh users can utilize a product such as VersTerm from Synergy Software. This product provides a TCP/IP stack, FTP client support, SMTP and POP mail, a Usenet newsreader, and several other TCP/IP applications for both LAN-based connections and dial-up access using SLIP.

Versions of the required software applications, such as FTP and newsreader, are included with several of the packages referenced in the preceding two paragraphs. In terms of the e-mail application, a product such as Qualcomm's Eudora warrants consideration because of its support for both the Windows and Macintosh platforms. Web browsers such as Netscape and NCSA Mosaic are also available for both Windows and Macintosh platforms. These applications can be downloaded from the Internet and from services such as CompuServe. NCSA Mosaic can be downloaded via anonymous FTP from ftp.ncsa.uiuc.edu, while Netscape can be downloaded from ftp.netscape.com.

IP Addressing Configuration and Implementation

Based on the size of the network and the number of users involved, the IAP provides its customer with a single class C address of 198.92.54.0 (note that this is an example—do not use this address in your implementation). Without subnetting, this network supports a total of 254 IP addresses on a single subnet or physical network segment. This is because the final octet can have addresses ranging from 0 to 255, with 0 and 255 being reserved addresses. The first three *octets*, or parts, of the address (198.92.54.) indicate the network address. The last octet of this address (0) indicates the host address, and needs to be determined by the network administrator.

Any devices that are connected to this network, including the router, file servers, and user workstations, will therefore have an address between 198.92.54.1 and 198.92.54.254. The address 198.92.54.0 denotes the subnet address, and the address 198.92.54.255 is reserved as the broadcast address. A *broadcast address* is used to transmit information to all of the devices on a network.

While it is not necessary to provide these host addresses to users in any particular order or method, some simple planning can make the management, administration, and troubleshooting of this network significantly easier. By implementing such a system, the network can readily recognize the type of computer, its location, and even its user by referring to the host portion of the IP address.

For purposes of this study, the model in table 11.1 is being used. The table illustrates a structured process for assigning host addresses to devices connected to the network. Keep in mind, however, that this model is provided as an example only. You will want to design your addressing scheme to your specific environment.

Table 11.1

Sample Host Address Distribution

Host Address Range	Function
1–5	Routers
6–20	File servers
21–50	Macintosh computers in the graphics/layout department
51–70	Macintosh computers in the production department
71–120	Windows computers in department A
121–160	Windows computers in department B
161–225	Windows computers in department C
226–254	Other devices requiring IP addresses (such as network management devices, LAN attached printers, and terminal servers)

Following the model displayed in the table, the router may be assigned an IP address of 198.92.54.1. The first file server may have an IP address of 198.92.54.6, the second file server an address of 198.92.54.7, and so on. The first Macintosh may have an address of 198.92.54.21, the second an address of 198.92.54.22, and so on. The first Windows computer may have an address of 198.92.54.71, the second an address of 198.92.54.72, and so on. Figure 11.3 shows a sample addressing scenario for the particular organization on which this case study focuses.

The router's IP address will have additional significance when configuring the individual workstations. One of the parameters that is specified on the workstation is the *default gateway*. This s the address of the device that will be the user workstation's "door" to the outside world—in this case, the router. The default gateway parameter should thus be set to the router's IP address for all workstations.

Security

In this type of organization, information is a very valuable commodity and must therefore be protected. Part of the network administrator's task is to ensure that unauthorized users will not have access to this data. This is frequently done by specifying appropriate filters on the router.

The router, for example, might be configured to enable users from within the organization to transmit e-mail, perform FTP file transfers, access Usenet, and access Web servers using a Web browser. The router might also be configured to only allow e-mail to come from the Internet into the administrator's network, thereby preventing outside users from being able to access corporate data using applications such as FTP or Telnet.

Not only should the router prevent unauthorized access to corporate resources, but it should also notify the network administrator of attempted violations to the security filters configured on the

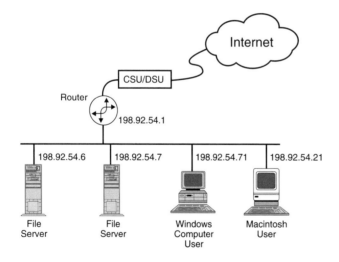

Figure 11.3

IP addressing within the local environment.

p a r t **IV** | **Administrative Issues**

router. This notification might be communicated as an alert on a network management workstation console, for example.

These filtering capabilities are found on many of the routers available in today's market, and should be considered as absolute requirements in the selection and specification of an Internet router.

Case Study Review

Once the Internet connection is implemented, there are two issues that require constant review—security and access to information on the Internet.

Security is not only considered when the Internet connection is installed—it must be constantly evaluated and assessed. It would be beneficial to track network traffic to and from the Internet on an ongoing basis. This practice, often called *protocol accounting*, is implemented in many of the routers available in today's market. Using this function, the network administrator can monitor network traffic by its source address, destination address, and protocol application to determine the heavier users of the Internet connection and even detect unauthorized access.

Access to information on the network also requires constant evaluation and action. There is a wealth of information available on the network, but is it accessible? One factor that should be reviewed is the user interface. Is the information that the users require accessible to them in a useful format and via methods that are easy to use?

The other issue that bears reevaluation is the *bandwidth*, or the capacity of the communications circuit to the IAP. While the 56 Kbps circuit may prove adequate initially, it may not be adequate as the use of the Internet connection increases. If this organization chooses to make their newsletter accessible to the Internet via a Web server, bandwidth to the Internet will become even more of an issue.

In these respects, the Internet connection is no different than any other part of the network. It requires frequent evaluation and assessment to ensure that it is providing the proper services to the user community, maintaining corporate standards and network performance, and meeting the objectives that were the catalyst for this project.

Case Study #2

The Current Environment

This case study deals with an organization that has a number of locations geographically distributed throughout North America. This organization is in the business of manufacturing and distributing components for the automotive industry.

The corporate office houses the administration functions, research and development, and manufacturing. The corporate office has six individual departmental networks, as follows:

→ Manufacturing Building #1 (150 computers)

→ Manufacturing Building #2 (150 computers)

→ Distribution and Shipping (50 computers)

→ Human Resources/Payroll (35 computers)

→ Finance (40 computers)

→ Data Processing (25 computers)

A small-scale version of one of these six departmental networks is shown in figure 11.4. It should be noted that the other five departmental networks within the corporate office are of similar network structure and design.

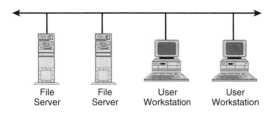

| File Server | File Server | User Workstation | User Workstation |

Figure 11.4

The current corporate office network environment.

The remote sites—totaling five sites—are primarily remote sales offices with approximately 15 to 20 users each. Currently, each remote office contains a network and a single Novell NetWare file server, as portrayed in figure 11.5.

Until this project, no communications links existed between any of the company locations.

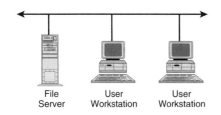

| File Server | User Workstation | User Workstation |

Figure 11.5

The current sales office environment.

Factors Necessitating the Internet Connection

The driving factor for this project is the communication requirements both within the company, as well as externally to outside vendors and customers.

Within the company, e-mail has been one of the most common requests from the users. After researching the potential benefits from electronic mail, it is found that electronic mail can save the company a significant amount of money in postage costs. In addition, it is evident that, on the average, the user productivity level increases with the use of e-mail. Furthermore, financial benefits can be demonstrated by being able to provide individuals with information immediately, rather than waiting for delivery via traditional methods.

Another internal function that will prove extremely beneficial is access to online computer data. Previously, representatives in sales offices were not immediately aware of price changes and did not have any means of verifying inventory of items available for shipment. This situation frequently caused sales of incorrectly priced items, and provided delivery schedules to customers that could not be met. The ramifications not only affected the financial bottom line, but also affected the quality of service provided to customers.

Services both to and from external organizations can also be improved. Electronic mail can be used as a means to more effectively communicate with vendors and customers. By transmitting information through the Internet, this organization is better able to procure materials through vendors on a timely basis and to provide products to customers.

Access to the Internet provides a new means of marketing this organization's products. By providing a Web server, customers and prospects are able to access marketing information, sales literature, and pricing with a highly graphical interface by using a Web browser, such as Netscape or Mosaic. Information can be updated frequently without the expense of page layout and printing.

Selecting the Method of Connecting to the Internet

This case study discusses a company whose communications requirements are more complex than those found in Case Study #1. The selection of an IAP will require communications within the company with obvious security requirements, as well as communications to vendors and customers.

Furthermore, it is vital to maintain suitable security within the organization. It is significant, for example, to provide adequate security to a network that might contain human resources and payroll computers.

The Internet Connection

Equipment Requirements

As in Case Study #1, two pieces of equipment must be selected in order to establish the connection to the IAP—a router and the equipment connecting the router to the communications circuit provided by the IAP. While both of these items may well be provided by the IAP, it is important nonetheless that the customer establish criteria to ensure that the services and products from the IAP meet both current and future requirements.

Initially, the router must support the transport of TCP/IP traffic to the IAP POP and provide adequate performance to utilize the communications circuit. As indicated in figure 11.6, the router needs to be configured with a minimum of six local LAN connections to connect each of the individual networks within the corporate offices. The router also needs appropriate wide-area communications ports to connect to the sales offices and the IAP.

Here, as in Case Study #1, filtering or security must be considered. This is discussed in more detail in the section "Security," found later in this case study. Figure 11.6 illustrates the new corporate network design. A router has been installed to connect each of the networks within the corporate offices. This router also provides the connections to the remote sales offices and the Internet.

Figure 11.7 illustrates the new network design for the remote sales offices. A router has been installed that provides connectivity from the LAN to the IAP, enabling access to the corporate offices and the Internet. The new corporate internetwork design is shown in figure 11.8.

Software Requirements

As in Case Study #1, software must be selected to address two issues: provision of a TCP/IP stack for the workstation, and provision of the applications to support e-mail, Telnet, FTP, and access to Web servers. Both types of software are discussed in detail in the "Software Requirements" section of Case Study #1.

IP Addressing Configuration and Implementation

This case study involves more complex addressing requirements than the earlier case study. This case study enables you to examine subnetting in detail, and provides an example that will make this somewhat mystifying task very understandable.

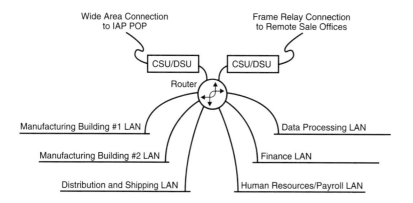

Figure 11.6

The new corporate network design.

Wide Area Connection to IAP POP

Frame Relay Connection to Remote Sale Offices

CSU/DSU

CSU/DSU

Router

Manufacturing Building #1 LAN

Data Processing LAN

Manufacturing Building #2 LAN

Finance LAN

Distribution and Shipping LAN

Human Resources/Payroll LAN

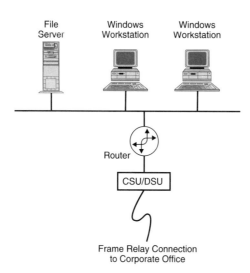

Figure 11.7

The new sales office network design.

File Server

Windows Workstation

Windows Workstation

Router

CSU/DSU

Frame Relay Connection to Corporate Office

This situation is not unique—in most cases, some level of subnetting will be required. It is highly unlikely that the IAP will provide a class C address for each remote site. Furthermore, given the limited pool of IP addresses under the current version of IP, providing a class C address for small sites such as this organization's sales offices would waste considerable amounts of address space.

To assist in this exercise, tables listing valid subnet information, including the subnet mask, the number of subnets provided, and the number of host/devices per subnet, have been provided in Appendix B, "IP Subnetting and Binary Conversion Tables." A table providing conversion between decimal and binary numbering has also been provided in the appendix.

Figure 11.8

The corporate internetwork design.

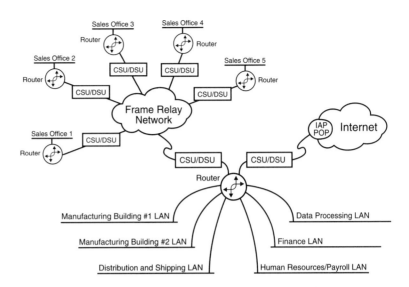

Given this environment, assume that the IAP provides a total of five class C addresses (one for each of the five departments), as follows:

> 198.92.54.0
>
> 198.92.55.0
>
> 198.92.56.0
>
> 198.92.57.0
>
> 198.92.58.0

First, you must determine how many devices on a single physical network or segment will require IP addresses. It is important to determine not only how many devices exist currently, but also what type of growth is expected. Any IP addressing scheme must be able to accommodate growth in order to be successful. The scheme must also be efficient and not waste addresses unnecessarily.

Let's start by addressing the networks in the corporate location. As you see in the table in the "Current Environment" section at the beginning of this case study, there are two manufacturing networks that both have approximately 150 computers. If you look at the IP address subnetting tables in Appendix B, it is evident that the only level of class C subnetting that would provide as many as 150 addresses per subnet would be 0 bits of subnetting. The subnet mask here would be 255.255.255.0. Therefore, you might assign the network number 198.92.54.0 to Manufacturing Building #1 and the network number 198.92.55.0 to Manufacturing Building #2. Each of these addresses permits host addresses from 1–254, which allows for a significant amount of growth within these two networks.

The networks in the other buildings have considerably fewer devices and therefore lend themselves to subnetting to optimize the use of your address space.

The Distribution and Shipping and Human Resources/Payroll networks currently have 45 computers and 35 computers installed respectively. If you refer to the IP address subnetting table, you find that by using a 2-bit mask or a mask of 255.255.255.192, each class C network provides for two subnets with 62 hosts per subnet. That will adequately meet the current requirements for these two networks, and yet still provide room for growth in the number of workstations. Let's then utilize the next class C network you have available—198.92.56.0—and utilize the 2-bit mask to determine the station addresses for these two networks.

As discussed in Chapter 3, "Understanding TCP/IP," in order to properly determine addresses using subnetting, it is necessary to convert these numbers to binary. A table of decimal to binary conversions has been provided in Appendix B.

If you take the subnet number 198.92.56.0 and convert it to binary representation, you have the following:

    11000110 . 01011100 . 00111000 .
    00000000

The subnet mask of 255.255.255.192 would be represented as follows:

    11111111 . 11111111 . 11111111 .
    11000000

Following the subnetting guidelines in Chapter 3, you know that the subnet portion of the mask cannot be either all 0s or all 1s. This would preclude the following subnets:

    11000110 . 01011100 . 00111000 .
    00000000

    11000110 . 01011100 . 00111000 .
    11000000

but would allow the following subnets:

    11000110 . 01011100 . 00111000 .
    01000000

    11000110 . 01011100 . 00111000 .
    10000000

Using this subnet mask, the two valid subnet numbers would be 198.92.56.64 and 198.92.56.128. Remember that this subnet number denotes the entire network segment, not any specific device on that segment.

The next step is to determine the broadcast address for this subnet. This is done by changing all of the bits in the host portion of the subnet address to 1s. Let's use the subnet 198.92.56.64 as an example. Converting this to binary representation results in the following:

    11000110 . 01011100 . 00111000 .
    01000000

The host bits are the final six bits of the final octet. If you convert all of the host bits to 1s, you have the following address:

    11000110 . 01011100 . 00111000 .
    01111111

If you refer to the decimal to binary conversion table in Appendix B, you see that this address in dotted decimal representation is 198.92.56.127. You now know your broadcast address for this subnet or network segment.

Using the guidelines illustrated in Chapter 3, you know that host addresses fall in the range between the subnet address and the broadcast address. Therefore, the devices on the Distribution and Shipping network would have addresses ranging from 198.92.56.65 to 198.92.56.126.

Now, focus your attention on the subnet 198.92.56.128 as the example. Converting this to binary representation results in the following:

11000110 . 01011100 . 00111000 . 10000000

If you convert the host bits of the address to 1s, you have the following address, which is your broadcast address in binary representation:

11000110 . 01011100 . 00111000 . 10111111

Referring to your decimal to binary conversion table in Appendix B, you find that this address in dotted decimal representation is 198.92.56.127.

Again, the host addresses fall in the range between the subnet address and the broadcast address. The devices on the Human Resources/Payroll network would therefore have addresses ranging from 198.92.56.129 to 198.92.56.190.

The addressing for both the Finance and Data Processing networks is handled in a similar function. The information has been provided in table 11.2. As in the example of the Distribution and Shipping network and the Human Resources/Payroll network, these two networks will also be using a 2-bit mask or a mask of 255.255.255.192.

Now, let's consider the remote sales offices. If you look at the IP address subnetting table in Appendix B, you see that by using a 3-bit subnet mask or a mask of 255.255.255.224, you have six subnet numbers with 30 hosts per subnet. This subnetting scheme is ideal because each of these offices has a maximum of 20 computers, and this scheme provides room for future growth.

If you take the subnet number 198.92.58.0 and convert it to binary representation, the result is as follows:

11000110 . 01011100 . 00111010 . 00000000

The subnet mask of 255.255.255.224 would be represented as the following:

11111111 . 11111111 . 11111111 . 11100000

Table 11.2 Addressing Ranges for the Finance and Data Processing Networks

	Finance Network	Data Processing Network
Subnet Number	198.92.57.64	198.92.57.128
First Host Address	198.92.57.65	198.92.57.129
Last Host Address	198.92.57.126	198.92.57.190
Broadcast Address	198.92.57.127	198.92.57.191

Using this subnet mask, your valid subnet numbers would be 198.92.58.32, 198.92.58.64, 198.92.58.96, 198.92.58.128, 198.92.58.160, and 198.92.58.192.

To determine the relevant addresses for the first subnet, you first convert the number to binary representation, as follows:

11000110 . 01011100 . 00111010 . 00100000

The host bits are the final five bits of the final octet. If you convert all of the host bits to 1s, you have the following address:

11000110 . 01011100 . 00111000 . 00111111

Referring to the decimal to binary conversion table in Appendix B, you find that this address in dotted decimal representation is 198.92.58.62. You know, therefore, that the valid host addresses range from 198.92.58.33 to 198.92.53.62.

For the second subnet, you again convert the subnet address 198.92.58.64 to binary representation, as follows:

11000110 . 01011100 . 00111010 . 01000000

The host bits are the final five bits of the final octet. If you convert all of the host bits to 1s, you have the following address:

11000110 . 01011100 . 00111000 . 01011111

The decimal to binary conversion table in Appendix B indicates that this address in dotted decimal rep-

resentation is 198.92.58.95. You know, therefore, that the valid host addresses range from 198.92.58.65 to 198.92.53.94.

This process would then be repeated for the remaining subnet addresses. Again, it is wise to establish some method to distributing host addresses to facilitate the administration and management of these devices. As an example, you could reserve the first four addresses within each subnet for file servers, the 5th through 7th addresses for network management devices, and the remaining addresses for user workstations.

To further clarify the concept of subnetting, let's reverse the process. Given the address of 198.92.58.135, how can you determine its subnet address and broadcast address?

First, you need to convert the address to binary representation, as follows:

11000110 . 01011100 . 00111010 . 10000111

Then, apply the subnet mask of 255.255.255.224 by comparing the corresponding bits within each octet, using the process explained in Chapter 3. If both of the corresponding bits in the address and the subnet mask are 1, then a 1 is placed in the corresponding bit in the resultant. This process is easiest if you display the address and the mask on successive lines, as follows:

Address	11000110 . 01011100 . 00111010 . 10000111
Subnet Mask	11111111 . 11111111 . 11111111 . 11100000
Resultant	11000110 . 01011100 . 00111010 . 10000000

By converting this entry to dotted decimal notation using the decimal to binary conversion table, you find that the result—your subnet—is 198.92.54.128.

Security

This case study brings the significance of security to bear not only in terms of access from the Internet, but from within the organization as well.

In this case study, the security requirements are implemented by appropriate configuration of the router. Network traffic within the company, for example, must be controlled to ensure the confidentiality of information maintained by the Human Resources and Payroll Departments. A possible configuration would be to allow electronic mail traffic to flow throughout the corporate network. Network traffic between the two manufacturing networks should be allowed to flow without restriction, but remain restricted from the other networks within the corporate network. Internet access traffic, such as electronic mail and HTTP for World Wide Web access, would be permitted to be transmitted to and from the Internet.

Network security is a critical component to the implementation of an internetwork. Before finalizing the selection of a router to connect to the Internet, determine what your security requirements are and ensure that the products selected meet all of your requirements.

Case Study Review

As in Case Study #1, access to information on the corporate network also requires constant evaluation and action. Information on the Internet must be accessible to the users within the corporate network. If this company chooses to implement a World Wide Web server to provide services and information to customers and prospects, the accessibility and useability of this information must be accessed. Depending on the volume of network both to and from the network, the bandwidth of the communications circuit may need to be reevaluated at a later date.

The objective of this case study was to illustrate the issues involved in connecting a more complex network to the Internet. Subnetting IP addresses is frequently required in real life as it was in this case study. Hopefully, the examples in this case study will assist in the implementation of your Internet connection.

12

Answers to Commonly Asked "New Internet User" Questions

New users joining the Internet community have the same questions as everyone else who has ever joined. The purpose of this chapter, which is in a question/answer type of format, is to provide new Internet users with up-to-date, basic Internet knowledge and experience. The information in this chapter, all of which has been drawn from RFC 1594 (FYI Q/A, FYI 4), might be beneficial as a training guide for new Internet users, as well as a reference for more experienced Internet users.

An additional RFC, called FYI Q/A, FYI 7, is also published that contains intermediate and advanced Internet user questions. This particular RFC, however, is not included as part of this chapter. If you are interested in obtaining this RFC or additional copies of the RFC presented in this chapter, both can be downloaded from the InterNIC (or any other of the several repositories around the world that maintain copies of RFCs) using the FTP application. Instructions on utilizing FTP can be found both in this chapter under the section, "How Do I Obtain RFCs?," as well as in Chapter 5, "Internet Applications."

 Future updates of the RFC presented in this chapter will be produced online as User Services members become aware of additional questions that should be included, and of deficiencies or inaccuracies that should be amended in this document. Although the RFC number of this document will change with each update, it will always have the designation of FYI 4.

Acknowledgments

The following people deserve thanks for their help and contributions to this FYI Q/A: Matti Aarnio (FUNET), Susan Calcari (InterNIC), Corinne Carroll (BBN), Vint Cerf (MCI), Peter Deutsch (Bunyip), Alan Emtage (Bunyip), John Klensin (UNU), Thomas Lenggenhager (Switch), Doug Mildram (Xylogics), Tracy LaQuey Parker (Cisco), Craig Partridge (BBN), Jon Postel (ISI), Matt Power (MIT), Karen Roubicek (BBN), Patricia Smith (Merit), Gene Spafford (Purdue), and Carol Ward (Sterling Software/NASA NAIC).

Questions About the Internet

What is the Internet?

The Internet is a collection of thousands of networks linked by a common set of technical protocols, which make it possible for users of any one of the networks to communicate with or use the services located on any of the other networks. These protocols are referred to as TCP/IP or the TCP/IP protocol suite. The Internet started with the ARPANET, but now includes such networks as the *National Science Foundation Network* (NSFnet), the *Australian Academic and Research Network* (AARnet), the *NASA Science Internet* (NSI), the *Swiss Academic and Research Network* (SWITCH), and about 10,000 other large and small, commercial and research, networks. There are other major wide area networks that are not based on the TCP/IP protocols, and are thus often not considered part of the Internet. It is possible to communicate between them and the Internet via electronic mail, however, because of mail gateways that act as "translators" between the different network protocols involved.

 You will often see "internet" with a small "i." This could refer to any network built based on TCP/IP, or might refer to networks using other protocol families that are composites built of smaller networks.

See FYI 20 (RFC 1462), "FYI on 'What is the Internet?'," for a lengthier description of the Internet [13].

I Just Got on the Internet. What Can I Do Now?

You now have access to all the resources you are authorized to use on your own Internet host, on any other Internet host on which you have an account, and on any other Internet host that offers publicly accessible information. The Internet gives you the ability to move information between these hosts via file transfers. Once you are logged into one host, you can use the Internet to open a connection to another, log in, and use its services interactively (this is known as *remote login* or *Telneting*). In addition, you can send electronic mail to users at any Internet site and to users on many non-Internet sites that are accessible via electronic mail.

There are various other services you can use. For example, some hosts provide access to specialized databases or to archives of information. The Internet Resource Guide provides information regarding some of these sites. This guide lists facilities on the Internet that are available to users. Such facilities include supercomputer centers, library catalogs, and specialized data collections. The guide is maintained by the Directory Services portion of the InterNIC, and is available online in a number of ways. It is available for anonymous FTP from the host ds.internic.net in the resource-guide directory. It is also readable via the InterNIC gopher (gopher internic.net). For more information, contact admin@ds.internic.net or call the InterNIC at (800)444-4345 or (908)668-6587.

Today, the trend for Internet information services is to strive to present the users with a friendly interface to a variety of services. The goal is to reduce the traditional needs for a user to know the source host of a service and the different command interfaces for different types of services. The Internet Gopher (discussed more in the "Questions about Internet Services" section) is one such service to which you have access when you join the Internet.

How Do I Find Out if a Site has a Computer on the Internet?

Frankly, it's almost impossible to find out if a site has a computer on the Internet by querying some Internet service itself. The most reliable way is to ask someone at the site you are interested in contacting.

It is sometimes possible to find whether or not a site has been assigned an IP network number, which is a prerequisite for connecting an IP network to the Internet (which is only one type of Internet access). To do so, query the WHOIS database, maintained by the Registration Services portion of the InterNIC. You have several options about how to do such a query. The most common currently are to Telnet to the host rs.internic.net and invoke one of the search interfaces provided, or to run a WHOIS client locally on your machine and use it to make a query across the network.

The *RIPE Network Coordination Center* (RIPE NCC) also maintains a large database of sites to whom they have assigned IP network numbers. You can query it by Telneting to info.ripe.net and stepping through the interactive interface they provide.

How Do I Get a List of All the Hosts on the Internet?

You really don't want that—the list includes more than 1.5 million hosts, and almost all of them require that you have access permission to actually use them. You may really want to know which of these hosts provide services to the Internet community. Investigate using some of the network resource discovery tools, such as Gopher, to gain easier access to Internet information.

Questions About TCP/IP

What is TCP/IP?

Transmission Control Protocol/Internet Protocol (TCP/IP) [4,5,6] is the common name for a family of over 100 data-communications protocols used to organize computers and data-communications equipment into computer networks. TCP/IP was developed to interconnect hosts on ARPANET, PRNET (packet radio), and SATNET (packet satellite). All three of these networks have since been retired, but TCP/IP lives on. It is currently used on a large international network of networks called the Internet, whose members include universities, other research institutions, government facilities, and many corporations. TCP/IP is also sometimes used for other networks, particularly *local area networks* (LANs) that tie together numerous different kinds of computers or tie together engineering workstations.

What are the Other Well-Known Standard Protocols in the TCP/IP Family?

Other than TCP and IP, the three main protocols in the TCP/IP suite are the *Simple Mail Transfer Protocol* (SMTP) [8], the *File Transfer Protocol* (FTP) [3], and the Telnet Protocol [9]. There are many other protocols in use on the Internet. The *Internet Ar-*

chitecture Board (IAB) regularly publishes an RFC [2] that describes the state of standardization of the various Internet protocols. This document is the best guide to the current status of Internet protocols and their recommended usage.

Questions About the Domain Name System

What is the Domain Name System?

The *Domain Name System* (DNS) is a hierarchical, distributed method of organizing the name space of the Internet. The DNS administratively groups hosts into a hierarchy of authority that allows addressing and other information to be widely distributed and maintained. A big advantage to the DNS is that using it eliminates dependence on a centrally maintained file that maps host names to addresses.

What is a Fully Qualified Domain Name?

A *Fully Qualified Domain Name* (FQDN) is a domain name that includes all higher level domains relevant to the entity named. If you think of the DNS as a tree-structure with each node having its own label, an FQDN for a specific node would be its label followed by the labels of all the other nodes between it and the root of the tree. For example, for a host, an FQDN would include the string that identifies the particular host, plus all domains of which the host is a part, up to and including the top-level domain (the root domain is always null). For example, atlas.arc.nasa.gov is an FQDN for the host at

128.102.128.50. In addition, arc.nasa.gov is the FQDN for the *Ames Research Center* (ARC) domain under nasa.gov.

Questions About Internet Documentation

What is an RFC?

The *Request for Comments* (RFC) documents are working notes of the Internet research and development community. A document in this series may be on essentially any topic related to computer communication, and may be anything from a meeting report to the specification of a standard. Submissions for Requests for Comments may be sent to the RFC Editor (RFC-EDITOR@ISI.EDU). The RFC Editor is Jon Postel.

Most RFCs are the descriptions of network protocols or services, often giving detailed procedures and formats for their implementation. Other RFCs report on the results of policy studies or summarize the work of technical committees or workshops. All RFCs are considered public domain unless explicitly marked otherwise.

While RFCs are not refereed publications, they do receive technical review from either the task forces, individual technical experts, or the RFC Editor, as appropriate. Currently, most standards are published as RFCs, but not all RFCs specify standards.

Anyone can submit a document for publication as an RFC. Submissions must be made via electronic mail to the RFC Editor. Please consult RFC 1543, "Instructions to RFC Authors," [10] for further information. RFCs are accessible online in public access files, and a short message is sent to a notification distribution list indicating the availability of the memo. Requests to be added to this distribution list should be sent to RFC-REQUEST@NIC.DDN.MIL.

The online files are copied by interested people and printed or displayed at their sites on their equipment. (An RFC may also be returned via electronic mail in response to an electronic mail query.) This means that the format of the online files must meet the constraints of a wide variety of printing and display equipment.

Once a document is assigned an RFC number and published, that RFC is never revised or re-issued with the same number. There is never a question of having the most recent version of a particular RFC. However, a protocol (such as *File Transfer Protocol* (FTP)) may be improved and re-documented many times in several different RFCs. It is important to verify that you have the most recent RFC on a particular protocol. The "Internet Official Protocol Standards" [2] memo is the reference for determining the correct RFC to refer to for the current specification of each protocol.

How Do I Obtain RFCs?

RFCs are available online at several repositories around the world. For a list of repositories, and instructions about how to obtain RFCs from each of the major U.S. repositories, send a message to rfc-info@isi.edu. As the text of the message, type **help: ways_to_get_rfcs**.

An example of obtaining RFCs online follows.

RFCs can be obtained via FTP from ds.internic.net with the path name rfc/rfcNNNN.txt (where "NNNN" refers to the number of the RFC). Log in using FTP, user name "anonymous," and your e-mail address as password. The Directory Services portion of the InterNIC also makes RFCs available via electronic mail, WAIS, and Gopher.

To obtain RFCs via electronic mail, send a mail message to mailserv@ds.internic.net and include any of the following commands in the message body:

document-by-name rfcnnnn	Where 'nnnn' is the RFC number. The text version is sent.
file /ftp/rfc/rfcnnnn.yyy	Where 'nnnn' is the RFC number and 'yyy' is 'txt' or 'ps'.
help	To get information on how to use the mail server.

How Do I Obtain a List of RFCs?

Several sites make an index of RFCs available. These sites are indicated in the ways_to_get_rfcs file, mentioned previously, and in the next question.

What is the RFC-INFO Service?

The *Information Sciences Institute* (ISI), University of Southern California, has a service called RFC-INFO. Even though this is a service, rather than a document, it is discussed in this section because it is so closely tied to RFC information.

RFC-INFO is an e-mail-based service to help in the locating and retrieval of RFCs, FYIs, STDs, and IMRs. Users can ask for "lists" of all RFCs and FYIs having certain attributes ("filters") such as their ID, keywords, title, author, issuing organization, and

date. Once an RFC is uniquely identified (e.g., by its RFC number), it may also be retrieved.

To use the service, send e-mail to RFC-INFO@ISI.EDU, with your requests as the text of the message. Feel free to put anything in the SUBJECT, the system ignores it. All input is case-independent. Report problems to RFC-MANAGER@ISI.EDU.

To get started, you may send a message to RFC-INFO@ISI.EDU, with requests such as in the following examples (without the explanations between brackets):

Help: Help	[To get this information]
List: FYI	[List the FYI notes]
List: RFC	[List RFCs with window as keyword or in title]
Keywords: window	
List: FYI	[List FYIs about windows]
Keywords: window	
List: *	[List both RFCs and FYIs about windows]
Keywords: window	
List: RFC	[List RFCs about ARPANET, ARPA NET WORK, etc.]
Title: ARPA*NET	
List: RFC	[List RFCs issued by MITRE, dated 1989-1991]
Organization: MITRE	
Dated-after: Jan-01-1989	
Dated-before: Dec-31-1991	

List: RFC	[List RFCs obsoleting a given RFC]
Obsoletes: RFC0010	
List: RFC	[List RFCs by authors, starting with "Bracken"]
Author: Bracken*	[* is a wild card]
List: RFC	[List RFCs by both Postel and Gillman]
Authors: J. Postel	[Note, the "filters" are ANDed]
Authors: R. Gillman	
List: RFC	[List RFCs by any Crocker]
Authors: Crocker	
List: RFC	[List only RFCs by S.D. Crocker]
Authors: S.D. Crocker	
List: RFC	[List only RFCs by D. Crocker]
Authors: D. Crocker	
Retrieve: RFC	[Retrieve RFC-822]
Doc-ID: RFC0822	[Note, always 4 digits in RFC#]
Help: Manual	[To retrieve the long user manual, 30+ pages]
Help: List	[How to use the List request]
Help: Retrieve	[How to use the Retrieve request]
Help: Topics	[List topics for which help is available]
Help: Dates	["Dates" is such a topic]
List: keywords	[List the keywords in use]
List: organizations	[List the organizations known to the system]

Which RFCs are Standards?

See "Internet Official Protocol Standards" (currently RFC 1540) [2]. This RFC documents the status of each RFC on the Internet standards track, as well as the status of RFCs of other types. It is updated periodically—make sure you are referring to the most recent version. In addition, the RFC Index maintained at the ds.internic.net repository notes the status of each RFC listed.

What is an FYI?

FYI stands for *For Your Information*. FYIs are a subset of the RFC series of online documents.

FYI 1 states, "The FYI series of notes is designed to provide Internet users with a central repository of information about any topics which relate to the Internet. FYI topics may range from historical memos on 'Why it was done this way' to answers to commonly asked operational questions. The FYIs are intended for a wide audience. Some FYIs will cater to beginners, while others will discuss more advanced topics."

In general, then, FYI documents tend to be more information oriented, while RFCs are usually (but not always) more technically oriented.

FYI documents are assigned both an FYI number and an RFC number.

As RFCs, if an FYI is ever updated, it is issued again with a new RFC number; however, its FYI number remains unchanged. This can be a little confusing at first, but the aim is to help users identify which FYIs are about which topics. For example, FYI 4 will always be FYI 4, even though it may be updated several times and during that process receive different RFC numbers. Thus, you need only to remember the FYI number to find the proper document. Of course, remembering titles often works as well.

FYIs can be obtained in the same way RFCs can and from the same repositories. In general, their path names are fyi/fyiNN.txt or fyi/fyiNN.ps, where NN is the number of the FYI without leading zeroes.

What is an STD?

The newest sub-series of RFCs are the *Standards* (STDs). RFC 1311 [12], which introduces this sub-series, states that the intent of STDs is to identify clearly those RFCs that document Internet standards. An STD number will be assigned only to those specifications that have completed the full process of standardization in the Internet. Existing Internet standards have been assigned STD numbers; a list of them can be found both in RFC 1311 and in the "Internet Official Protocol Standards" RFC.

Like FYIs, once a standard has been assigned an STD number, that number will not change, even if the standard is reworked and re-specified and later issued with a new RFC number.

It is important to differentiate between a "standard" and "document." Different RFC documents will always have different RFC numbers. However, sometimes the complete specification for a standard will be contained in more than one RFC document. When this happens, each of the RFC documents that is part of the specification for that standard will carry the same STD number. For example, the *Domain Name System* (DNS) is specified by the combination of RFC 1034 and RFC 1035; therefore, both of those RFCs are labeled STD 13.

What is the Internet Monthly Report?

The *Internet Monthly Report* (IMR) communicates online to the Internet community the accomplishments, milestones reached, or problems discovered by the participating organizations. Many organizations involved in the Internet provide monthly updates of their activities for inclusion in this report. The IMR is for Internet information purposes only.

You can receive the report online by joining the mailing list that distributes the report. Requests to be added or deleted from the Internet Monthly Report list should be sent to imr- request@isi.edu.

In addition, back issues of the Report are available for anonymous FTP from the host ftp.isi.edu in the in-notes/imr directory, with the file names in the form imryymm.txt, where yy is the last two digits of the year and mm two digits for the month. For example, the July 1992 Report is in the file imr9207.txt.

What is an Internet Draft? Are There any Guidelines Available for Writing One?

Internet Drafts (I-Ds) are the current working documents of the IETF. Internet Drafts are generally in the format of an RFC, with some key differences:

➜ The Internet Drafts are not RFCs and are not a numbered document series.

➜ The words INTERNET-DRAFT appear in place of RFC XXXX in the upper left-hand corner.

➜ The document does not refer to itself as an RFC or as a Draft RFC.

➜ An Internet Draft does not state nor imply that it is a proposed standard. To do so conflicts with the role of the IAB, the RFC Editor, and the *Internet Engineering Steering Group* (IESG).

An Internet Drafts directory has been installed to make draft documents available for review and comment by the IETF members. These draft documents that will ultimately be submitted to the IAB and the RFC Editor to be considered for publishing as RFCs. The Internet Drafts Directories are maintained on several Internet sites. There are also several "shadow" machines that contain the IETF and Internet Drafts Directories. They are as follows:

West Coast (U.S.) Address: ftp.isi.edu (128.9.0.32)

East Coast (U.S.) Address: ds.internic.net (198.49.45.10)

Europe Address: nic.nordu.net (192.36.148.17)

Pacific Rim Address: munnari.oz.au (128.250.1.21)

To access these directories, use anonymous FTP. Log in with user name "anonymous" and your e-mail address as password (or "guest" if that fails). Once logged in, change to the desired directory with "cd internet-drafts." Internet Draft files can then be retrieved. Once logged in, if you change to the directory "ietf," you can retrieve a file called "1id-guidelines.txt," which explains how to write and submit an Internet Draft.

How Do I Obtain OSI Standards Documents?

OSI Standards documents are NOT available from the Internet via anonymous FTP, due to copyright restrictions. These are available from the following:

Omnicom Information Service
501 Church Street NE
Suite 304
Vienna, VA 22180 USA
Telephone: (800) 666-4266 or (703) 281-1135
Fax: (703) 281-1505

American National Standards Institute
11 West 42nd Street
New York, NY 10036 USA
Telephone: (212) 642-4900

However, the GOSIP specification that covers the use of OSI protocols within the U.S. Government is available from the *National Institute of Standards and Technology* (NIST). The final text of GOSIP Version 2 is now available from both sites.

Online Sources

These are available through anonymous FTP from osi.ncsl.nist.gov (129.6.48.100) as the following:

./pub/gosip/gosip_v2.txt — ascii

./pub/gosip/gosip_v2.txt.Z — ascii compressed

./pub/gosip/gosip_v2.ps — PostScript

./pub/gosip/gosip_v2.ps.Z — PostScript compressed

Hard Copy Source:

Standards Processing Coordinator (ADP)
National Institute of Standards and Technology
Technology Building, Room B-64
Gaithersburg, MD 20899
(301) 975-2816

Questions about Internet Organizations and Contacts

What is the IAB?

The *Internet Architecture Board* (IAB) is concerned with technical and policy issues involving the evolution of the Internet architecture [7]. IAB members are deeply committed to making the Internet function effectively and evolve to meet a large scale, high speed future. The chairman serves a term of two years and is elected by the members of the IAB. The IAB focuses on the TCP/IP protocol suite, and extensions to the Internet system to support multiple protocol suites.

The IAB performs the following functions:

→ Reviews Internet Standards

→ Manages the RFC publication process

→ Reviews the operation of the IETF and IRTF

→ Performs strategic planning for the Internet, identifying long-range problems and opportunities

→ Acts as an international technical policy liaison and representative for the Internet community

→ Resolves technical issues that cannot be treated within the IETF or IRTF frameworks

The IAB has two principal subsidiary task forces, as follows:

→ Internet Engineering Task Force (IETF)

→ Internet Research Task Force (IRTF)

Each of these Task Forces is led by a chairman and guided by a Steering Group, which reports to the IAB through its chairman. For the most part, a collection of research or working groups carries out the work program of each Task Force.

All decisions of the IAB are made public. The principal vehicle by which IAB decisions are propagated to the parties interested in the Internet and its TCP/IP protocol suite is the *Request for Comments* (RFC) note series and the Internet Monthly Report.

What is the IETF?

The Internet has grown to encompass a large number of widely geographically dispersed networks in academic and research communities. It now provides an infrastructure for a broad community with various interests. Moreover, the family of Internet protocols and system components has moved from experimental to commercial development. To help coordinate the operation, management, and evolution of the Internet, the IAB established the *Internet Engineering Task Force* (IETF).

The IETF is a large open community of network designers, operators, vendors, and researchers concerned with the Internet and the Internet protocol suite. The activity is performed in a number of working groups organized around a set of several technical areas, each working group has a chair, and each area is managed by a technical area director. The IETF overall is managed by its chair and the *Internet Engineering Steering Group* (IESG), which is made up of the area directors.

The IAB has delegated to the IESG the general responsibility for the resolution of short- and mid-range protocol and architectural issues required to make the Internet function effectively, and the development of Internet standards.

What is the IRTF?

To promote research in networking and the development of new technology, the IAB established the *Internet Research Task Force* (IRTF). The IRTF is a set of research groups, generally with an Internet focus. The work of the IRTF is governed by its *Internet Research Steering Group* (IRSG).

In the area of network protocols, the distinction between research and engineering is not always clear, so there will sometimes be overlap between activities of the IETF and the IRTF. There is, in fact, considerable overlap in membership between the two groups. This overlap is regarded as vital for cross-fertilization and technology transfer.

What is the Internet Society?

The Internet Society is a relatively new, professional, non-profit organization with the general goal of fostering the well-being and continued interest in, and evolution and use of the Internet. The Society (often abbreviated ISOC) is integrating the IAB, IETF, and IRTF functions into its operation.

The following goals of the Society are taken from its charter:

→ To facilitate and support the technical evolution of the Internet as a research and education infrastructure, and to stimulate the involvement of the scientific community, industry, government, and others in the evolution of the Internet

→ To educate the scientific community, industry, and the public at large concerning the technology, use, and application of the Internet

→ To promote educational applications of Internet technology for the benefit of government, colleges and universities, industry, and the public at large

→ To provide a forum for exploration of new Internet applications, and to stimulate collaboration among organizations in their operational use of the global Internet

More information about the Internet Society is available for anonymous FTP from the host: isoc.org in the directory: isoc. Information is also available via the ISOC Gopher, accessible via "gopher isoc.org" if you are running a Gopher client.

What is the IANA?

The task of coordinating the assignment of values to the parameters of protocols is delegated by the

Internet Architecture Board (IAB) to the *Internet Assigned Numbers Authority* (IANA). These protocol parameters include op-codes, type fields, terminal types, system names, object identifiers, and so on. The "Assigned Numbers" RFC [1] documents the currently assigned values from several series of numbers used in network protocol implementations. Internet addresses and autonomous system numbers are assigned by the Registration Services portion of the InterNIC. The IANA is located at USC/Information Sciences Institute.

Current types of assignments listed in Assigned Numbers and maintained by the IANA are as follows:

Address Resolution Protocol Parameters

BOOTP Parameters and BOOTP Extension Codes

Character Sets

Domain System Parameters

Encoding Header Field Keywords

ESMTP Mail Keywords

Ethernet Multicast Addresses

Ethernet Numbers of Interest

Ethernet Vendor Address Components

IANA Ethernet Address Block

ICMP Type Numbers

IEEE 802 Numbers of Interest

Internet Protocol Numbers

Internet Version Numbers

IP Option Numbers

IP Time to Live Parameter

IP TOS Parameters

Internet Multicast Addresses

Inverse Address Resolution Protocol

Machine Names

Mail Encryption Types

Mail System Names

Mail Transmission Types

MILNET X.25 Address Mappings

MILNET Logical Addresses

MILNET Link Numbers

MIME Types

MIME/X.400 Mapping Tables

Network Management Parameters

Novell Numbers

Operating System Names

OSPF Authentication Codes

Point-to-Point Protocol Field Assignments

Protocol Numbers

Protocol and Service Names

Protocol/Type Field Assignments

Public Data Network Numbers

Reverse Address Resolution Protocol Operation Codes

SUN RPC Numbers

TCP Option Numbers

TCP Alternate Checksum Numbers

Telnet Options

Terminal Type Names

Version Numbers

Well-Known and Registered Port Numbers

X.25 Type Numbers

XNS Protocol Types

For more information on number assignments, contact IANA@ISI.EDU.

What is an NIC? What is an NOC?

"NIC" stands for *Network Information Center*. It is an organization that provides network users with information about services provided by the network.

"NOC" stands for *Network Operations Center*. It is an organization that is responsible for maintaining a network.

For many networks, especially smaller, local networks, the functions of the NIC and NOC are combined. For larger networks, such as mid-level and backbone networks, the NIC and NOC organizations are separate, yet they do need to interact to fully perform their functions.

What is the InterNIC?

The InterNIC is a five year project partially supported by the National Science Foundation to provide network information services to the networking community. The InterNIC began operations in April of 1993 and is a collaborative project of three organizations—General Atomics provides Information Services from their location in San Diego, CA; AT&T provides Directory and Database Services from South Plainsfield, NJ; and Network Solutions, Inc. provides Registration Services from their headquar-

ters in Herndon, VA. Services are provided via the network electronically, and by telephone, FAX, and hardcopy documentation.

General Atomics offers Information Services acting as the "NIC of first and last resort" by providing a Reference Desk for new and experienced users, and midlevel and campus NICs. The InterNIC Reference Desk offers introductory materials and pointers to network resources and tools.

AT&T services include the Directory of Directories, Directory Services, and Database Services to store data available to all Internet users.

Network Solutions, Inc. (NSI), provides Internet registration services, including IP address allocation, domain registration, and autonomous system number assignments. NSI also tracks points of contact for networks and domain servers, and provides online and telephone support for questions related to IP address or domain name registration.

All three portions of the InterNIC can be reached by calling (800)444-4345 or by sending a message to info@internic.net. Callers from outside the U.S. can telephone +1 (619)445-4600. Extensive online information is available at host is.internic.net, accessible via Gopher or Telnet.

What is the DDN NIC (nic.ddn.mil)?

The DDN NIC is the *Defense Data Network NIC*. Until the formation of the InterNIC, the DDN NIC had been responsible for many services to the whole Internet, especially for registration services. Now the DDN NIC focuses on serving its primary constituency of MILNET users. Its host is nic.ddn.mil; the address hostmaster@nic.ddn.mil may still be in older Internet registration documentation. The DDN NIC maintains close ties to the newer InterNIC.

What is the IR?

The *Internet Registry* (IR) is the organization that is responsible for assigning identifiers, such as IP network numbers and autonomous system numbers, to networks. The IR also gathers and registers such assigned information. The IR delegates some number assignment authority to regional registries (such as NCC@RIPE.NET and APNIC-STAFF@APNIC.NET). It will continue to gather data regarding such assignments, however. At present, the Registration Services portion of the InterNIC at Network Solutions, Inc. serves as the IR.

Questions About Services

How Do I Find Someone's Electronic Mail Address?

There are a number of directories on the Internet; however, all of them are far from complete. Many people can be found via the InterNIC WHOIS services, or Knowbot. Generally, though, it is still necessary to ask the person for his or her e-mail address.

How Do I Use the WHOIS Program at the InterNIC Registration Services?

There are several ways to search the WHOIS database. You can Telnet to the InterNIC registration host, rs.internic.net. There is no need to log in. Type **whois** to call up the information retrieval program, or choose one of the other options presented to you. Help is available for each option. You can also run a client of the WHOIS server and point it at any whois database you'd like to search. Pointing a client at the whois server ds.internic.net will enable you to query the databases at three hosts: ds.internic.net, rs.internic.net, and nic.ddn.mil.

For more information, contact the InterNIC at (800)444-4345 or the registration services group at (703)742-4777.

How Do I Use the Knowbot Information Service?

The Knowbot Information Service is a white pages "meta-service" that provides a uniform interface to heterogeneous white pages services in the Internet. Using the Knowbot Information Service, you can form a single query that can search for white pages information from the NIC WHOIS service, the PSI White Pages Pilot Project, and MCI Mail, among others, and have the responses displayed in a single, uniform format.

Currently, the Knowbot Information Service can be accessed through Telnet to port 185 on hosts cnri.reston.va.us and sol.bucknell.edu. From a UNIX host, use "telnet cnri.reston.va.us 185". There is also an electronic mail interface available by sending mail to netaddress at either cnri.reston.va.us or sol.bucknell.edu.

The commands "help" and "man" summarize the command interface. Simply entering a user name at the prompt searches a default list of Internet directory services for the requested information. Organization and country information can be included through the syntax: "userid@organization.country."

For example, the queries "droms@bucknell" and "kille@ucl.gb" are both valid. Note that these are not domain names, but rather a syntax to specify an organization and a country for the search.

What is the White Pages at PSI?

Performance Systems International, Inc. (PSI), sponsors a White Pages Project that collects personnel information from member organizations into a database and provides online access to that data. This effort is based on the OSI X.500 Directory standard.

To access the data, Telnet to WP.PSI.COM and log in as "fred" (no password is necessary). You may now look up information on participating organizations. The program provides help on usage. For example, typing **help** will show you a list of commands, **manual** will give detailed documentation, and **whois** will provide information regarding how to find references to people.

For a list of the organizations that are participating in the pilot project by providing information regarding their members, type **whois -org ***. Access to the White Pages data is also possible via programs that act as X.500 *Directory User Agent* (DUA) clients.

For more information, send a message to WP-INFO@PSI.COM.

What is Usenet? What is Netnews?

Usenet is the formal name—and Netnews a common informal name—for a distributed computer information service used by some hosts on the Internet. Usenet handles only news and not mail,

and uses a variety of underlying networks for transport, including parts of the Internet, BITNET, and others. Netnews can be a valuable tool to economically transport traffic that would otherwise be sent via mail. Usenet has no central administration.

How Do I Get a Netnews Feed?

To get a Netnews feed, you must acquire the server software, which is available for some computers at no cost from some anonymous FTP sites across the Internet, and you must find an existing Usenet site that is willing to support a connection to your computer. In many cases, this "connection" merely represents additional traffic over existing Internet access channels.

One well-known anonymous FTP archive site for software and information regarding Usenet is ftp.uu.net. There is a "news" directory that contains many software distribution and information subdirectories.

It is recommended that new users subscribe to and read news.announce.newusers—it will help them to become oriented to Usenet and the Internet.

What is a Newsgroup?

A newsgroup is a bulletin board focused on a particular topic from which readers can read and respond to messages posted by other readers. Generally, there will be a few "threads" of discussion going on at the same time, but they all share some common theme. There are approximately 900 newsgroups, and there are more being added all the time.

There are two types of newsgroups—moderated and unmoderated. A *moderated* newsgroup does not enable individuals to post directly to the newsgroup. Rather, the postings go to the newsgroup's moderator, who determines whether or not to pass the posting to the entire group. An *unmoderated* newsgroup enables a reader to post directly to the other readers.

How Do I Subscribe to a Newsgroup?

You don't subscribe to a newsgroup. Either you get it on your machine or you don't. If there's one you want, all you can do is ask the systems administrator to try to get it for you.

What is Anonymous FTP?

Anonymous FTP is a conventional way of enabling you to sign on to a computer on the Internet and copy specified public files from it [3]. Some sites offer anonymous FTP to distribute software and various kinds of information. You use it like any FTP, but the user name is "anonymous." Many systems will request that the password you choose is your e-mail address. If this fails, the generic password is usually "guest."

What is Archie?

The Archie system was created to automatically track anonymous FTP archive sites, and this is still its primary function. The system currently makes available the names and locations of some 2,100,000 files at some 1,000 archive sites.

Archie's User Access component enables you to search the "files" database for these file names. When matches are found, you are presented with the appropriate archive site name, IP address, the location within the archive, and other useful information.

You can also use Archie to "browse" through a site's complete listing in search of information of interest, or to obtain a complete list of the archive sites known to that server.

The Archie server also offers a *package descriptions* (or "whatis") database. This is a collection of names and descriptions gathered from a variety of sources and can be used to identify files located throughout the Internet, as well as other useful information. Files identified in the whatis database can then be found by searching the files database as described above.

How Do I Connect to Archie?

You can connect to Archie in a variety of ways. There is a conventional Telnet interface, an electronic mail interface, and a variety of client programs available. The use of a client is strongly encouraged. There are currently 22 Archie servers located throughout the world.

To try the Telnet interface to Archie, you can Telnet to one of the 22 Archie servers (preferably the one nearest you, and during non-peak hours). Log in as "archie" (no password is required). Type **help** to get you started.

The following is a list of Archie servers as of the date this was written:

archie.au*	139.130.4.6	Australia
archie.edvz.uni-linz.ac.at*	140.78.3.8	Austria
archie.univie.ac.at*	131.130.1.23	Austria
archie.uqam.ca*	132.208.250.10	Canada
archie.funet.fi	128.214.6.100	Finland
archie.th-darmstadt.de*	130.83.22.60	Germany
archie.ac.il*	132.65.6.15	Israel
archie.unipi.it*	131.114.21.10	Italy
archie.wide.ad.jp	133.4.3.6	Japan
archie.hana.nm.kr*	128.134.1.1	Korea
archie.sogang.ac.kr*	163.239.1.11	Korea
archie.uninett.no*	128.39.2.20	Norway
archie.rediris.es*	130.206.1.2	Spain
archie.luth.se*	130.240.18.4	Sweden
archie.switch.ch*	130.59.1.40	Switzerland
archie.ncu.edu.tw*	140.115.19.24	Taiwan
archie.doc.ic.ac.uk*	146.169.11.3	United Kingdom
archie.unl.edu	129.93.1.14	USA (NE)
archie.internic.net*	198.48.45.10	USA (NJ)
archie.rutgers.edu*	128.6.18.15	USA (NJ)
archie.ans.net	147.225.1.10	USA (NY)
archie.sura.net*	128.167.254.179	USA (MD)

Note: Sites marked with an asterisk "*" run Archie version 3.0.

You can obtain details on using the electronic mail interface by sending mail to Archie at any of the preceding server hosts. Put the word "help" as the text of your message for directions.

Questions, comments, and suggestions can be sent to the Archie development group by sending mail to info@bunyip.com.

What is Gopher?

The Internet Gopher presents an extremely wide variety of diverse types of information in an easy to use menu-driven interface. Gopher servers link information from all around the Internet in a manner that can be transparent to the user. (Users can easily discover the source of any piece of information, however, if they want.) For example, Gopher links databases of every type, applications, white pages directories, sounds, and pictures.

Some Gophers are available via Telnet. Since most Gophers are linked to other Gophers, if you can get to one, you can get to many. You can, for example, Telnet to naic.nasa.gov and use their public Gopher.

The best way to use the Gopher service, as with all client/server type services, is by running your own Gopher client. The Internet Gopher was developed at the University of Minnesota. More information is available for anonymous FTP on the host boombox.micro.umn.edu.

What is the World Wide Web? What is Mosaic?

The World Wide Web is a distributed, hypermedia-based Internet information browser. It presents users with a friendly point-and-click interface to a wide variety of types of information (text, graphics, sounds, movies, etc.) and Internet services. It is possible to use the Web to access FTP archives, databases, and even Gopher servers.

The most familiar implementations of the World Wide Web are the Mosaic clients developed by the *National Center for Supercomputing Applications* (NCSA). Mosaic software is available online at ftp.ncsa.uiuc.edu.

How Do I Find Out about Other Internet Resource Discovery Tools?

The field of Internet resource discovery tools is one of the most dynamic on the Internet today. In addition to those discussed here, there are several tools that are useful for discovering or searching Internet resources. The *European Academic and Research Network* (EARN) Association has compiled an excellent document that introduces many of these services and provides information about how to find out more about them. To obtain the document, send a message to listserv@earncc.bitnet or listserve%earncc.bitnet@cunyvm.cuny.edu. As the text of your message, type **GET filename**, where the file name is either "nettools ps" or "nettols memo." The former is in PostScript format. This document is also available for anonymous FTP on some hosts, including naic.nasa.gov, where it is available in the files/general_info directory as earn-resource-tool-guide.ps and earn-resource-tool-guide.txt.

What is Telnet?

The term "Telnet" refers to the remote login that is possible on the Internet because of the Telnet protocol [9]. The use of this term as a verb, as in "Telnet to a host" means to establish a connection across the Internet from one host to another. Usually, you must have an account on the remote host to be able to log in to it once you've made a connection. Some hosts, however, such as those offering white pages directories, provide public services that do not require a personal account.

If your host supports Telnet, your command to connect to a remote host would probably be "telnet <hostname>" or "telnet <host IP address>." For example, "telnet rs.internic.net" or "telnet 198.41.0.5."

Mailing Lists and Sending Mail

What is a Mailing List?

A *mailing list* is an e-mail address that stands for a group of people rather than for an individual. Mailing lists are usually created to discuss specific topics. Anybody interested in that topic, may (usually) join that list. Some mailing lists have membership restrictions, others have message content restrictions, and still others are moderated. Most "public" mailing lists have a second e-mail address to handle administrative matters, such as requests to be added to or deleted from the list. All subscription requests should be sent to the administrative address, rather than to the list itself!

How Do I Contact the Administrator of a Mailing List rather than Posting to the Entire List?

Today, there are two main methods used by mailing list administrators to handle requests to subscribe or unsubscribe from their lists. The administrative address for many lists has the same name as the list itself, but with "-request" appended to the list name. So, to join the ietf-announce@cnri.reston.va.us list, you would send a message to ietf-announce request@cnri.reston.va.us. Most often, requests to a "-request" mailbox are handled by a human, and you can phrase your request as a normal message.

More often today, especially for lists with many readers, administrators prefer to have a program handle routine list administration. Many lists are accessible via LISTSERVE programs or other mailing list manager programs. If this is the case, the administrative address will usually be something like "listserv@host.domain," where the address for the mailing list itself will be "list@host.domain." The same listserve address can handle requests for all mailing lists at that host. When talking with a program, your subscription request will often be in the form, "subscribe ListName YourFirstName YourLastName" where you substitute the name of the list for ListName and add your real name at the end.

The important thing to remember is that all administrative messages regarding using, joining, or quitting a list should be sent to the administrative mailbox instead of to the whole list so that the readers of the list don't have to read them.

How Do I Send Mail to Other Networks?

Mail to the Internet is addressed in the form user@host.domain. Remember that a domain name can have several components and the name of each host is a node on the domain tree. So, an example of an Internet mail address is june@nisc.sri.com.

There are several networks accessible via e-mail from the Internet, but many of these networks do not use the same addressing conventions the Internet does. Often you must route mail to these networks through specific gateways as well, thus further complicating the address.

Here are a few conventions you can use for sending mail from the Internet to three networks with which Internet users often correspond:

Internet user to Internet user:

username@hostname.subdomain.toplevel domain

for example, gsmith@nisc.sri.COM

Internet user to BITNET user:

user%site.BITNET@BITNET-GATEWAY

for example, gsmith%emoryu1.BITNET@cunyvm.cuny.edu.

gsmith%emoryu1@CORNELLC.CIT.

CORNELL.EDU

Internet user to UUCP user:

user%host.UUCP@uunet.uu.net

user%domain@uunet.uu.net

Internet user to SprintMail user:

/G=Mary/S=Anderson/O=co.abc/ ADMD=SprintMail/C=US/@SPRINT.COM

or

/PN=Mary.Anderson/O=co.abc/ ADMD=SprintMail/C=US/@SPRINT.COM (Case is significant.)

Internet user to CompuServe user:

Replace the comma in the CompuServe user ID (represented here with xs) with a period, and add the compuserve.com domain name:

xxxx.xxxx@compuserve.com

CompuServe user to Internet user:

>Internet:user@host

Insert >internet: before an Internet address.

Internet user to MCIMail user:

accountname@mcimail.com

mci_id@mcimail.com

full_user_name@mcimail.com.

Miscellaneous "Internet Lore" Questions

What Does :-) Mean?

In many electronic mail messages, it is sometimes useful to indicate that part of a message is meant in jest. It is also sometimes useful to communicate emotion that simple words do not readily convey. To provide these nuances, a collection of "smiley faces" has evolved. If you turn your head sideways to the left, :-) appears as a smiling face. Some of the more common faces are the following:

:-)	smile	:-(	frown
:)	also a smile	;-)	wink
:-D	laughing	8-)	wide-eyed
:-}	grin	:-X	close mouthed
:-]	smirk	:-o	oh, no!

What Do "btw," "fyi," "imho," "wrt," and "rtfm" Mean?

Often common expressions are abbreviated in informal network postings. These abbreviations stand for "by the way," "for your information," "in my humble [or honest] opinion," "with respect to," and "read the f*ing manual" –with the "f" word varying according to the vehemence of the reader :-).

What is the "FAQ" List?

This list provides answers to *Frequently Asked Questions* (FAQs) that often appear on various Usenet newsgroups. The list is posted every four to six weeks to the news.announce.newusers group. It is intended to provide a background for new users learning how to use the news. As the FAQ list provides new users with the answers to such questions, it helps keep the newsgroups themselves comparatively free of repetition. Often, specific newsgroups will post versions of a FAQ list that are specific to their topics. The term FAQ has become generalized so that any topic may have its FAQ even if it is not a newsgroup.

The following is information about obtaining the USENET FAQs, courtesy of Gene Spafford.

Many questions can be answered by consulting the most recent postings in the news.announce.newusers and news.lists groups. If those postings have expired from your site, or you do not get news, you can get archived postings from the FTP server on the host rtfm.mit.edu.

These archived postings include all the Frequently Asked Questions posted to the news.answers newsgroups, as well as the most recent lists of Usenet newsgroups, Usenet-accessible mailing lists, group moderators, and other Usenet-related information posted to the news.announce.newusers and news.lists groups.

To get the material by FTP, log in using anonymous FTP (user id of anonymous and your e-mail address as password).

The archived files, and FAQ files from other newsgroups, are all in the following directory:

/pub/usenet/news.answers

Archived files from news.announce.newusers and news.lists are in:

/pub/usenet/news.announce.newusers

/pub/usenet/news.lists

respectively.

To get the information by mail, send an e-mail message to: mail- server@pit-manager.mit.edu containing the following:

send usenet/news.answers/TITLE/PART

where TITLE is the archive title, and PART is the portion of the posting you want.

Send a message containing "help" to get general information about the mail server, including information on how to get a list of archive titles to use in further send commands.

Administrative Issues

part

Appendixes

Examining Internet Access Providers

This appendix contains a list of some of the *Internet Access Providers* (IAPs) within the U.S. that offer Internet access for LAN users. This list was derived by surveying various list members and sending questionnaires to IAPs. In some cases, information has been derived with permission from the Web servers of the IAPs. The IAPs who only, or predominantly, offer single user dial-up access are not included in this list.

There is no implied or stated guarantee of the accuracy of this information since it is constantly changing. Therefore, readers are advised to check directly with the IAPs in their area.

The various items that have been specified for each IAP in this appendix are shown in the following. These items appear in the order indicated for each IAP unless the information was not supplied by the IAP.

→ Company name

→ Company address

→ Telephone number

→ E-mail address

→ Web server address

Internet Access Providers Listing

Aimnet Corporation

20410 Town Center Lane #290
Cupertino, CA 95014

408-257-0900

info@aimnet.com

http://www.aimnet.com

ANS

1875 Campus Commons Dr., Ste. 220
Reston, VA 22091

703-758-7700 or 800-456-8267

info@ans.net

B3NET

B3 Corporation

715-387-1700

info@free.org

BBN Internet Services Corp.

BARRNET—San Francisco Bay Area

415-725-1790

info@barrnet.net

http://www.barrnet.net

NEARNET—Northeast U.S.

800-NEARNET

nearnet-join@near.net

http://www.near.net

Beckemeyer Development

P.O. Box 21575, Oakland, CA 94620

510-530-9637

info@bolt.com

http://www.bolt.com

Branch Information Services

2901 Hubbard, Ann Arbor, MI 48105

313-741-4442

branch-info@branch.com

http://branch.com

CERFnet

    800-876-2373

    sales@cerf.net

    http://www.cerf.net

    info@onramp.net

CICNet, Inc.

    2901 Hubbard, Ann Arbor, MI 48105

    313-998-6703 or 800-947-4754

    info@cic.net

Cloud 9 Consulting

    15 Lake Street, White Plains, NY 10603

    914-682-0626

    staff@cloud9.net

Colorado SuperNet, Inc.

    303-296-8202

    info@csn.org

    http://www.csn.org

CyberGate, Inc.

    662 S. Military Trail

    Deerfield Beach, FL 33442

    305-428-GATE or 800-NET-GATE

    sales@gate.net

    http://www.gate.net

Datatex Corporation

    Dallas, TX

    sales@datanet.net

    http://www.datanet.net

DFW Internet Services, Inc.

    204 E. Belknap, Ste. 101, Fort Worth, TX

    817-429-3520 or 800-2DFWNet

    info@dfw.net

Digital Express Group, Inc.

    6800 Virginia Manor Dr.
    Beltsville, MD 20705

    301-847-5000 or 800-969-9090

    info@digex.net

Earthlink Network, Inc.

    213-644-9500

    sales@earthlink.net

    http://www.earthlink.net

EMI Communications, Inc.

    Syracuse, NY

    800-456-2001

    info@emi.com

    http://www.emi.com

Exodus Communications, Inc.

>948 Benecia Ave., Sunnyvale, CA 94086

>800-263-8872

>sales@exodus.com

>http://www.exodus.com

Fullfeed Communications

>359 Raven Lane, Madison, WI 53705

>608-246-4239

>info@msn.fullfeed.com

Fullfeed Communications, Fox Valley

>611 N. Lynndale Dr., Suite K
>Appleton, WI 54914

>414-954-0444 or 800-840-8205

>info@atw.fullfeed.com

Galaxy StarSystems

>P.O. Box 580782, Tulsa, OK 74158-0782

>918-835-3655 or 918-TEL-INET

>mlester@galstar.com

Global Enterprise Services

>3 Independent Way, Princeton, NJ 08540

>800-358-4437

>market@jvnc.net

>http://www.jvnc.net

ICNet

>2901 Hubbard, Ann Arbor, MI 48105

>313-998-0090

>info@ic.net

>http://www.ic.net

IgLou Internet Services

>3315 Gilmore Industrial Blvd., Louisville, KY

>800-I-DO-IGLOU or 502-966-3848

>info@iglou.com

Infinite Systems

>274 Marconi Blvd., Ste. 410
>Columbus, OH 43215

>614-268-9941

>sales@infinet.com

INTAC Web Services

>256 Broad Ave., Palisades Park, NJ 07650

>201-944-1417

>info@intac.com

Internet Atlanta

>340 Knoll Ridge Ct., Alpharetta, GA 30202

>404-410-9000

>info@atlanta.com

Internetworks, Inc.

>503-233-4774

>info@i.net

>http://www.i.net

Internex Information Services, Inc.

>1050 Chestnut St., Ste. 201
>Menlo Park, CA 94025
>
>415-473-3060
>
>info@internex.net
>
>http://www.internex.net

Interpath

>711 Hillsborough St.
>Raleigh, NC 27605-2800
>
>800-849-6319
>
>info@interpath.net

Interport Communications

>1133 Broadway, New York, NY 10010
>
>212-989-1128
>
>info@interport.net
>
>http://www.interport.net

InterQuest

>Huntsville, AL 35824
>
>205-464-8280
>
>info@iquest.com
>
>http://www.iquest.com

Intuitive Information, Inc.

>1 Oak Hill Rd., Fitchburg, MA 01420
>
>508-342-1100 or 800-405-4495
>
>info@iii.net
>
>http://www.iii.net

Iquest Network Services

>2035 E. 46th St., Indianapolis, IN 46205-1472
>
>317-259-5050
>
>info@iquest.net

MCI Telecommunications

>800-955-6505
>
>moreinfo@networkmci.com
>
>http://www.mci.com

MCS Net, Inc.

>Chicago, IL
>
>312-248-8649
>
>info@mcs.net
>
>http://www.mcs.net

MIDnet

>201 N. 8th St., Ste. 421
>Lincoln, NE 68508
>
>800-682-5550
>
>sales@mid.net

NETCOM On-Line Communications Services

>3031 Tisch Way, San Jose, CA 95128
>
>408-983-5950 or 800-353-6600
>
>sales@netcom.com
>
>http://www.netcom.com

Network Access Services

P.O. Box 28085, Bellingham, WA 98228-0085

360-733-9279

info@nas.com

http://www.nas.com

New York Net

82-04-218th Street
Hollis Hills, NY 11427-1416

718-776-6811

sales@newyork.net

Northcoast Internet

518 E. St., Eureka, CA 95501

707-443-8696

support@northcoast.com

OARnet

2455 N. Star Rd., Columbus, OH 43221

614-728-8100

info@oar.net

PSI, Inc.

P.O. Box 592, Herndon, VA 22070

703-709-0300 or 800-82PSI82

info@psi.com

http://www.psi.net

QuakeNet

830 Wilmington Rd., San Mateo, CA 94402

415-655-6607

info@quake.net

http://www.Quake.Net

Santa Cruz Community Internet

903 Pacific Ave., #203-A
Santa Cruz, CA 95060

800-319-5555

info@scruz.net

http://www.scruz.net

SEANET

Columbia SeaFirst Center

701 Fifth Ave., Ste. 6801, Seattle, WA 98104

206-343-7828

seanet@seanet.com

http://www.seanet.com

SIMS, Inc.

701 E. Bay St., Ste. 1-123, PCC Box 1011,
Charleston, SC 29403

803-853-4333

info@sims.com

SprintLink

12502 Sunrise Valley, Reston, VA 22096

703-827-7240

info@sprint.net

http://www.sprintlink

SRMC

San Jose, CA

408-437-1800

info@srmc.com

Structured Network Systems, Inc.

15635 SE 114th Ave., Ste. 201
Clarkamas, OR 97015

503-656-3530

info@structured.net

Suranet

8400 Baltimore Blvd.
College Park, MD 20740

301-982-4600 or 800-SURANET

marketing@sura.net

http://www.sura.net

The Black Box

P.O. Box 591822, Houston, TX 772590-1822

713-480-2684

info@blkbox.com

TIAC

The Internet Access Company, Inc.

P.O. Box 1098, Bedford, MA 01730

617-276-7200

sales@tiac.net

http://www.tiac.net

Transport Logic

13500 SW Pacific Hwy #513
Portland, OR 97223

503-243-1940

sales@transport.com

UltraNet Communications, Inc.

910 Boston Post Rd., Ste. 220, Marlboro, MA

508-229-8400

info@ultranet.com

http://www.ultranet.com

US Net

301-572-5926

info@us.net

http://www.us.net

UUNET Technologies, Inc.

3060 Williams Dr., Ste. 601, Fairfax VA 22031

800-488-6383

sales@alter.net

http://www.alter.net

IP Subnetting and Binary Conversion Tables

Implementing an Internet connection presents the

network administrator with many new tasks. One

of these tasks is the design and implementation of

an IP addressing scheme. The tables in this appen-

dix provide information for two critical issues in this

process—determining valid IP subnet masks and

converting IP addresses both to and from dotted

decimal notation and binary representation.

IP Address Subnetting Tables

In the following tables, the valid options for subnetting for both class B and class C addresses are listed. The number of bits and the subnet mask for each option is provided. By using these tables, you can determine what subnet mask is appropriate for your environment based on the number of subnets and the number of hosts or devices per subnet that are required in your network.

# Bits	Subnet Mask	# Subnets	# Hosts
2	255.255.192.0	2	16382
3	255.255.224.0	6	8190
4	255.255.240.0	14	4094
5	255.255.248.0	30	2046
6	255.255.252.0	62	1022
7	255.255.254.0	126	510
8	255.255.255.0	254	254
9	255.255.255.128	510	126
10	255.255.255.192	1022	62
11	255.255.255.224	2046	30
12	255.255.255.240	4094	14
13	255.255.255.248	8190	6
14	255.255.255.252	16382	2

Table B.1

Class B Subnetting

Table B.2	# Bits	Subnet Mask	# Subnets	# Hosts
Class C Subnetting	0	255.255.255.0	1	254
	2	255.255.255.192	2	62
	3	255.255.255.224	6	30
	4	255.255.255.240	14	14
	5	255.255.255.248	30	6
	6	255.255.255.252	62	2

Decimal to Binary Conversion Table

While IP addresses are often depicted in dotted decimal notation (i.e., 198.92.54.65), network devices view these addresses in binary representation. Binary representation also helps the network administrator in the process of designing and implementing an IP addressing scheme. This assists in determining subnet numbers, broadcast addresses, and host addresses using the processes explained in Chapter 3, "Understanding TCP/IP," and illustrated in detail in Case Study #2 of Chapter 11, "Case Studies."

In table B.3, the equivalent binary representation of the decimal numbers 0 to 255 have been provided as an aid. Make use of this table to convert dotted decimal numbers to binary and binary numbers to dotted decimal notation until you are comfortable doing the conversion yourself.

Table B.3 Decimal to Binary Conversion for Numbers 0 to 255

Decimal	Binary	Decimal	Binary	Decimal	Binary
0	00000000	86	01010110	172	10101100
1	00000001	87	01010111	173	10101101
2	00000010	88	01011000	174	10101110
3	00000011	89	01011001	175	10101111
4	00000100	90	01011010	176	10110000
5	00000101	91	01011011	177	10110001

continues

Table B.3, Continued

Decimal	Binary	Decimal	Binary	Decimal	Binary
6	00000110	92	01011100	178	10110010
7	00000111	93	01011101	179	10110011
8	00001000	94	01011110	180	10110100
9	00001001	95	01011111	181	10110101
10	00001010	96	01100000	182	10110110
11	00001011	97	01100001	183	10110111
12	00001100	98	01100010	184	10111000
13	00001101	99	01100011	185	10111001
14	00001110	100	01100100	186	10111010
15	00001111	101	01100101	187	10111011
16	00010000	102	01100110	188	10111100
17	00010001	103	01100111	189	10111101
18	00010010	104	01101000	190	10111110
19	00010011	105	01101001	191	10111111
20	00010100	106	01101010	192	11000000
21	00010101	107	01101011	193	11000001
22	00010110	108	01101100	194	11000010
23	00010111	109	01101101	195	11000011
24	00011000	110	01101110	196	11000100
25	00011001	111	01101111	197	11000101
26	00011010	112	01110000	198	11000110
27	00011011	113	01110001	199	11000111

Decimal	Binary	Decimal	Binary	Decimal	Binary
28	00011100	114	01110010	200	11001000
29	00011101	115	01110011	201	11001001
30	00011110	116	01110100	202	11001010
31	00011111	117	01110101	203	11001011
32	00100000	118	01110110	204	11001100
33	00100001	119	01110111	205	11001101
34	00100010	120	01111000	206	11001110
35	00100011	121	01111001	207	11001111
36	00100100	122	01111010	208	11010000
37	00100101	123	01111011	209	11010001
38	00100110	124	01111100	210	11010010
39	00100111	125	01111101	211	11010011
40	00101000	126	01111110	212	11010100
41	00101001	127	01111111	213	11010101
42	00101010	128	10000000	214	11010110
43	00101011	129	10000001	215	11010111
44	00101100	130	10000010	216	11011000
45	00101101	131	10000011	217	11011001
46	00101110	132	10000100	218	11011010
47	00101111	133	10000101	219	11011011
48	00110000	134	10000110	220	11011100
49	00110001	135	10000111	221	11011101
50	00110010	136	10001000	222	11011110

continues

Decimal	Binary	Decimal	Binary	Decimal	Binary
52	00110100	138	10001010	224	11100000
53	00110101	139	10001011	225	11100001
54	00110110	140	10001100	226	11100010
55	00110111	141	10001101	227	11100011
56	00111000	142	10001110	228	11100100
57	00111001	143	10001111	229	11100101
58	00111010	144	10010000	230	11100110
59	00111011	145	10010001	231	11100111
60	00111100	146	10010010	232	11101000
61	00111101	147	10010011	233	11101001
62	00111110	148	10010100	234	11101010
63	00111111	149	10010101	235	11101011
64	01000000	150	10010110	236	11101100
65	01000001	151	10010111	237	11101101
66	01000010	152	10011000	238	11101110
67	01000011	153	10011001	239	11101111
68	01000100	154	10011010	240	11110000
69	01000101	155	10011011	241	11110001
70	01000110	156	10011100	242	11110010
71	01000111	157	10011101	243	11110011
72	01001000	158	10011110	244	11110100
73	01001001	159	10011111	245	11110101

Decimal	Binary	Decimal	Binary	Decimal	Binary
74	01001010	160	10100000	246	11110110
75	01001011	161	10100001	247	11110111
76	01001100	162	10100010	248	11111000
77	01001101	163	10100011	249	11111001
78	01001110	164	10100100	250	11111010
79	01001111	165	10100101	251	11111011
80	01010000	166	10100110	252	11111100
81	01010001	167	10100111	253	11111101
82	01010010	168	10101000	254	11111110
83	01010011	169	10101001	255	11111111
84	01010100	170	10101010		
85	01010101	171	10101011		

Glossary

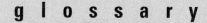

ACK *acknowledgment.* A response from a receiving computer to a sending computer to indicate successful reception of information. TCP requires that packets be acknowledged before it considers the transmission safe.

active open An action taken by a client to initiate a TCP connection with a server.

address classes Grouping of IP addresses with each class, defining the maximum number of networks and hosts available. The first octet of the address determines the class. Class A networks (first octet value between 1-126) can have 16,777,214 hosts per network. Class B networks (128-191) can have 65,534 hosts per network. Class C networks (192-223) can have up to 254 hosts per network.

address mask A 32-bit binary number used to select bits from an IP address for subnet addressing.

address resolution A translation of an IP address to a corresponding physical address. See *ARP.*

agent The software routine in an SNMP-managed device that responds to get and set requests and sends trap messages.

ANSI *American National Standards Institute.* The membership organization responsible for defining U.S. standards in the information technology industry. ANSI is a member of ISO and participates in defining network protocol standards.

API *Application Programming Interface.* A language and message format that enables a programmer to use functions in another program or in the hardware.

ARP *Address Resolution Protocol.* A protocol in the TCP/IP suite used to bind an IP address to a physical hardware address.

ARPAnet *Advanced Research Projects Agency Network.* A research network funded by ARPA (later DARPA), a government agency, and built by BBN, Inc. in 1969. It was the first packet switching network and served as the central Internet backbone for many years.

AS *Autonomous System.* A collection of routers and gateways that falls under the control of a single administrative entity. The collection cooperates closely to provide network routing information using a common Interior Gateway Protocol.

baseband A network technology that requires all nodes attached to the network to participate in every transmission. Ethernet is a baseband technology.

best-effort delivery Characteristic of a network technology that does not ensure link level reliability. IP and UDP protocols work together to provide best-effort delivery service to applications.

BGP *Border Gateway Protocol.* A protocol that advertises the networks that can be reached within an Autonomous System.

big endian A format for storage or transmission of data in which the most significant byte (or bit) comes first. See also *little endian.*

BOOTP *Bootstrap Protocol.* A protocol used to configure systems across internetworks.

bps *bits per second.* A measure of the rate of data transmission.

bridge A computer device that connects two or more physical networks and forwards packets among them. Bridges usually operate at the physical level.

broadband A network technology that multiplexes multiple network carriers onto a single cable. The technology uses less cable, but equipment is more expensive.

broadcast A packet destined for all hosts on the network.

brouter A computer device that works as both a bridge and a router. Some traffic may be bridged, while other traffic is routed.

buffer A storage area used to hold input or output data.

checksum A computed value used to verify the accuracy of data in TCP/IP packets and check for errors.

CMIP *Common Management Information Protocol.* An OSI network management protocol.

connection A logical path between two protocol modules that provides a reliable delivery service.

connectionless service A delivery service that treats each packet as a separate entity. Often results in lost packets or packets out of sequence.

CRC *Cyclic Redundancy Check.* A computation about a frame of which the result is a small integer.

The value is appended to the end of the frame and recalculated when the frame is received. If the results differ from the appended value, the frame has presumably been corrupted and is therefore discarded. Used to detect errors in transmission.

CSMA *Carrier Sense Multiple Access.* A simple media access control protocol that enables multiple stations to contend for access to the medium. If no traffic is detected on the medium, the station may send a transmission.

CSMA/CD *Carrier Sense Multiple Access with Collision Detection.* A characteristic of network hardware that uses CSMA in conjunction with a process that detects when two stations transmit simultaneously. If that happens, both back off and retry the transmission after a random time period has elapsed.

datagram A packet of data and delivery information.

DHCP *Dynamic Host Configuration Protocol.* A protocol that provides dynamic address allocation and automatic TCP/IP configuration.

directed broadcast address An IP address that specifies all hosts on a network.

DNS *Domain Name System.* A distributed database system used to map IP addresses to their system names. DNS also provides the location of mail exchangers.

DNS name servers The servers that contain information about a portion of the DNS database.

domain name space The database structure used by DNS.

EBONE *European IP Backbone.*

EGP *Exterior Gateway Protocol.* A protocol that advertises the networks that can be reached within an autonomous system.

fair queuing A technique used to control traffic in gateways by restricting every host to an equal share of gateway bandwidth.

FCS *Frame Check Sequence.* A computation about the bits in a frame of which the result is appended to the end of the frame and recalculated when the frame is received. If the results differ from the appended value, the frame has presumably been corrupted and is therefore discarded. Used to detect errors in transmission.

FDM *Frequency Division Multiplexing.* A technique of passing multiple signals across a single medium by assigning each signal a unique carrier frequency.

flow control A mechanism that controls the rate that hosts may transmit at any time. Used to avoid congestion on the network, which may exhaust memory buffers.

FQDN *Fully Qualified Domain Name.* A combination of the host name and domain name.

fragment A piece that results when a datagram is partitioned into smaller pieces. Used to facilitate datagrams that are too large for the network technology it must traverse.

frame A packet as transmitted across a medium. Differing frame types have unique characteristics.

FTP *File Transfer Protocol.* A high-level protocol that supports file copying between systems. Requires client and server components.

gateway A computer that attaches multiple TCP/IP networks for the purpose of routing or delivering IP packets between them. Used interchangeably with IP router.

GOSIP *Government Open Systems Interconnection Profile.* A U.S. Government document that defines a specification of a set of OSI protocols that agencies may use.

hardware address The physical address of a host used by networks.

HDLC *High-Level Data Link Control.* A standard data link level protocol.

header Data inserted at the beginning of a packet that contains control information.

hop count A measure of distance that measures the number of gateways that separate two hosts.

host Any computer system or device attached to the internetwork.

host ID The portion of an IP address that identifies the host in a particular network. Used in conjunction with network IDs to form a complete IP address.

HOSTS file A text file that contains mappings of IP addresses to host names.

IAB *Internet Architecture Board.* An independent group responsible for policies and standards for TCP/IP and the Internet.

ICMP *Internet Control Message Protocol.* A maintenance protocol that handles error messages to be sent when datagrams are discarded or when systems experience congestion.

IGMP *Internet Group Management Protocol.* A protocol used to carry group membership information in a multicast system.

IGP *Interior Gateway Protocol.* A generic term that applies to any routing protocol used within an autonomous system.

internet A collection of packet-switching networks connected by IP routers and appearing to users as a single network.

Internet The world's largest collection of networks that reaches universities, government research labs, business organizations, and military installations in many countries.

IP *Internet Protocol.* Along with TCP, one of the most fundamental protocols in TCP/IP networking. IP is responsible for addressing and sending datagrams across an internet.

IP address The 32-bit address assigned to hosts that identifies a node on the network and specifies routing information on an internetwork.

IS-IS *Intermediate System to Intermediate System* protocol. A protocol that can be used to route both OSI and IP traffic.

ISO *International Standards Organization.* An international body founded to draft standards for network protocols.

LAN *Local Area Network.* A physical communications network that operates over short geographical areas.

little endian A format for storage or transmission of data in which the least significant byte (or bit) comes first. See also *big endian*.

LLC   *Logical Link Control.* A protocol that provides a common interface point to the MAC layers.

MAC   *Media Access Control.* A protocol that governs the access method a station has to the network.

mail bridge   A gateway that screens mail between two networks to make sure it meets administrative constraints.

MAN   *Metropolitan Area Network.* A physical communications network that operates across a metropolitan area.

MIB   *Management Information Base.* A database made up of a set of objects that represent various types of information about a device. Used by SNMP to manage devices.

MSS   *Maximum Segment Size.* The largest amount of data that can be transmitted at one time. Negotiated by sender and receiver.

MTU   *Maximum Transmission Unit.* The largest datagram that can be sent across a given physical network.

multihomed host   A TCP/IP host that is attached to two or more networks, requiring multiple IP addresses.

name resolution   The process of mapping a computer name to an IP address. DNS and DHCP are two tools for resolving names.

network ID   The portion of an IP address that identifies the network. Used in conjunction with host IDs to form a complete IP address.

NFS   *Network File System.* A distributed file system developed by Sun Microsystems that uses IP to enable clients to mount remote directories on their local file systems, regardless of machine or operating system. Users can access remote files as if they were local.

NIC   *Network Information Center.* A central administration facility responsible for providing users with information about TCP/IP and the Internet.

NIS   *Network Information Service.* A naming service from SunSoft used to provide a directory service for network information.

NSFnet   *National Science Foundation Network.* A network that serves as part of the current Internet backbone funded by the NSF.

NVT   *Network Virtual Terminal.* A set of rules that define a very simple virtual terminal interaction used at the start of a telnet session.

OSF   *Open Software Foundation.* A nonprofit organization comprised of hardware manufacturers who attempt to produce standard technologies for open systems.

OSI   *Open Systems Interconnection.* A set of ISO standards that define the framework for implementing protocols in seven layers.

packet   The unit of protocol data sent across a packet switching network.

ping   *Packet internet groper.* A program used in TCP/IP internetworks to test reachability of other hosts. A ping is simply an ICMP echo request that waits for a reply.

port ID   The method used by TCP and UDP to specify which application is sending or receiving data.

PPP *Point-to-Point Protocol.* An industry standard protocol for data transfer across serial links. It allows for several protocols to be multiplexed across the link.

protocol A set of rules used to govern the transmission and receiving of data.

RARP *Reverse Address Resolution Protocol.* A protocol that enables a computer to find its IP address by broadcasting a request. Used by a diskless workstation at startup to find its logical IP address.

repeater A device that amplifies or regenerates the data signal in order to extend the transmission distance. Only two repeaters can appear between any two machines on an Ethernet network.

resolver Client software that enables access to the DNS database.

RFC *Request for Comment.* Official documents containing Internet protocols, surveys, measurements, ideas, and observations. These documents are available online from the Network Information Center.

RIP *Routing Information Protocol.* A router-to-router protocol used to exchange information between routers. RIP supports dynamic routing.

RMON *Remote Network Monitor.* A device that collects information about network communication.

route The path that network traffic takes from its source to its destination.

router A computer responsible for deciding the routes network traffic will follow, and then sending traffic from one network to another.

RPC *Remote Procedure Call.* An interface that allows an application to call a routine that executes on another machine in a remote location.

segment A protocol data unit consisting of part of a stream of bytes being sent between two machines. Also includes information about the current position in the stream and a checksum value.

SLIP *Serial Line Internet Protocol.* A simple protocol used to transmit datagrams across a serial line.

SMTP *Simple Mail Transfer Protocol.* A protocol used to transfer electronic mail messages from one machine to another.

SNA *System Network Architecture.* A protocol suite developed and used by IBM.

SNMP *Simple Network Management Protocol.* A protocol used for network management data. SNMP enables a management station to configure, monitor, and receive trap messages from gateways and the networks to which they are attached.

socket A bidirectional pipe for incoming and outgoing data that allows an application program to access the TCP/IP protocols.

source route A route identifying the path a datagram must follow, determined by the source device.

subnet Any lower network, identified by the network ID, that is part of the logical network.

subnet mask A 32-bit value that distinguishes the network ID from the host ID in an IP address.

TCP *Transmission Control Protocol.* Along with IP, one of the most fundamental protocols in TCP/IP networking. TCP is a connection-based protocol that provides reliable, full duplex data transmission between a pair of applications.

Telnet Remote terminal protocol that allows a terminal attached to one host to log into other hosts, as if directly connected to the remote machine.

TFTP *Trivial File Transfer Protocol.* A basic, standard protocol used to upload or download files with minimal overhead. TFTP depends on UDP and is often used to initialize diskless workstations. It has no directory or password capability.

TLI *Transport Layer Interface.* An AT&T-developed interface that enables applications to interface to both TCP/IP and OSI protocols.

transceiver A device that connects a host interface to a network. Used to apply signals to the cable and sense collisions.

trap A block of data that indicates some request failed to authenticate. An SNMP service sends a trap when it receives a request for information with an incorrect community name.

TTL *Time-To-Live.* A measurement of time, usually defined by a number of hops, that a datagram can exist on a network before being discarded. Used to prevent endlessly looping packets.

UDP *User Datagram Protocol.* A simple protocol that enables an application program on one machine to send a datagram to an application program on another machine. Delivery is not guaranteed, nor is it guaranteed the datagrams will be delivered in the proper order.

universal time An international standard time reference, formerly called Greenwich Mean Time.

UTC Coordinated Universal Time. See also *universal time.*

UUCP *UNIX-to-UNIX Copy.* An application that allows one UNIX system to copy files to or from another UNIX system over a single link. UUCP is the basis for electronic mail transfer in UNIX.

WAN *Wide Area Network.* A physical communications network that operates across large geographical distances. WANs usually operate at slower speeds than LANs or MANs.

X.25 A CCITT standard for connecting computers to a network that provides a reliable stream transmission service, which can support remote login.

X.400 A CCITT standard for message transfer and interpersonal messaging, like electronic mail.

XDR *External Data Representation.* A data format standard developed by Sun that defines datatypes used as parameters, and encodes these parameters for transmission.

X Windows System A software system developed at MIT that enables a user to run applications on other computers and view the output on their own screen. Window placement and size are controlled by a window manager program.

D

E

F

J-L

M

N

Q-R

QUOTED-PRINTABLE encoding (MIME), 123

RARP (Reverse Address Resolution Protocol), 42, 274
raw socket support (WINSOCK), 61
RBOCs (regional bell operating companies) and WANs, 136-138
readers, e-mail, 75, 77
receiving e-mail, 80
regional IAPs (Internet Access Providers), 171-172
   compared to national IAPs, 185
registering domain names and IP addresses, 47-48
reliability
   e-mail, 82
   IAPs (Internet Access Providers), 185-186
remote access servers, 157-158, 165
remote logins, 229
Remote Network Monitors (RMONs), 274
Remote Procedure Calls (RPCs), 274
renting Web space, 133
repeaters, 274
research on the Internet, 16
reselling hardware/software (IAPs), 177
resolvers, 274
retrieving e-mail, 116
Reverse Address Resolution Protocol (RARP), 42, 274
RFC 822 (e-mail addressing), 118-119
RFC-INFO, 232-233
RFCs (Requests for Comments), 11, 14, 231-234, 274
RFPs (requests for proposals), 187-191
.rhosts file (security), 196
RIP (Routing Information Protocol), 274
   IP/IPX, 56
RIPE NCC (RIPE Network Coordination Center), 229
RMONs (Remote Network Monitors), 274

routers, 10, 274
   application relays, 203-204
   external dial-up routers, 158-159
   external routers
      ISDN service, 162
      leased-line services, 164-165
   integrated ISDN routers, 162-163
   internal routers
      dial-up analog services, 158
      ISDN service, 160-161
      leased-line services, 164
   packet filtering (security), 198-199
routes, 274
routing e-mail, 124-125
   to other networks, 246
routing tables, 46
RPCs (Remote Procedure Calls), 274

S

SAPs (Service Access Points), 33
screening routers (security), 198-199
screens (Web browsers), 93
security, 7, 193-207
   access reporting, 202
   access restrictions, 197
   anonymous FTP, 196
   application relays, 203-204
   application type access, 202
   authentication, 205
   bindery integration, 201
   break-ins, 195-196
   case studies, 211-225
   CERT (Computer Emergency Response Team), 196, 206
   cost, 197
   daemons, 195-196
   electronic commerce, 205-206
   encryption, 205
   Finger, 196
   firewalls, 199-203

telephone systems
    WANs (wide area networks), 136
    WAN access devices, 155
Telnet, 100-103, 245, 275
    Archie, 99, 242-244
    NetWare, 57
    terminal emulation, 101
terminal adapters (ISDN), 145-146
terminate-and-stay resident (TSR)
    programs, 62
TFTP (Trivial File Transfer Protocol), 275
third-party TCP/IP in the server, 68
time of day access, 202
time-sharing accounts (Internet connectivity),
    181-182
TLI (Transport Layer Interface), 275
topologies for e-mail systems, 110-112
training services for IAPs, 179
transceivers, 275
Transmission Control Protocol (TCP),
    49-50, 274
Transmission Control Protocol/Internet
    Protocol, *see* TCP/IP
transport layer
    SPX/IPX, 56-57
    TCP/IP, 48-50, 56-57
traps, 275
Trumpet (newsreader), 89
TSR (terminate-and-stay resident)
    programs, 62
TTL (Time-To-Live), 275
turnkey services (IAPs), 178

U

UDP (User Datagram Protocol), 48-49, 275
    compared to IPX, 56
unauthorized newsgroups, 89-90
universal time, 275
UNIX
    BSD UNIX (TCP/IP), 29
    SMTP, 117-118

UNIX-to-UNIX Copy Program (UUCP),
    127, 275
unmoderated newsgroups, 242
unreliable protocols (IP), 34
URLs (Uniform Resource Locators), 92
Usenet, 89-91, 128
    e-mail-only access (Internet connectivity),
        180-181
    FAQs (Frequently Asked Questions), 90-91,
        247-248
    NNTP (Network News Transport Protocol), 89
user agents (e-mail), 109
User Datagram Protocol (UDP), 48-49, 275
    compared to IPX, 56
UTC (Coordinated Universal Time), 275
UUCP (UNIX-to-UNIX Copy Program),
    127, 275
uuencoding e-mail, 77-78

V

value added services (IAPs), 178-179
VARs (value added resellers), 175
Veronica, 100
video conferencing, 18
View Source command (File menu), 131
VXDs (virtual device drivers), 62

W

WAN access devices
    combined access, 165-167
    dial-up analog service, 156-159
    direct attached modems, 156
    external dial-up routers, 158-159
    external routers
        ISDN service, 162
        leased-line services, 164-165
    integrated ISDN routers, 162-163
    internal routers

X-Y-Z

PLUG YOURSELF INTO...

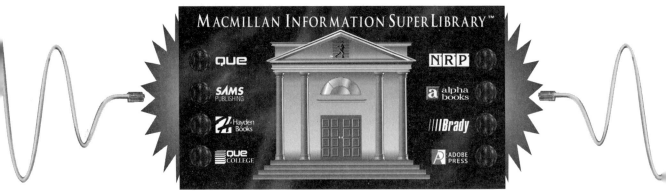

THE MACMILLAN INFORMATION SUPERLIBRARY™

Free information and vast computer resources from the world's leading computer book publisher—online!

FIND THE BOOKS THAT ARE RIGHT FOR YOU!

A complete online catalog, plus sample chapters and tables of contents give you an in-depth look at *all* of our books, including hard-to-find titles. It's the best way to find the books you need!

- **STAY INFORMED** with the latest computer industry news through our online newsletter, press releases, and customized Information SuperLibrary Reports.

- **GET FAST ANSWERS** to your questions about MCP books and software.

- **VISIT** our online bookstore for the latest information and editions!

- **COMMUNICATE** with our expert authors through e-mail and conferences.

- **DOWNLOAD SOFTWARE** from the immense MCP library:
    - Source code and files from MCP books
    - The best shareware, freeware, and demos

- **DISCOVER HOT SPOTS** on other parts of the Internet.

- **WIN BOOKS** in ongoing contests and giveaways!

TO PLUG INTO MCP: →   WORLD WIDE WEB: **http://www.mcp.com**

GOPHER: gopher.mcp.com

FTP: ftp.mcp.com

INFORMATION?

CHECK OUT THESE RELATED TOPICS OR SEE YOUR LOCAL BOOKSTORE

CAD and 3D Studio

As the number one CAD publisher in the world, and as a Registered Publisher of Autodesk, New Riders Publishing provides unequaled content on this complex topic. Industry-leading products include AutoCAD and 3D Studio.

Networking

As the leading Novell NetWare publisher, New Riders Publishing delivers cutting-edge products for network professionals. We publish books for all levels of users, from those wanting to gain NetWare Certification, to those administering or installing a network. Leading books in this category include *Inside NetWare 3.12*, *CNE Training Guide: Managing NetWare Systems*, *Inside TCP/IP*, and *NetWare: The Professional Reference*.

Graphics

New Riders provides readers with the most comprehensive product tutorials and references available for the graphics market. Bestsellers include *Inside CorelDRAW! 5*, *Inside Photoshop 3*, and *Adobe Photoshop NOW!*

Internet and Communications

As one of the fastest growing publishers in the communications market, New Riders provides unparalleled information and detail on this ever-changing topic area. We publish international bestsellers such as *New Riders' Official Internet Yellow Pages, 2nd Edition*, a directory of over 10,000 listings of Internet sites and resources from around the world, and *Riding the Internet Highway, Deluxe Edition*.

Operating Systems

Expanding off our expertise in technical markets, and driven by the needs of the computing and business professional, New Riders offers comprehensive references for experienced and advanced users of today's most popular operating systems, including *Understanding Windows 95*, *Inside Unix*, *Inside Windows 3.11 Platinum Edition*, *Inside OS/2 Warp Version 3*, and *Inside MS-DOS 6.22*.

Other Markets

Professionals looking to increase productivity and maxmize the potential of their software and hardware should spend time discovering our line of products for Word, Excel, and Lotus 1-2-3. These titles include *Inside Word 6 for Windows*, *Inside Excel 5 for Windows*, *Inside 1-2-3 Release 5*, and *Inside WordPerfect for Windows*.

Orders/Customer Service **1-800-653-6156**   Source Code **NRP95**

New Riders Publishing   201 West 103rd Street ◆ Indianapolis, Indiana 46290 USA

REGISTRATION CARD

Connecting NetWare to the Internet

Name _____ Title _____

Company_____ Type of business _____

Address _____

City/State/ZIP _____

Have you used these types of books before? ☐ yes ☐ no

If yes, which ones? _____

_____

How many computer books do you purchase each year? ☐ 1–5 ☐ 6 or more

How did you learn about this book? _____

Where did you purchase this book? _____

Which applications do you currently use? _____

_____

Which computer magazines do you subscribe to? _____

_____

What trade shows do you attend? _____

_____

Comments: _____

_____

_____

Would you like to be placed on our preferred mailing list? ☐ yes ☐ no

☐ **I would like to see my name in print!** You may use my name and quote me in future New Riders products and promotions. My daytime phone number is: _____

New Riders Publishing 201 West 103rd Street ◆ Indianapolis, Indiana 46290 USA

Fax to 317-581-4670   Orders/Customer Service 1-800-653-6156   Source Code NRP95

Fold Here

NO POSTAGE
NECESSARY
IF MAILED
IN THE
UNITED STATES

BUSINESS REPLY MAIL
FIRST-CLASS MAIL PERMIT NO. 9918 INDIANAPOLIS IN

POSTAGE WILL BE PAID BY THE ADDRESSEE

NEW RIDERS PUBLISHING
201 W 103RD ST
INDIANAPOLIS IN 46290-9058